Crazy for Corn

Also by Betty Fussell

....

Mabel: Hollywood's First I-Don't-Care Girl

Masters of American Cookery

I Hear America Cooking

Eating In

Food in Good Season

Home Plates

The Story of Corn

Crazy for Corn

BETTY FUSSELL

HarperPerennial

A Division of HarperCollins*Publishers*

Copyright acknowledgments follow page 237.

HarperCollins books may be purchased for educational, business, or sales promotional use. For information please write Special Markets Department, HarperCollins Publishers, Inc., 10 East 53rd Street, New York, NY 10022.

FIRST EDITION

DESIGNED BY JOEL AVIROM & JASON SNYDER
ILLUSTRATIONS BY JULIA LaPINE

Library of Congress Cataloging-in-Publication Data
Fussell, Betty Harper
  Crazy for corn / Betty Fussell. — 1st ed.
      p.   cm.
    Includes bibliographical references and index.
    ISBN: 0-06-095028-5
    1. Cookery (Corn)   2. Corn.   I. Title.
  TX809.M3F87   1995
  641.6'567—dc20   94-49683

95 96 97 98 99 ❖/RRD 10 9 8 7 6 5 4 3 2 1

For Fleury and Don

....

They can be prepared in 42 styles, each of which has its special name. . . . There is made of it bread, porridge (bouillie), cold meal (farine froide), ground corn (farine grolée), smoke-dried meal or meal dried in the fire and smoke, which when cooked has the same taste as our small peas and is sugary. That is also made which is called gruel (grut), that is to say that having beaten and pounded it for some time in a wooden mortar, along with a little water, the skin or envelope with which it is covered is removed. The grain thus beaten and dried is transported to great distances and keeps perfectly. The finest of that left behind is used in making hominy (sagamite), which is a kind of porridge cooked with oil or meat. It is a very good and nourishing aliment.

—*Dumont de Montigny*, Mémoires historiques sur la Louisiane, *1753*

Crazy for Corn

CONTENTS

....

....

ACKNOWLEDGMENTS

A COMMUNITY OF CORN

For a decade I've quizzed friends and strangers, combed bookstores, haunted libraries, scrutinized menus, pestered chefs, and interrogated farmers for corn. By now there are a small number of books devoted to nothing but corn recipes (see the bibliography, "A List of Corn Cookery"), and a vast number of books that contain interesting corn recipes whatever their subject. I've drawn on every source I could for this collection of recipes to show two things: the scope of corn cookery as it traveled from America to the rest of the world and the current flowering of corn cookery at the hands of some of our best and brightest American chefs, both those who were born here and those who have come here from elsewhere. In other words, I want to show both how wide are corn's global fields and how deep are corn's American roots.

Because I believe cooking, as well as eating, is a communal enterprise, I have been delighted to have corn as an excuse to talk with friends and strangers, to eat with strangers who then became friends, to travel to places I'd never been, to learn from chefs and marketers and farmers, to tell others what I've learned. I've mentioned many names in these recipes and I've adapted many recipes from the works of others because I want to acknowledge my pleasure in discovering with this person a particular combination of ingredients, or with that person a particular method that suddenly illuminates a dish. And there are many names I've not mentioned who have nonetheless contributed much to my knowledge and pleasure: Lydia Bastianich, Toni Chiappetta, Travis Clark, Sophie Coe, Deborah Madison, Waldy Malouf, Zarela Martinez, Carol Peck, Joel Porte, Richard Sax.

I'm heavily indebted to cooks who've given me permission to use recipes which they've culled individually from countries as far apart as Moldavia and Ecuador. The corn connection turns regional cuisines into a global one, and I've tried to incorporate

as many dialects as possible into the common language of corn. Corn embraces an international community, whether or not we are aware of the rest of the group and whether or not we are conscious of the ancient and continuous traditions that feed our individual imaginations.

I'm heavily indebted to a whole generation of American chefs who have come of age while I've been working on corn, and part of my excitement with the subject is the way these chefs continue to explore with their particular creative skills this basic staple of American cookery, rediscovering it in their own kitchens the way a home cook rediscovers and re-creates the primal art of cooking each time she cooks a meal, making an art as old as fire forever new.

As numberless as kernels of corn are the people I would like to thank person by person but can't, so here are three. Thank you Leah Holzel, who helped begin this book, and Lauren Deen, who helped end it, and Fern Berman, in between. Thanks also to Susan Friedland and to the James Beard House for embracing corn madness.

INTRODUCTION

W hen corn looked me straight in the eye about a decade ago, I had no notion that corn would take over my life. Now as I look about my kitchen, at the plastic corn magnets on the refrigerator, the shelves of bagged cornmeal in the refrigerator, the crocheted corn pot holders and tea cozies, the printed corn dish towels, the corn apron and oven mitts, the ceramic corn plates-platters-pitchers and salt and pepper shakers from Ohio, the molded corn candles from Guatemala, the papier-mâché corn ears from Mexico, the dried purple corn ears for real from Peru—I wonder, was there life before corn?

Not life in this hemisphere—not at any rate civilized life—rooted in planting and staying put, rather than hunting and gathering the wild. Corn, as I discovered when I set out to tell *The Story of Corn,* built the civilizations of the ancient New World as it built that of our own modern industrial world, connecting past to present by the peculiarities of a staple that feeds not only men and animals but also a giant industrial machine. Today, we speak of corn as a $20 billion crop. Anciently, Pueblo Indians spoke of corn as the fifth element: there was earth, air, fire, water—and corn.

We don't just eat and drink corn as a vegetable and a grain. We eat it converted through fodder into pork chops and beef steaks, chickens and eggs, milk and cheese. We drink it as beer and whiskey and soda pop. Corn is the base not just of our food chain but of our industrial chain. Industry eats corn chemically as an oil, a starch, and a sugar. Anything petroleum can do, corn can do better. We use this industrially converted corn in thousands of different products from cradle to grave, from talcum powder to embalming fluid. Every one of our lives is touched every day by an invisible network of corn.

But that's another story from the one I want to tell here through recipes that use the many different kinds of corn that you eat and drink and make merry with. This is not a short story but a global epic. That's the trouble with this quintessentially native

American crop. Wherever you touch corn, it takes you not only into every part of the food chain and into every segment of a menu, but also around the world. The gold Columbus discovered was corn and, after Columbus, corn went everywhere because it would grow everywhere. Corn became the poor man's staple from Beijing to Timbuktu, so it surfaces in recipes from Indonesia, Spain, India, Africa, Japan, as well as from Ecuador, Bolivia, Guatemala, and Brazil.

Corn also takes you deep into the American past, into a highly sophisticated corn cuisine created by the royal dynasties of Maya, Aztec, and Inca. The banquets of Moctezuma dazzled Cortés, and the inheritors of the cooking skills that produced them still dazzle visitors to Mexico with the quality and variety of their corn breads. North of the border we don't understand that corn traditions south of the border are directly connected to ours. Because their breads are called tortillas and tamales, we don't associate them with our spoon breads and jonnycakes and muffins. We don't realize that we too are the inheritors of an ancient body of corn knowledge cradled in the middle of the Americas and disseminated north and south.

We don't understand because all of us who are not Native Americans came to America from elsewhere, from all the cultures of the Old World founded on wheat and more recently from the many Asian cultures founded on rice. At whatever time our ancestors came, whether to New England in 1640 or to the Great Lakes in 1840 or to New York in 1940, they had to adapt what they already knew to what was new to them, a culture founded on corn. The original colonists survived only by absorbing corn into their wheat vocabulary, which accounts for the comedy of calling corn "Turkish wheat," or corn mush "hasty pudding." The result has been a hybrid language and a hybrid cuisine, befitting the polyglot culture America has evolved. Still, with all the vernaculars and ethnic dialects of American cooking, corn is the base of our multiple stocks and it behooves us to know all we can about what we've inherited and what we've lost.

Through the beginning of this century, much of that inheritance was still intact. Across the country American farmers grew hundreds of varieties of corn in their fields and gardens. Farmers' wives knew how to dry, grind, toast, pickle, and parch the kernels they also knew how to shell from the cob. Families knew how to cook it with lye from wood ashes in order to make hominy and knew how to grind that hominy into grits. Men and women knew how to make yeasted breads, quick breads, oven cakes, and battercakes with cornmeals and corn flours. They knew how to boil and fry mush,

how to roast or boil whole ears of field corn as well as sweet corn, how to grate fresh corn and squeeze out milk from the cobs, how to smooth fresh kernels with butter and cream, how to turn popcorn into candies, how to ferment corn mash into whiskey and beer.

Today we know little about corn kinds and less about how to use them. Today most Americans know corn only as three generic types: the sweet kind you eat on the cob, the field kind pigs eat in the trough, and the other kind everybody eats popped. Even if we were skilled in our ancestors' lore and knew how to choose different varieties of corn for different culinary uses, today we would be unable to get those varieties unless we grew them ourselves and even then we'd have to search hard to find heritage seeds. Usually we know sweet corn only by the kind our local green-market farmer sells in summer, or by the kind our local supermarket imports from Florida in winter. We know popcorn only by the name of our favorite brand.

As for field corn, we know it only when it's been commercially milled and packaged as cornmeal, most of which is degermed in the milling for the sake of long shelf life and is thus denuded of taste. If we find stone-ground meal in our local health food store, we don't know how long it's been on the shelf and whether it's fresh or stale. Even here we don't know what varieties of corn are being used or where they're grown. We are so removed from the roots of the corn plant and of the food chain that springs from it that we don't know what the choices are. When I asked an excellent baker recently what kind of cornmeal he was using in his vegetable tart crust, he was puzzled and asked, "Is there more than one kind?"

Yes, there's more than one kind, there's a whole world of corn kinds that wait, like ruined temples in the rainforest, to be rediscovered in our own modern kitchens and tasted on our own eclectic palates and plates. The purpose of this book is to open up that world, so that anyone grazing these pages can see at once both how vast it is and how particular, how ancient and how modern, how earthy and how urbane. Above all I want to open up our kitchens to the multiplicity of that world so that we can more fully enjoy and savor the bounty of a plant that more than any other nourishes our lives.

Corn can do this because it's a crazy plant, unlike any other of the world's staple grains. All grains evolved from grass, but corn is the world's oldest genetically engineered grass. Geneticists call it "a botanical monster" because the seeds on an ear of corn are so tightly wrapped and closely packed that they cannot seed themselves without man's help. The plant cannot grow in the wild. How it got that way is a puzzle, but so is the fact that corn has "jumping genes" that enable it to hybridize more readily than any other plant, with or without the aid of man.

Because it can hybridize so easily, it has adapted itself to more extremes of climate and ecology than any staple plant and exists everywhere but the North and South Poles. Its varieties are so numerous that they must be divided and subdivided into "races" of corn, with some genetic lines dating back thousands of years. It can be bred to produce kernels of any color in the rainbow, kernels of different kinds of starches, different degrees of sweetness, different sizes and shapes.

Because corn varieties are constantly evolving, it's hard to keep our cooking methods current with the latest developments in corn breeding. A century ago our great-grandmothers boiled fresh corn on the cob for 30 minutes to an hour because they were cooking types of field corn, when it was young or "green." When sweet corn types became popular at the turn of the century, our grandmothers reduced cooking time to 20 minutes and then to 10. As sweet types were engineered to have ever less starch and ever more sugar, our mothers reduced cooking time to a formulaic "3 minutes." Nowadays, with supersweet types that seem to be all sugar and no starch, savvy corn lovers cut the time from 3 minutes to 1 to none.

As a rule, I'm against rules, but I'm all for suggestions. And I suggest that when you buy fresh corn, at a country stand or in a supermarket, you ask the seller what kind it is and where it was grown, as well as when it was picked. If it's a farmer, ask if the corn was grown organically. Let him know that you'd rather have a worm in the corn-cob than chemical pesticides and fertilizers in the cornfield. When you buy cornmeals, try to find out what kind of corn was used, how it was ground, and when it was shipped. The same people who are fanatics about the freshness of sweet corn are often undiscriminating and even indifferent to the freshness of cornmeals. Many don't even know there's a choice. The more you know about the corn you eat, the better you can cook it and the more you will savor its taste.

As an edible plant, corn is an oddity because its fruit, large as a child's forearm, is composed entirely of seeds, and those seeds can be eaten raw or cooked, fresh or dried, whole or ground. Because corn always contains some sugar as well as starch, it can run the flavor gamut from savory to sweet and the menu gamut from snacks to desserts. That's why popcorn tastes good whether it's seasoned with salt (and peppers

and herbs) or sweetened with molasses or brown sugar. That's why the taste of cornmeal can blend as perfectly with fruits and chocolate and sugared creams as with chilies and cheese and meat and game.

Every summer, for a number of years now, I've celebrated corn's infinite variety with an all-corn dinner at the James Beard House in Manhattan. In this city I've been lucky to be able to draw on the talent and expertise of a whole generation of stellar young American chefs and caterers—Bobby Flay, Brendan Walsh, Ruth Bronz, Michael Lomonaco, Ali Barker, David Turk, Stuart Taborin, among many others. On a hot August night, sitting under the leafy trees in the garden of Beard's townhouse in Greenwich Village, candles lit, faces aglow with memories and expectation, I feel a chill up my spine at the thought that on this very spot Canarsees and Wappingers once celebrated corn in their annual midsummer rites, roasting their young green ears in the embers of a fire, laughing, dancing, praying, and making merry because the renewal of corn meant life would go on, and an abundant crop meant life would go on more abundantly.

What I asked of myself I could ask of this city—was there life before corn? None that I know of, and I hope this book will show how much life there is *in* corn, how it feeds and nourishes our communal memories and joys as well as our bodies, how it connects our childhoods of popcorn and Cracker Jacks to our adult tastes for polenta and posole, and how it aligns kernels of pleasure like kernels on a cob.

I begin my midsummer corn rite every year by invoking the sacred words of Garrison Keillor: "People have tried and they have tried but sex is not better than sweet corn." Is it better, I wonder, than popcorn or polenta or hominy or grits or hot buttered corn bread or creamy corn pudding or salty corn chips or crispy corn fritters or lobster corn chowders or sweet corn flapjacks or blueberry blue corn muffins or spring-garden succotash or fresh peach corn ice cream? After my corn-crazed decade, I'd say it's a toss-up. At this very moment, I'd say corn's got the edge.

A CORN ANATOMY

Before geneticists in the 1940s began to group corn by ancestral races, with names like Palomero Toluqueño and Confite Morocho, corn was grouped by the nature of its endosperm, the interior of the kernel containing protein and starch. Thus all corn was divided into five distinct types: pop, sweet, dent, flint, and flour. (Recently they've added an additional generic type, "waxy.") The oldest known corn, the original corn, was popcorn, and it grew on a cob no bigger than your little fingernail.

As this ancestral corn evolved under man's cultivation some seven thousand years ago, corn's ability to hybridize produced these basic types very quickly, so that sweet, dent, flint, and flour types are nearly as ancient as pop. Both pop and flint types contain hard starch and high protein. Dent contains a pocket of soft waxy starch at the crown, which causes it to "indent" when dried. Flour varieties contain waxy starch, which makes them easy to grind. Sweet varieties contain more sugar than starch and so have translucent kernels that wrinkle when dried.

Each of these types serves a different purpose. Any kind of corn kernel will pop slightly when heated, but only a popcorn type will explode and turn itself inside out to make a little white ball. Any kind of corn will taste slightly sweet when young, but only a sweet corn type will maintain sweetness when mature. In this country, most Americans eat only sweet varieties as a vegetable, either on the cob or with kernels cut off. Many Native Americans, however, north and south of the border, prefer other types, especially dent, for boiling or roasting immature (or "green") ears on the cob.

Most of us in this country find dent, flint, and flour types only in dried form, either in whole kernels as hominy or ground into meal and flour. Dent varieties have been favored in the South for hominy and grits. Flour varieties have been favored in the Southwest for posole and tortillas because of easier grinding; many crosses of flint and flour types are, as Southwesterners say, "good for everything." Flint varieties have been favored in the colder regions of the North for batters like jonnycake, because the flint type evolved to withstand hard winters and short summers.

Every corn type can be grown in any color. Color by itself is no indication of flavor or of kind. Except for yellow corn, color is usually only skin deep and doesn't affect the starch core, but the chemical nature of the pigmentation may have a slight effect on flavor. A red-skinned corn, like a red-skinned grape, will have some tannins. But by the time the corn is cooked, the tannins will have largely burned off or disappeared. Color may, however, indicate vitamin and mineral content. Yellow corns contain carotene, and therefore vitamin A, while white corns do not. Both white and yellow corns are rich in vitamins B and C and in potassium. Generally, blue corn types are higher in lysine and iron.

It's the particular variety, not the color, that is the main indicator of flavor and texture. Varietal flavor depends on texture (hard, soft, chalky, flaky, crisp, moist), aroma (fruity, earthy, herby), and the relation of starch to sugar to oil in the kernel. A sweet corn with white kernels, for example, is not sweeter or crisper than one with all yellow or bicolored kernels. It's the variety that counts, whether it's Silver Queen or Butter 'N Eggs or Hidatsa Gummy, a heritage strain you're not apt to find in your local market.

Here are a few current varieties of the five kinds, some of them recent hybrids, the seed of which you can buy in mainstream seed catalogs. Others are heirloom strains that are called "nonhybrid," meaning they have evolved perhaps over centuries, and are now available through Seed Savers Exchange or Native Seeds/SEARCH. (See "A Source List," page 223.) Multiply each of these strains by triple digits and you'll begin to see just how big the corn world is.

Pop: Burpee's Peppy Hybrid, Creme-Puff Hybrid, Pretty Pops, Bearpaw, Chapalote, Lady Finger, Tom Thumb Yellow, Reventador

Sweet: Golden Cross Bantam, Kandy Korn, Silver Queen, Honey and Cream, Honey 'N Pearl, How Sweet It Is, Black Aztec, Hooker's Sweet Indian, Paiute, Six Shooter, Cocopah, Mohave, Hopi Bantam, Hidatsa Gummy, Howling Mob

Dent: Bloody Butcher, Cherokee Princess, Hickory King, Texas Gourdseed, Tarahumara Pepitillo, Yaqui June, Cónico Norteño Pepitillo, Bloody Mary, Skyscraper, Preacher Hill

Flint: Rhode Island Whitecap, Garland Flint, Mandan Black, Purple Husk, Indian Ornamental, Squaw Corn, Tarahumara Apachito, Tepehuan Maíz Colorado, Longfellow, Seneca Blue Bear Dance

Flour: Blue Tortilla, Chichito, Hopi Blue, Papago, African Zulu Maize, Mandan Bride, Hopi Greasy Hair, Navajo Robin's Egg, Taos White, Osage Red, Winnebago Grey

Not only each type but each variety within a type has its own flavor and texture, and that too will vary according to soil, water, climate, the weather of that particular growing season, and the farmer of that particular field. In the 1920s Henry Wallace created the world's first commercial crop by crossing a Northern Flint with a Southern Dent to produce Corn Belt Dent. This hybrid provided the highest yield and therefore made money for the corn industry but it had nothing to do with taste. Not until the 1970s did farmers, and others, become alarmed that we were in danger of destroying the diversity of the corn world by a single monolithic factory crop.

Recently seed savers have become saviors of heritage strains at the growing level. Now it's time for cooks and eaters to explore the tastes of different corns and to encourage farmers to grow them. As Kent Whealy of Seed Savers Exchange said of the 325 varieties of heritage corn he had accumulated for their 1992 *Garden Seed Inventory,* "Try to imagine what it would cost, in terms of time and energy and money, to develop this many outstanding varieties. But they already exist. All we have to do is save them." But we must also savor them.

FRESH SWEET CORN
AND HOW TO COOK IT

This is our first crop of corn.

We don't appreciate

any tales about

Nebraska's corn

Iowa's corn

Kansas's corn

Nor your father's corn.

— Sign hand-printed on a brown paper bag
at the Union Square Greenmarket in New York City, July 19, 1989

In America, cooking and eating corn on the cob are sacred matters and you don't mess around with somebody's religion. I've demonstrated ways to cook fresh corn at country fairs and city markets from coast to coast, and while nobody yet has actually pelted me with corncobs, sometimes it's a near thing. People get mad. Or at least sullen, and certainly resistant, if you merely suggest (remember I'm against rules) any variation in their personal orthodox liturgy of cooking corn on the cob. So be it.

These suggestions are not for them. But they are for those who recognize that corn engineering has revolutionized sweet corn types during the last decade and that only now are chefs and home cooks beginning to catch up with that change. Sweet corns are classified by the percentage of sugar in their kernels. "Sweet" has 5 to 10 percent, "Sugar-Enhanced" 15 to 18 percent, and "Supersweet" 25 to 30 percent. Each season brings a new batch of supersweet varieties with names like Kandy Korn, Peaches & Cream, Phenomenal, Incredible, and doubtless the sugar percentage and names to match will continue to inflate.

Normally the sugar in an ear of corn begins to convert to starch the moment it's picked. That accounts for the "rule" to have your water boiling on the stove before the corn is picked in the field. But today many supersweet varieties are being bred to delay conversion of sugar to starch for 2 weeks or longer. That is why you are now getting fresh corn grown in Florida and shipped nationwide all winter long, corn bred to retain sweetness while being transported around the country. The sweetness stays but moisture is lost and therefore texture. Winter sweet corn does not have the creaminess of seasonal summer corn freshly picked. Anyone can tell you that, but fresh winter sweet corn is a good alternative to either frozen or canned corn.

Canned sweet corn is a product unto itself, like corn flakes, because it is packed in sugar and salt. Canned creamed corn is even more a processed product with its own distinct taste quite different from fresh corn kernels. Frozen corn brands vary in price and quality (currently priced from around $1.00 to $2.00 per 10-ounce box), according to the kind of corn and its packaging. Birds Eye Deluxe Sweet corn is a supersweet type about twice as sweet and twice as costly as Birdseye Sweet corn. Fresh winter ears of corn are priced currently at around 30 to 50 cents an ear, which makes them competitive with frozen corn and to my mind a better value because they have better texture than frozen corn.

To Buy It

My first suggestion about buying fresh sweet corn is to respect its chastity within the protection God gave it. It is the husk tightly closed that keeps the seeds within at maximum freshness. And yet I have seen people at markets do violence to ear after ear, stripping back the husks with frenzy and tossing the cobs back in the pile as if they were discarding so many ravished virgins. Presumably they do this to see that the kernels are filled out all the way to the top of each cob and that the husks hide no nasty worms. But you can tell whether a cob is completely filled by feeling the top from the outside of the husk. As for a worm, it will not only do you no harm, granted that you remove it when you take the silks from the cobs, but today it may testify that the corn has been grown without the pervasive chemicals that do us all harm. Be tender with the corn and it will repay you in kind.

TO EAT IT RAW

My first suggestion about cooking sweet corn is not to cook it at all but to eat it raw. At least sample it raw, nibbling at the top of an ear to see what kind you've got, how sweet it is, how fresh it is. The freshest and sweetest is best eaten raw. The first year I demonstrated raw sweet corn at the Union Square Greenmarket in New York, raw corn was a hard sell. Even when it was free. I would chop cobs in thirds with a cleaver and offer samples to passersby, but many looked at me as if I'd offered them a live snake. This last year it was different. I could hardly keep up with the samplers, so maybe the word has gotten out that the sweeter and sweetest types of sweet corn when picked fresh are at their best *au naturel*.

My hope is not to convert America to eating raw corn on the cob the way they'd eat sushi, but to remove any fear of using raw sweet corn in salads or purees or in vegetable mixes or pastas or as garnishes. Once you adjust to the idea that raw sweet corn is good, the way an apple, a raw carrot, or a raw oyster is good, then cooking sweet corn as briefly as possible, depending on its ratio of sugar to starch, seems a reasonable idea. Heat speeds the conversion of sugar to starch, so the longer you cook sweet corn the tougher and starchier you're making it.

TO BOIL OR STEAM IT

Salt toughens the skins of the kernels, so don't salt the water you boil for corn. Sugar was once added to corn water to help sweeten it, but with supersweets that's really overdoing it. With supersweets, the briefer the dip into boiling water the better. Forget "the 3-minute rule." I don't dip a corn ear for more than 30 seconds, just long enough to give it a quick zap. You don't need even that zap for digestibility, as you don't need it for taste. But you do need it if you like your corn, as I do, with melted butter.

Think of cooking corn the way you cook pasta. Don't put ears in cold water and bring them slowly to the boil. Don't even put ears in boiling water and turn the fire off and leave them there covered for 3 or 5 or any number of arbitrary minutes. Put on a big kettle of boiling water so there'll be plenty of room for your corn ears. Then dip them in and take them out.

However you're cooking corn on the cob, I suggest you cook it with the husks on. The green husks intensify corn flavor and, until the Victorian age genteelized table manners, fresh ears were always cooked in their husks. The husks not only increase flavor, they steam the corn rather than boil it and they retain heat, so that your ears will stay warmer in their wrappers once they've had their hot water bath.

Simply remove the coarse outer husks. You don't need to remove the inner silks before cooking because most of them will stick to the husks when you pull them off. (If you insist on removing the silks first, push the husks back over the top and tie them with a strip of husk, a piece of string, a wire twist, or nothing at all; even if the husks aren't tight, they'll still help the steaming process.) Cooking corn with the husks on does not increase cooking time if your pot of boiling water is large enough to maintain heat when filling it with ears. Here's a quick summary:

30-SECOND CORN STEAMED IN THE HUSK

Take your largest pot, fill it with water (do *not* add salt), and bring it to a vigorous boil. Remove a layer of outer husks and drop the ears four to six at a time in the boiling water. Leave for no more than 30 *seconds*. Drain the ears well and place them on a platter.

With the husks on you are in fact steaming the kernels inside, but if you prefer to use a conventional steamer to avoid immersing the ears in water, don't steam too long. Place the ears in a single layer on the steamer rack, or pack them upright against each other, so that the steam will get to them as quickly and evenly as possible. Length of time depends on how many ears in what size steamer, but it may take as much as 5 to 10 minutes for the ears to heat through. I find no advantage to this method. On the contrary, timing is harder.

To show off the beauty of corn when you serve the ears, pull back the husks to the base of each ear (with a towel or pot holder for protection), remove any remaining silks, and serve the ears with their greenery. Eaters can break off the ear at the base if they wish or hold onto the husks at one end and the kerneled tip at the other. Because I like to display corn as a work of art in itself, and serve it with a number of flavored butters, I usually make corn on the cob a course in itself, most often a first course because it is too filling to serve after the entree. Some people regard corn as the entree, and I am one of them.

To Grill or Roast It

Because I like the flavor of grilled corn, I've experimented a lot to find the best and easiest ways to get a grilled taste without overcooking the corn. And I mean a grilled taste, not a steamed one. I don't like to soak the husks first in cold water as many do, because that steams the corn on the grill. I prefer to either grill the corn in the husks without soaking (again, you don't need to remove the silks first because they'll come off with the husks) so that the husks char a bit on the outside and transmit some of that flavor to the kernels. Or to husk it and grill the nude ears directly over the heat. This tends to caramelize the sugar in the corn and give it a wonderful color and taste, intensifying sweetness. Husks-on corn takes about twice as long as husks off. On a hot grill the corn takes about 6 to 8 minutes with the husks on and about 3 minutes with the husks off.

For city dwellers like myself who can seldom use an outdoor grill, I get that same caramelized taste by roasting an ear, husks removed, directly over the flame of a gas stove, the way you would roast a pepper. Hold the ear with a pair of tongs and turn it so that it scorches slightly on all sides, about 3 to 4 minutes. The corn is so flavorful that you need no seasoning and no oil or butter, but all the same I go for a sprinkling of herbed olive oil, or fresh lime juice and a little pure ground chili, or any number of flavored butters.

I also love the taste of smoked corn, which I do in a wok, again because I don't have an outdoor smoker. For smoking materials, you can use wet husks and silks (see recipe on page 66) or wood chips. Put a handful of wet wood chips (hickory, apple, cherry, mesquite, etc.), which you've soaked about 10 minutes, into the bottom of a wok. Put a rack on top, cover the wok tightly with a lid, and start the chips smoking by putting the wok on high heat for about 5 minutes. Remove the lid and lay ears of husked corn on the rack without their sides touching. Cover the wok again, lower the heat to medium, and smoke the corn for about 5 to 8 minutes.

Roasting corn in a hot oven, 450 to 500 degrees, works better than most oven broilers. If you roast the ears in their husks you are again steaming the kernels and it takes about 6 to 8 minutes to get the corn hot all the way through. Should you want to rub the ears with a little seasoned butter, you need to first pull back the husks, remove the silks, then spread on the butter, and finally pull the husks back over the tops.

By all accounts microwave ovens do well with corn if you are cooking only one or two ears. I never am, but if *you* are, cook them with the husk on and at the highest setting (100 percent power). Again, you will be "steaming" them in their husks, and you can rub them with olive oil or butter before cooking if you wish. For microwaving, I follow Barbara Kafka's chart: At 700 watts, cook one ear for 2 minutes and two ears for 5; at 400 watts, cook one ear for 3 minutes and two ears for 8. If cooking more than two ears, to hell with the microwave, the times are too long.

If you are cooking quantities of sweet corn and for whatever reason are husking the ears first, you can ease the labor of removing corn silks by running a damp paper towel over the ear so that the silks will stick to the towel. Some stores sell a "corn silk remover," which is a small nylon brush with soft plastic bristles to comb the kernels. Personally, I like the feel of the silks on my fingers and so I remove them by hand; it reminds me that each single silk was once attached to a single kernel and furnished the route for a speck of pollen to do its work and turn an embryo into a plump juicy youth.

To Season It

Sweet corn needs no addition, but there are too many delicious seasonings not to mention some. In Southeast Asia they dip or brush roasted cobs with salted coconut milk; in India's Punjabi, with curry and lime; in Mexico, with lime, chili, and salt or with chili and *queso fresco*. Think of the possibilities. James Beard liked butter and bacon crumbs, mustard mayonnaise, or green mayonnaise. Many Southern cooks like to flavor their roasting ears by wrapping them in bacon or by brushing them with their favorite barbecue sauce before grilling.

I like the taste of olive oil on grilled corn and herbed or chilied butters on boiled corn. Now that flavored oils are popular, consider truffled oil or garlic oil for roasted ears. In season, chopped basil is good to use with either olive oil or butter. But so are other fresh herbs like thyme, rosemary, sage, tarragon. And of course any kind of chili is kin to corn.

My favorite recipe puts tarragon and chili together in a butter flavored with fresh orange:

Orange-Tarragon-Chili Butter

MAKES ABOUT ½ CUP.

Peel from ½ orange
¼ cup fresh orange juice
1 teaspoon anchovy paste
½ teaspoon chipotle chili puree
1 teaspoon fresh lemon juice
2 tablespoons chopped green onions
½ teaspoon dried tarragon
8 tablespoons (1 stick) butter
2 tablespoons chopped fresh tarragon leaves

Put all the ingredients but the butter and fresh tarragon leaves in a blender and mix well. In a saucepan, heat the butter until bubbling. With the motor turned on, pour the butter slowly through the opening of the blender lid until the mixture begins to thicken. Remove from the blender and stir in the tarragon leaves.

SWEET CORN MUSHROOMS, OR HUITLACOCHE

When I first got interested in corn, I never met an American corn farmer who called the black-blue fungus that occasionally balloons on sweet corn anything but "corn smut." That was the nicest thing he called it. A mere decade later a number of farmers from Pennsylvania to Florida have learned to call the fungus "corn mushrooms" and occasionally, if they've lived near the Mexican border, they call it by its original Nahuatl name, pronounced "wheat-la-co-che." Not only that, some farmers no longer exterminate the fungus as a blight that will ruin their sweet corn crop, but grow it in a controlled area for chefs who can't get enough of it.

Not many do this, of course, but for the first time there is a market for this delicacy in fine restaurants in the States, a delicacy long treasured in Mexico and among natives of the Southwest. The credit for introducing Americans to huitlacoche goes single-handedly to Christina Arnold, who initiated a company and an agricultural program to promulgate this extraordinary corn food. It is now being cultivated on a small scale by inoculating young sweet corn ears with the fungus. Where once you could only get it canned from Mexico, now you can get it year-round, fresh in the summer season and flash-frozen the rest of the year. The texture is best fresh, but its color and flavor are intense and are well preserved frozen.

What is unusual about this mushroom is that it surrounds and incorporates the kernels of sweet corn it grows on, so that the mushroom always has a sweetness to it as well as a dark earthy taste. It also has a rich black glossy color, blacker than a truffle, so depending on what you mix it with in the cooking, the color can range from raven's-wing black to a kind of decorator taupe or greige. Think of what this can do to color a pasta or a sauce.

In Mexico I've eaten huitlacoche in soups, sauces, tamales, sautés, stews, you name it. In New York I've tasted a number of all-huitlacoche dinners, beginning with appetizers and ending with mousses or ice creams. I've tried to show something of the range of huitlacoche in the recipes in this book, particularly by incorporating it into breads, but it's ripe for exploration in all kinds of culinary ways and I hope this is one ancestral corn edible we'll rediscover in our home kitchens.

DRIED CORN AND CORNMEALS

DRIED SWEET CORN

I hope also we'll rediscover dried sweet corn, which was once as much a farmhouse kitchen staple as dried cornmeal. Today few would go to the trouble of drying their own, although it is perfectly possible to do so. Here are two ways taken from Mary L. Wade's *The Book of Corn Cookery* of 1917:

Mother's Way of Drying Sweet Corn on the Cob

1. *Turn back the husks all but the last layer. Then hang in the sun or a very warm room.*
2. *Cut from the ear. Spread in shallow boxes or tin pans. Cover with cheesecloth and dry in the sun or on the shelf over the stove or in the warming oven. When dry put up in jars and cover closely. Or if you prefer the old-fashioned way, put in paper bags, tie tight and hang in the attic until needed.*

Today mothers and others buy dried sweet corn from a mail-order catalog, since few specialty markets handle it. Sometimes it comes whole kernel and sometimes cracked kernel, but either way drying intensifies the sweetness of corn just the way it does the sweetness of fruit. You can reconstitute dried kernels with warm water the way you do dried chilies or dried fruit. I find dried corn useful for mixing with other things when you would like little nuggets of corn flavor, as in a yeasted bread. In the Southwest, dried whole-kernel sweet corn is called "chicos" and is a staple of winter stews.

WHOLE-KERNEL DRIED CORN

The other whole-kernel dried corn is usually not a sweet type but a flint, dent, or flour type, used for hominy or posole. Hominy and posole are two words for the same

thing: dried whole kernels that have been boiled with some form of alkali (lye from wood ash or lime slaked from limestone) to remove the kernel's tough outer skins. This is a process almost as ancient as corn, for it not only makes the kernels easier to grind but it also completes the protein chain of corn, which is weak in tryptophan and lysine. (Today you can buy a Hi-Lysine cornmeal, but most of us are getting lysine in plenty of other ways.) Since the daily bread of ancient Native American civilizations was made of alkali-processed corn, corn can be said to be the world's oldest chemically processed food.

Until this century, hominy was a staple of the American kitchen, ever since colonists learned from Native Americans how to grind and cook corn. Today hominy makers have all but disappeared, except among a few remote Appalachians, and even store-bought canned hominy has all but disappeared from grocery shelves, except among Spanish specialty stores. Fortunately, however, hominy has come to life again in the form of Southwestern or Mexican posole, which gives its name to different hearty stews composed usually of hominy and meats like pork and chicken, in a broth flavored by red chilies or green chilies, red tomatoes or green tomatillos.

GROUND CORN

In this country hominy was ground dry to make grits. Today grits often means simply coarsely ground cornmeal, but properly grits means ground skinned corn, or ground hominy. In Mexico freshly boiled hominy (or *nixtamal*) is ground wet to make *masa,* the soft wet dough for tortillas and tamales. This wet dough can be dried and pulverized as *masa harina,* or (alkali-processed) corn flour. This flour is much more finely ground than most of our cornmeals. Because of its fine texture and because it has already been cooked, it works as a kind of "instant" flour, for use as an all-purpose thickener. It can substitute wonderfully for wheat flour in a roux, a cream sauce, a soup, a casserole, a dessert. Because alkali is a good preservative, this is one whole-grain meal that keeps well without refrigeration.

In our own country ground corn comes in many different kinds and qualities, ranging from corn cracked in large fragments and called "samp," to commercially processed cornstarch. The trouble is that you have to search out these kinds and qualities because they are not in your supermarket. The deeper trouble is that 99 percent of our cornmeal is dead, because it has been stripped of the living germ that contains oil. Whole-grain meal

will go rancid more quickly than degermed meal because of the oil in that embryonic germ. But if you strip the meal of oil, you strip it of flavor, leaving only a slightly sweet starch.

Standard commercial corn has almost twice as much oil in its kernel as a standard wheat berry does, so that the flavor of cornmeal suffers twice the loss when the oil is removed by industrial milling. While corn has 3.9 grams of oil per 100 grams of whole-grain meal, wheat has only 2. In addition, the oil in corn is largely unsaturated fat, which is more subject to oxidation than the oil in wheat and therefore goes rancid more quickly.

Because of its larger percentage of oil, corn requires more care in the milling than wheat does and so again has suffered more than wheat from the industrial milling that, over a century ago, replaced grinding stones with steel rollers. Steel rollers created mass-produced milling and marketing, which for corn has been as destructive of flavor and quality as any other method that puts volume and efficiency above excellence. Oil-rich kernels scorch easily and, in milling as in storage, heat is the enemy.

Steel rollers displaced not just grinding stones but good millers. Good millers know the individual qualities of the corn they grind and they grind their corn in small enough quantities to control the process at every point from the cornfield to the cornmeal buyer. Good millers are particular. They are people like Diane and Robert Smith on Moonstone Beach Road in Perryville, Rhode Island, whose Whitecap flint corn is grown by Harry Records in nearby Exeter and who grind it in the 1703 Carpenter's Grist Mill they have lovingly restored. It's not the old-fashioned mill that makes their flint cornmeal good, it's the care they give it.

Even if you find a whole-grain meal like Arrowhead or Indian Head or White Lily in your supermarket, our distribution chains are such that you cannot know how long the grain has been on the shelf. And that matters. Boy, does that matter. Any whole-grain cornmeal should be dated and kept chilled the way milk is dated and refrigerated. That's why in my recipes I call always for "freshly ground" meal the way recipes, ever since Julia Child's first volumes, call for "freshly ground" pepper. Even though most of us are not going to grind our corn at home (although you can do so in domestic electric mills), you can make sure that the meal you buy is fresh and you can keep it that way by cold storage. Once you've smelled and tasted the difference between "freshly ground" whole-grain meal and an industrial brand, you'll want the quality that only freshness brings.

Grinding with buhrstones does not in itself guarantee quality or freshness, nor does it guarantee less heat than rollers or spinning hammers. But "stone-ground" is a sort of shorthand for a miller who cares, who grinds small enough quantities to get the meal to you while it is optimally fresh. After that it is up to you to keep it that way as carefully as you would eggs or dairy products, which means keeping meal refrigerated in kitchens without larders and with central heating.

Fortunately, the lost art of grain milling is being revived in restored mills and new mills at different points of the map across the country. Last time I counted there were about 125 such mills grinding cornmeal, along with other grains. The South still has the greatest number, as befitting our most traditionally agricultural region, but mills are everywhere. You just have to hunt out one in your region or one that is a reliable shipper. I've supplied a very brief list in "A Source List" (page 223) of those that I have used and found excellent, but there are dozens more. And you can help create a climate for them by asking the mail-order distributors who do not grind their own meals but whose products you trust where they got the meals they're selling—what kind of corn, where grown, how milled, and how stored. The more you want to know the more they'll need to know to help you. As the ads say, you *can* make a difference.

Corn can be ground in any texture from very coarse to very fine. That's why I've tried to specify the ideal grind of meal for any particular dish. A finely ground corn flour is very different from cornstarch, which is simply the starch element of a kernel industrially extracted, refined, and powdered. Cornstarch has almost no flavor because, like arrowroot, its function is to thicken without flavoring. Corn flour, on the other hand, should be ground whole-grain so that all the flavor is there. *Masa harina* is simply one type of very finely ground corn flour, but by its processing one with a distinctive flavor and distinctive behavior. This is the flour that anciently was toasted, reground, and retoasted, to use as "journeying" corn for instant food and drink while traveling.

Grits too can range from coarse to fine, depending on the miller. "Speckled" or "speckled heart" grits will show tiny black dots in the meal, which indicates that the meal is whole grain with the hardened black tip of the germ included. In preparing posole, recipes often instruct the cook to remove that tiny hardened tip so that the kernel will "blossom," or swell up full and round and even when it absorbs water under heat. Those who want their grits pure white, or without speckles, prefer the germ removed.

Through mail-order catalogs, we can buy cornmeals in many colors and forms. We can buy toasted cornmeal, which I highly recommend, both yellow and blue. We

can buy blue corn posole and blue cornmeal and blue corn *masa harina*. One Santa Fe grower is now starting to market red corn posole and red corn *masa*. We can buy parched corn grown by the Hopi of the Second Mesa in Arizona or jonnycake meal from Whitecap flint grown exclusively in Rhode Island or yellow whole-grain grits from a mill in Greenwood, Mississippi, called Yellow Dog after "Yellow Dog Blues." Cornmeals are one way to taste at home the regional flavors of America.

POLENTA, THE MUSH OF ROMANCE

In our imaginations, polenta tastes of Italy. In fact, polenta and cornmeal are two words for the same thing. The corn grown in Italy for cornmeal does not differ in kind from the corn grown in the States for meal, although where and how it is grown, and above all how it is milled, matter just as much as here. Just like our cornmeal, polenta can range from coarse to fine. And just like our meal, 99 percent of Italian cornmeal is industrially milled. Because the polenta tradition is still strong in Italy, however, market turnover is high and your chances of getting fresh packaged meal in an Italian supermarket are better than here. You can even get a slab of polenta already cooked and molded in the chilled foods section.

When you buy imported cornmeal as "polenta," you will be paying more than for any good domestic stone-ground meal, so make sure that you are getting the highest quality and that shipping time is commensurate with freshness. Don't buy polenta just for the name or you'll be throwing your money away. Remember that polenta is no more than the Italian name for both cornmeal and corn mush.

HOW TO COOK POLENTA OR MUSH

But with food as with sex, words are everything. Have you tried recently to entice someone over to a delicious dinner of mush? Try again with Polenta al Forno. That's why I call polenta the Mush of Romance. I asked a couple of young American friends recently to tell me what they most liked to eat for breakfast. Sue told me she ate "cornmeal mush with soy sauce, plum vinegar, and tahini," which suggests that her romance is with China. Her sister Eileen ate "polenta with pesto and Parmesan cheese," which tells you her heart is north of the Tiber.

As someone has said, making polenta is a quasi-mystical rite like baking bread or treading grapes. You can make polenta in the traditional copper pan called a *paiolo*, stirring it for at least half an hour to an hour with the traditional wooden spoon of

chestnut or acacia. Or you can make it in a microwave. Or you can steam it in a double boiler, as I nearly always do with any kind of mush.

For the record, the traditional way of cooking polenta is to add cornmeal to a pot of water in a slow steady stream, stirring constantly until all the liquid is absorbed and until the mush pulls away from the side of the pan. It is then turned onto a slab and cut with a taut string into portions. This seems to me a lot of work and so is the microwave version. For a microwave, you pour cornmeal into water in a microwave-safe bowl, cover and cook it on high power for anything from 10 to 30 minutes, depending on wattage and quantity. But you also have to take it out every 5 or 6 minutes and stir it and put it back.

I want to avoid all that fuss. For me the easiest and most consistent way to cook mush is to scald the meal by pouring on boiling liquid, stir well to dissolve lumps, then steam it in the top of a double boiler. The advantage of steaming is that the even heat gives the grain time to absorb the liquid evenly without the cook ever having to worry about the meal lumping. The other advantage is that it saves work.

In general, milled corn of any kind seems to absorb more liquid than milled wheat. This difference does not stem from a difference in starch content but from a difference in the protein matrix characteristic of each grain. Working with cornmeals, I learned that they could soak up liquids to an alarming degree if one were not prepared for that fact. I also found myself constantly thirsty when eating a sequence of cornmeal dishes, which suggested that corn's absorptive powers were great. Because there is so much more variety in cornmeals than in wheat flours, anyone cooking with cornmeal must be flexible in his approach.

Cooking times depend entirely on the proportion of liquid to meal and to the coarseness or fineness of the meal. Coarse cornmeals take more liquid and take longer. Some meals require no more than 20 or 30 minutes, some coarse grinds may take 1 or 2 hours. *Masa harina,* because it has been cooked in the processing, works like an instant flour that requires no "cooking" time at all. You can control the thickness of a cornmeal mush by cooking time, cooking it longer and uncovered for a final period if you want it stiffer. If it gets too thick, simply add more liquid. Cornmeal is not temperamental. It is sturdy and reliable and simply needs to be treated as a partner in your culinary explorations.

A Corn Glossary

Atole: Finely ground and toasted cornmeal stirred into a liquid, usually water or milk, with or without flavorings like chili, chocolate, sugar, and usually for a drink or dessert. In the Southwest blue corn atole is common. Pinole is an interchangeable term.

Chicos: Dried sweet corn kernels, usually used in stews. A term common in the Southwest.

Corn flour: Finely ground cornmeal of any kind. *Masa harina* is an alkali-processed corn flour.

Cornmeal: Ground kernels of any kind of corn, usually a dent, flint, or flour type. The corn can be ground to any degree of coarseness or fineness. Commercial "wet milling" removes the hull and germ of the corn kernel and fragments the kernel into its components of starch, sugar, and oil. Commercial "dry milling" removes the germ before grinding the rest of the kernel. The best meal is whole-grain meal with the germ in.

Cornstarch: Industrially processed starch extracted from the starch components of corn.

Grits: Ground cornmeal, coarse or fine, white or yellow, and the mush that is made from that meal. Originally the meal was ground from dried hominy, or whole kernels processed with alkali. The term and the mush are most popular in the South.

Hominy: Dried whole-kernel corn, yellow or white, that has been cooked in water with an alkali to remove the skins. Today hominy is found most frequently canned and packed in a light brine.

Huitlacoche: Mexican term (originally Nahuatl for "raven's shit") for the sweet corn mushroom, or fungus, that Americans call "corn smut."

Maize or maíz: Historically, the proper generic name for the grain native to the Western Hemisphere. Latin name, *Zea mays*. America's use of the word "corn" for maize comes from British English, where corn means any kind of grain.

Masa: Mexican term for the dough produced by grinding wet corn kernels processed with alkali.

Masa harina: Mexican term for this same dough, dried and pulverized into fine corn flour. Works like an "instant" flour.

Nixtamal: Mexican term (from Nahuatl) for wet whole kernels freshly processed with alkali.

Polenta: Italian term for cornmeal and for the mush or porridge made with that meal.

Posole: Mexican term for dried whole kernels processed with alkali and for the soup/stews made with those kernels.

Samp: Coarsely cracked corn.

Taxcalate: A Mexican term for an atole or pinole that is premixed with *achiote*, sugar, cinnamon, and powdered chocolate. Used for both drinks and desserts.

Appetizers & Side Dishes

Crazy for Corn

Creamed Corn in Chili Butter

Zucchini and Pumpkin Seed Succotash

Country Fried Corn with Bacon

Mashed Potatoes with Corn

Grated Corn and Potato Pancakes

Corn and Blueberry Tomatoes

Sea Vegetable and Corn Sauté

Corn Curry with Goat's Milk

Scallop Corn Salad

Ecuadorian Corn and Pineapple Salad
   (*Ensalada Cecilia*)

Classic Corn Custard

Chili-Corn Ramekin

Corn and Goat Cheese Flan

Corn Mushroom in Chèvre Sauce
   (*Huitlacoche con Queso*)

Corn "Hollandaise"

Orange Shrimp Seviche with Popcorn
   (*Cebiche de Camarones*)

Salmon-Polenta Terrine with Corn
   and Caviar Salsa

Hominy Primavera

Good Grits

Hominy and Broccoli Rabe

Chicos and Bean Cakes

West Indian Fungie

Pennsylvania Scrapple

"There's certain things," one of the hired men once observed at such a feast [of roast corn], "that ort to be et out of doors and corn's one of 'em. If you want to drizzle butter all down the sides of your mouth, the' ain't nobody settin' acrost the table to scowl. And watermelon's another."

—Della Lutes, The Country Kitchen, 1936

There are certain things that ought to be called Small Dishes, whether they're eaten in or out-of-doors, because they can be eaten at any point in a meal or in a day if you're a chronic grazer. There are fresh corn salads and light sautées, potato pancakes studded with corn, flans creamy with chèvre and corn puree, hominy with spring vegetables, grits with yogurt and cheese. There are even such unexpected but healthy innovations as a hollandaise sauce made entirely of corn. It's time to let your imaginations fly.

Creamed Corn in Chili Butter

SERVES 4

The marriage of corn and chili was made in heaven and on earth. The grain and the spice shared the same cradle millennia ago in Mesoamerica and together they ventured around the world on the same Portuguese and Spanish galleons. Among many foods, corn, chili, tomatoes, and potatoes are the Big Four that the Americas gave to the world, and these four have an affinity with each other. This recipe uses three of them, turning the classic colonial dish of fresh corn kernels stewed in butter or cream into a slightly spicier version.

This is a wonderful first course to serve in individual dishes, and because it's rich and flavorful, you can also serve it as a main dish by increasing the quantity.

   4 dried chilies, such as ancho,
       mulato, pasilla, chipotle
   8 tablespoons (1 stick) butter
   1 small onion, chopped fine
  12 cherry tomatoes, halved
   1 teaspoon dried oregano
       Salt and freshly ground
           black pepper
   1 cup half-and-half
6 to 8 ears fresh sweet corn (to make 3
           to 4 cups kernels) (see Note)

Discard the stems of the chilies. Break them open, shake out the seeds, and tear out the veins. Tear the chilies in large pieces and toast them in a heavy skillet over low heat, holding the pieces flat with a spatula as you toast (1 or 2 minutes a side). Pulverize them in a spice grinder and reserve.

Melt the butter in the skillet, add the onion, and sauté until softened, about 3 to 5 minutes. Add the tomatoes, oregano, seasonings, and the half-and-half and mix well. Stir in the pulverized chilies and let the mixture simmer 2 or 3 minutes. Add the corn kernels and simmer 2 or 3 minutes more.

Note: Throughout I've estimated that one ear of corn will produce ½ cup of raw kernels, but know that this is very approximate. Some corn ears will yield as much as 1 cup of kernels.

Zucchini and Pumpkin Seed Succotash

SERVES 4 TO 6

Succotash was a Native American dish that was readily embraced by colonists because it mixed in the pot the trio of vegetables that grew entwined as a complete food chain in Indian gardens—corn, beans, and squash. In the summer when all these were fresh instead of dried, they were particularly prized and nowhere more than in the desert mesas of the Southwest, where natives added pumpkin and sunflower seeds to make more savory their summer stew.

The mix of vegetables and textures makes this a good accompaniment for fish, chicken, or meats but clearly it works well also as a main dish or, at room temperature, as a salad.

1½ cups fresh beans (lima, cranberry, fava, flageolet)

4 to 6 ears fresh sweet corn (to make 2 to 3 cups kernels)

½ cup pumpkin seeds, toasted

½ cup chicken or vegetable stock

½ to 1 teaspoon salt

¼ teaspoon freshly ground black pepper

Pinch of cayenne

1 medium onion, chopped fine

1 clove garlic, minced

2 tablespoons butter

2 tablespoons olive oil

2 small zucchini, diced

1 poblano or Anaheim chili, roasted, seeded, and chopped (see Note)

2 plum tomatoes, seeded and diced

½ cup sunflower seeds, toasted

Parboil the beans in salted water to cover until just tender, 5 to 10 minutes, drain and set aside.

Husk the corn, cut the kernels from the cobs, and scrape the cobs to extract all the milk. Put 1 cup of the kernels and milk mixture in a blender with the pumpkin seeds, chicken stock, salt, and peppers and puree. Reserve.

Sauté the onion and garlic in the butter and oil until softened. Turn up the heat, add the zucchini, chili, and tomatoes and sauté for only 1 or 2 minutes to keep the squash crunchy.

Add the reserved corn kernels and the beans and mix well. Stir in the reserved puree and cook just until the sauce is heated. Garnish the mixture with the sunflower seeds.

Note: To roast fresh chilies, char their skins by holding them over a gas flame or by putting them under a broiler, turning them to char evenly. Remove skins and stems and cut the chilies open to remove the seeds.

Country Fried Corn with Bacon

SERVES 4 TO 6

Southern folk and Southern cookbooks were once full of recipes for fried corn. It goes with fried country ham and red-eye gravy and fried green tomatoes. Midwestern creamed corn is a gentler, not to say a genteel, version of what a Deep South country cook with a hot iron skillet full of good ham or bacon fat would consider decent fried corn. Nowadays you have to go to books like Ibbie Ledford's 1991 *Hill Country Cookin' and Memoirs* to find a dish that calls for "meat grease" and "fresh field corn," but the complementary taste of corn and bacon or ham is so fundamental that you scarcely need a recipe to guide you. This makes a fine breakfast or light supper dish, especially accompanied by eggs and broiled tomatoes.

4 slices smoked country bacon
½ small onion, chopped fine
6 to 8 ears fresh sweet corn (to make 3 to 4 cups kernels)
Salt and freshly ground black pepper

Fry the bacon until crisp, drain it on paper towels, and pour off all but 2 tablespoons of the fat. Cut the bacon into small strips or crumble it and reserve.

Add the onion to the fat in the skillet and fry it until it softens.

Husk the corn, cut the kernels from the ears, and scrape the cobs to get all the milk. Add the kernels and milk mixture to the onions in the skillet and cook for 2 or 3 minutes. Add the bacon, season as needed, and serve.

Mashed Potatoes with Corn

SERVES 4

What could be sweeter or homier or more comforting than potatoes mashed, whipped, riced, beaten—whatever word you choose—with golden nuggets of corn? The texture is creamy with a slight crunch not due to lumpy potatoes, and the flavor is subtle and addictive. To turn this into a main dish, add cooked salt cod pureed with cream and oil for a variant *brandade de morue*. It also makes good potato pancakes for frying the next day.

4 medium baking potatoes
½ cup milk
2 ears fresh sweet corn (to make
    1 cup kernels)
4 tablespoons butter
   Salt, freshly ground black pepper,
    and cayenne

Peel and quarter the potatoes.

Bring a saucepan of salted water to the boil, add the potatoes and boil them, partially covered, for 15 to 20 minutes, until the potatoes are tender.

While the potatoes are cooking, heat the milk in a small saucepan, add the raw corn kernels, butter, and seasonings, and heat until the butter melts.

When the potatoes are done, put them through a ricer or coarse strainer. Mix in the corn and milk mixture and beat until fluffy. If the potatoes are too stiff, add a little more milk.

Grated Corn and Potato Pancakes

SERVES 4

The grated potato pancake may be a staple of Jewish cuisine in its fine form of latkes, but it was also a staple of my Presbyterian childhood that followed me wherever I went. When I went heavily into corn, I found my beloved potato pancake was happy to embrace this new sibling. The grated corn lends both sweetness and texture and the starch in the corn augments the starch in the potato to help the pancake stick together without the use of eggs.

I like to eat potato pancakes for lunch, as a single main dish, but more usually they are used to accompany meats and are excellent with beef or ham.

4	ears fresh sweet corn (to make 2 cups kernels)
1	large baking potato
½	cup grated onion
1	tablespoon fresh thyme leaves
1	teaspoon salt
¼	teaspoon freshly ground black pepper
1 to 2	tablespoons vegetable oil

Husk the corn and grate the ears over a bowl to catch the grated kernels (if using frozen corn, puree the kernels in a food processor).

Peel and grate the potato over the same bowl. Mix with the kernels. If the mixture is watery, gently squeeze out any excess liquid with your hands.

Add the grated onion, thyme, and seasonings. Mix well and shape the mixture into four flat cakes.

Heat a heavy skillet over high heat, add oil to film the bottom. When the oil is hot but not smoking, add the potato cakes and flatten them with a spatula so each will form a good bottom crust. Turn the heat down to medium.

When the bottom crusts have formed (3 or 4 minutes), turn each cake to brown on the other side. Serve immediately.

Corn and Blueberry Tomatoes

SERVES 4

In the East, where the sun season is short, there is a blissful moment in August when tomatoes on the vine are as plump and juicy as corn kernels on the cob and blueberries on the bush. This is the moment when I contrive every possible excuse to put them together. If you remember that tomatoes and corn are fruits as much as they are vegetables, combining their flavors with blueberries will not seem strange. The natural sweetness of corn complements the tartness of the berries, accented by the acid of tomatoes. And besides, the colors are terrific.

Depending on your summer mood and temperature, you can skin the tomatoes, stuff them with raw kernels and berries, and bind them with a fruited vinegar and oil for a salad. If it's not too hot, I prefer to bake the tomatoes and their filling at a very low temperature to distill and blend flavors. Their flavors are excellent with pork or lamb or any barbecued meats.

4 large ripe tomatoes
1 ear fresh sweet corn (to make
     ½ cup kernels)
½ cup fresh blueberries
¼ cup olive oil
1 tablespoon blueberry vinegar
   Salt and freshly ground black
     pepper
   Fresh basil leaves for garnish

Preheat oven to 200 degrees.

Cut the tomatoes in half and gently squeeze out the seeds from their "pockets." Put the halves, cut side up, in a baking pan.

Husk the corn, cut the kernels from the cob, and mix them with the blueberries. Stuff the mixture into the emptied tomato pockets. (If you want to be fancier, keep the kernels and berries separate, and fill pockets alternately.)

Beat the oil with vinegar, salt, and pepper and pour a little of the dressing over each tomato half.

Bake for about an hour to heat the tomatoes. Garnish each half with a couple of basil leaves and serve warm or cold.

Sea Vegetable and Corn Sauté

SERVES 4

Once we called them seaweeds and now we call them sea vegetables, but the taste of the sea is there either way. For most of us it's simple ignorance that keeps us from using in any number of ways this highly nutritious, ecologically thrifty, pungent and rich-flavored vegetation. Frank Arcuri, long associated with the Natural Gourmet Cookery School in Manhattan, has taught me much about sea vegetables and suggested this corn mix. Frank favors black sea vegetables like hijiki because "the corn pops out like little jewels," but certainly you could use other kinds like alaria, dulse, or arame. In addition to Japanese imports at high prices, my local health food stores now carry at about half the cost excellent quality home-grown sea vegetation from Maine Coast Sea Vegetables in Franklin, Maine.

I like to use this as a luncheon dish or a salad, served at room temperature.

1½ ounces hijiki or other sea vegetable
¼ cup dark sesame oil
4 medium onions, sliced
⅛ to ¼ cup tamari or soy sauce
4 to 5 ears fresh sweet corn
　　　(to make 2 to 2½ cups kernels)

Wash and drain the hijiki.

Heat the oil in a sauté pan, add the onions and sauté for 2 or 3 minutes, stirring to coat them evenly with oil.

Put the hijiki on top of the onions and add water to barely cover. Bring to the simmer over medium heat, turn the heat to low, and add half the tamari. Cover tightly and simmer 20 to 30 minutes. Check occasionally and add more water if the pan is dry.

Simmer uncovered for about 10 minutes until most of the liquid has evaporated. Taste and add more tamari if wanted.

Add the corn kernels, stir well, and continue cooking another 2 to 3 minutes.

Corn Curry with Goat's Milk

SERVES 4

Because of the increasing number of Americans who have started raising goats to produce goat-milk cheese, you can now get fresh goat's milk in green markets and health food stores. I find it the most delicious of all milks. In this curry it lends to the sweetness of corn and caramelized onions an earthy tang. Corn curries using coconut milk are common to the Saurashtra region of western India, as Madhur Jaffrey tells us in *A Taste of India,* and curry of this kind can be flavored with any number of spices such as fresh ginger, cumin, chili, cilantro. I've used curry powder here to save time.

Serve this in little side dishes or, if you want it for a main dish, add some cubed chicken, or white fish such as cod or haddock, or lentils and beans.

4 ears fresh sweet corn
  (to make 2 cups kernels)
3 cups thinly sliced red Bermuda
  onions
2 tablespoons vegetable oil
1 large clove garlic, minced
1 teaspoon grated fresh ginger
1 teaspoon curry powder
  Salt and freshly ground black
  pepper
1 cup goat's milk

Husk the corn, cut kernels from the cobs, and set aside.

In a heavy skillet caramelize the onions in the oil over high heat for 8 to 10 minutes, until the onions are crisply browned.

Lower heat, stir in the garlic, ginger, and curry powder. Add the corn, salt, and pepper; mix well.

Pour in the goat's milk, let the mixture boil up once and serve hot or at room temperature.

Scallop Corn Salad

SERVES 4 AS A FIRST COURSE

I picked this up from a lifelong cooking pal, Glenna Campbell, when we were sitting over a dinner table in Guatemala after a meal so good the talk could only be of other perfect meals. One of them was this orange-spiked salad of potatoes, scallops, and corn. In small portions the salad makes a good first course, but double the portions and it's a full meal.

1 pound tiny new potatoes
2 tablespoons olive oil
2 ears fresh sweet corn
    (to make 1 cup kernels)
2 red Bermuda onions, sliced
1 pound sea scallops
½ pound mesclun or baby lettuces
    Salt

FOR THE DRESSING:

¼ cup olive oil
1 teaspoon Dijon mustard
1 tablespoon grated orange zest
1 tablespoon fresh orange juice
2 teaspoons rice wine vinegar
1 teaspoon salt
    Cayenne

Preheat oven to 450 degrees.

Dribble about a tablespoon of the olive oil on the potatoes, wrap them in a single layer in foil, and roast them for 30 to 40 minutes.

Husk the corn and cut the kernels from their cobs. Heat a heavy skillet over high heat, add the kernels and pan-grill them 2 or 3 minutes until they are slightly charred. Remove and reserve.

Add the remaining oil to the skillet and grill the red onions 6 to 8 minutes until they are slightly charred. Remove and reserve.

Pan-grill the scallops, browning them for just a minute or two on each side until they are barely cooked. Remove and reserve.

Assemble the salad by arranging a bed of mesclun on a platter. Arrange the potatoes on top (and slice them if they're larger than an inch in diameter). Salt the potatoes lightly and on top of them pile the onions, corn kernels, and scallops.

Beat together all the ingredients for the dressing, in order, and pour the dressing over the top of the salad.

Ecuadorian Corn and Pineapple Salad
(*Ensalada Cecilia*)

SERVES 4 TO 6

This is a fresh garden salad where all the vegetables should be, as Michelle Fried's cookbook *Comidas del Ecuador* puts it, "al dente." If you live in Ecuador it's easy to get purple potatoes and fresh pineapple; in the States pineapples appear more often green than ripe. Fortunately, Fried prefers a tart green pineapple for this salad, although I've also used a ripe one and liked the taste. If you think that pineapple is an exotic fruit to mix in a vegetable salad, think of avocados, papayas, and oranges, all of which we use happily in vegetable salads. Because pineapple is acidic, this salad has a very fresh taste, and because it includes both corn and potatoes, it easily makes a one-dish meal for lunch or supper.

Boston or bibb lettuce leaves
1 pound purple potatoes, precooked
    and sliced
4 ears fresh sweet corn
    (to make 2 cups kernels)
1 cup grated peeled carrots
1 cup snowpeas, cut in thirds
½ cup diced celery
1 cup cubed fresh pineapple
2 hard-cooked eggs, chopped
2 tablespoons chopped fresh cilantro

FOR THE DRESSING:

⅓ cup olive oil
2 tablespoons lime or lemon juice
2 tablespoons pineapple juice
1 teaspoon pure ground chili,
    New Mexican type
Salt and freshly ground black
    pepper

Assemble the salad ingredients on lettuce leaves in a colorful mixture, sprinkling the chopped eggs and cilantro leaves on top.

Beat together the ingredients for the dressing, taste for seasoning, and pour over the whole.

Classic Corn Custard

SERVES 4

One colonial classic of "green" corn, as colonists called the first tender ears of the season, was a baked custard "pudding" of eggs, cream, and butter, highly sweetened but served as a side dish to an entree. The eighteenth-century British pudding tradition, which incorporated everything from carrots and potatoes to apples and whortleberries, simply added corn to its imperial reach. Colonists in the American South added to the corn local ingredients like shrimp, okra, and green peppers. Northerners stuck to a pure corn custard like the one Maria Parloa in her *New Cook Book* of 1881 called New Bedford Corn Pudding, where she adds ¼ cup of sugar (an unusually small amount) to 3 cups of milk and 12 ears of corn. She warns the housewife, however, that if the corn is old, it may take a quart of milk; "if very young and milky," a pint may be enough. The corn Miss Parloa was using was not nearly as sweet as our current sweet corn, so I've omitted sugar entirely.

The traditional method of making corn custard was to score the kernels, cutting down the center of each row, then scraping them with the back of the knife to get all the milk without any of the "skins." Today it's much easier to puree the kernels in a food processor, then rub them through a strainer to get the milk (4 cups kernels will produce about 2 cups milk). The result is worth the effort because the texture of the custard is meltingly creamy and delicate. I can't resist flavoring it with a little fresh tarragon because the herb illuminates eggs and cream.

The custard best complements white meats like veal or chicken, or seafood like scallops or shrimp. You can prepare it ahead and serve it warm or at room temperature. It's easier to cook in a single dish, but easier to serve in individual soufflé dishes or ramekins (see recipe opposite for another kind of corn custard in ramekins).

8	**ears fresh sweet corn**
	(to make 4 cups kernels)
3	**eggs**
1½	**cups half-and-half**
3	**tablespoons butter, melted**
1	**teaspoon salt**
½	**teaspoon white pepper**
2	**tablespoons chopped fresh tarragon**

Preheat the oven to 350 degrees and heat water to pour into a baking pan large enough to hold a 1½-quart baking dish (or six 8-ounce soufflé dishes).

Cut the kernels from the cobs and puree them in a food processor. Scoop the puree into a strainer placed over a large bowl and

rub the liquid through with a large spoon. Discard the skins in the strainer.

Beat the eggs and add them to the corn milk. Stir in the half-and-half. Add the melted butter, seasonings, and tarragon and mix well.

Butter the baking dish and pour in the corn mixture. Set the dish in a larger pan, place it in the oven, and pour in enough hot water to come halfway up the sides of the dish. Bake about 35 to 45 minutes, until the top is browned at the edges and a tester inserted in the center comes out clean.

Chili-Corn Ramekin

SERVES 4

A good healthy way to lighten the classic corn pudding is to increase the proportion of corn puree so that no eggs, butter, or cream are needed for thickening. I puree only half the kernels and leave the rest whole to create a texture less like an egg custard and more like creamed corn. I like a little chili pepper for flavor and to give the dish a pale sunset color.

You can use any kind of individual baking dishes or a single dish if you prefer. Adjust cooking time according to the depth of the dish. A large dish may take 35 to 45 minutes to bake. Because of the chili, this dish goes particularly well with game like quail, duck, or pheasant.

8 ears fresh sweet corn
   (to make 4 cups kernels)
1 cup whole milk
1 tablespoon pure ground red chili,
   New Mexican type
   Salt and freshly ground black
     pepper

Preheat oven to 350 degrees and heat water for a baking pan large enough to hold four ramekins 6 inches in diameter. Butter the ramekins.

Put half the kernels in a blender with the milk and seasonings. Puree as smooth as possible.

Mix the puree with the remaining kernels and ladle the mixture into the ramekins. Set the ramekins into a baking pan and place in the oven. Add enough hot water to the baking pan to cover the bottom by ½ inch. Bake for 25 to 30 minutes until the mixture is soft but not runny.

Corn and Goat Cheese Flan

SERVES 4 TO 6 AS A SIDE DISH

Corn and cheese pair in every possible way, but for an extraordinarily creamy texture, try pairing a fresh corn puree with fresh goat's cheese. Because of the eggs, this is a kind of custard, but one that is thickened only by corn and cheese and therefore easier to bake; you don't need a pan of hot water to protect it against direct heat.

If I want to use this flan as a side dish with chicken or fish, I bake it in timbales or custard cups. If I want to use it as a main dish for a light supper, with roasted vegetables or a salad, I bake it in individual soufflé dishes.

8 ears fresh sweet corn
       (to make 4 cups kernels)
½ pound fresh goat's cheese (chèvre)
6 eggs
   Salt and freshly ground
       black pepper
   Cayenne or pure ground chili,
       New Mexican type (optional)

Preheat the oven to 325 degrees and butter six timbales or small soufflé dishes.

Put the kernels into a food processor and puree. Crumble the cheese over the top and puree again.

Add the eggs one at a time through the lid, with the machine running. Add the seasonings and puree again.

Scoop the mixture into the baking dish or dishes and bake 20 to 30 minutes, or until the center is set.

Corn Mushroom in Chèvre Sauce
(*Huitlacoche con Queso*)

SERVES 4 TO 6 AS A FIRST COURSE

This is a very dramatic black-and-white dish where the color contrast is primary, but so is the tangy taste of chèvre that echoes the rich earthy taste of corn mushrooms. Here I've made a simple mushroom sauté and placed it on a pool of smooth creamy chèvre thickened with corn puree. If you want to be *muy elegante,* puree the mushroom mixture, add an egg and cream, and bake it in timbales to unmold as little black circles on the white chèvre. The dish makes a spectacular first course.

1 small finely chopped onion
1 clove garlic, minced
¼ cup olive oil
½ pound chopped fresh corn
   mushrooms (drain well, if frozen)
1 poblano or 2 jalapeño chilies,
    roasted (see Note, page 5)
    seeded, and diced
2 tablespoons chopped fresh
    epazote or oregano
   Salt and freshly ground black
   pepper

FOR THE SAUCE:

4 ears fresh sweet corn
    (to make 2 cups)
¼ pound fresh goat's cheese (chèvre)
   Salt and freshly ground black
    pepper
   Grated peel of 1 lemon

Preheat the oven to 250 degrees.

Sauté the onion and garlic in the oil for 3 to 5 minutes until softened. Add the mushrooms, chilies, herb, and seasonings and sauté over medium heat for 5 or 10 minutes until all the liquid has evaporated. Keep warm in the preheated oven.

To make the sauce, husk the corn, cut the kernels from the cobs, and put them in a food processor. Scoop the puree into a strainer over a bowl, and press the liquid through with a large spoon. Discard the skins in the strainer.

Put the corn milk into a saucepan with the chèvre and seasonings, and stir constantly over low heat until the cheese melts and the milk thickens slightly, about 4 to 6 minutes. Stir in the lemon peel.

Put a pool of sauce on each plate and a mound of corn mushroom in the middle of the sauce.

Orange Shrimp Seviche with Popcorn
(Cebiche de Camarones)

SERVES 4 TO 6

In Ecuador, seviche is served with a garnish of popped corn. The corn absorbs some of that powerful hot and tart juice that has "cooked" the fish or shellfish and makes the distinctiveness of the dish. Here the shrimp are parboiled briefly in a milk "bouillon" before the citrus marinade. Latin America's bitter oranges are not available here, so I've used a combination of fresh orange juice with lemon.

Serve with a copious bowl of popcorn for each diner to sprinkle over the top of his shrimp. Good for a first course or a light meal.

2   pounds raw large shrimp
    in the shell
2   cups milk
1   carrot, chopped
1   stalk celery, chopped
2   scallions, chopped
1½ cups fresh orange juice
¼   cup fresh lemon juice
3   tablespoons tomato concentrate
    or paste
3   tablespoons olive oil
2   tablespoons chopped fresh cilantro
    Salsa, Tabasco, or other hot sauce
1   red onion, sliced thin
2   cups popped corn for garnish

Rinse the shrimp and drain them.

In a saucepan, bring the milk to the simmer. Add the carrot, celery, scallions, and then the shrimp. Return the liquid to the simmer, cover the pan, remove from the heat, and let sit 3 minutes. Drain the mixture over a bowl to save the liquid. Cool the shrimp and discard the vegetables. Return the milk to the saucepan.

Put the orange and lemon juice, tomato concentrate, oil, cilantro, and salsa in a blender and puree until smooth.

Bring the milk again to the simmer and blanch the onion slices in the milk for 1 minute. Drain the onion well and use the milk for sauce or soup at another time.

Shell and devein the shrimp and discard the shells (or boil the shells in the milk and intensify the shrimp flavor for that later sauce or soup). Mix the shrimp meat with the onions, pour on the orange marinade. Cover with plastic wrap and refrigerate for at least 2 hours.

Serve with the bowl of popcorn.

Corn "Hollandaise"

MAKES 1½ CUPS

For those who love the creamy texture of hollandaise but eschew butter and eggs, I've adapted a "hollandaise" of pureed corn from one devised by Frank Arcuri, using corn "milk." Many recipes in nineteenth-century American cookbooks advise the housewife to "milk" the cob by scoring the top of the kernels with a sharp knife, then scraping down the kernels with the back of the knife to get "milk" without any of the kernels' skins.

Naturally corn milk has a sweetness to it that hollandaise, with its butter, eggs, and lemon juice, does not. I like to balance the sweetness of corn milk not only with a little lemon but also with a white wine vinegar, especially an herbed vinegar like tarragon. This sauce is good on broiled fish, chicken, vegetable soufflés, fresh asparagus, or artichokes, where an undertone of sweetness is interesting rather than off-putting.

6 ears fresh sweet corn
    (to make 3 cups kernels)
½ teaspoon salt
¼ teaspoon white pepper
    Small pinch of nutmeg
2 teaspoons fresh lemon juice,
1 teaspoon white wine vinegar

Put the corn kernels in a blender with the seasonings, lemon juice, and vinegar and liquefy until the mixture is as smooth as possible. Pour the mixture through a strainer into a heavy-bottomed saucepan. Don't press the mixture too vigorously because you want to eliminate any corn skins. Taste for seasoning and adjust.

Place the saucepan over very low heat and stir constantly for 2 or 3 minutes until it thickens slightly.

Salmon-Polenta Terrine with Corn and Caviar Salsa

SERVES 8

You can make this beautiful polenta loaf in two ways, one by layering cornmeal with the salmon mixture, the other by mixing the cornmeal and salmon together in the loaf. I've done the latter here because sometimes I like to pan-grill the slices and serve them with a salsa that mixes sweet corn with salmon caviar. If you use a finely ground cornmeal, you don't have to cook it first; simply scald it with the boiling liquid to dissolve it, then let it bake with the salmon, where it forms a binder for the fish. If you have leftover salmon, start with that instead of raw fish. Slow-baking the cornmeal and fish together produces a full-bodied flavor to match the color of this salmon-pink loaf.

This makes a decorative terrine for a cold buffet, but the flavor is best if you grill or sauté slices as you would slices of polenta.

FOR THE LOAF:

1 cup freshly ground cornmeal,
    fine grind (or corn flour or *masa*)
1 teaspoon salt
1½ cups strong fish stock, boiling
1 tablespoon butter or olive oil
6 green onions, chopped
½ teaspoon ground cumin seeds
1 tablespoon chipotle chili in adobo
    sauce or pure ground chili,
    New Mexican type
2 cups chopped raw salmon
½ cup sour cream
    Juice of ½ lemon
    Salt, freshly ground black pepper,
    and cayenne

FOR THE SALSA:

4 ears fresh sweet corn
    (to make 2 cups kernels)
1 cup salmon caviar
¼ cup minced Vidalia or other sweet
    onion
    Freshly ground black pepper

Preheat the oven to 325 degrees and oil a 9 × 4-inch loaf pan.

Put the cornmeal with the salt in a saucepan and scald it with the boiling fish stock, stirring until smooth. Let sit.

Heat the butter in a heavy skillet and sauté the green onions, cumin, and chili for 2 or 3 minutes. Remove from the heat and stir in the salmon, sour cream, lemon, and seasonings.

Scrape the mixture into a food processor and pulse until the mixture is pureed. Taste for seasoning and adjust. Because mush absorbs flavor, the salmon should be highly seasoned.

Stir the salmon mixture into the cornmeal and mix thoroughly. Then scrape the mixture into the loaf pan and smooth the top. Cover tightly with foil.

Bake the loaf for 2 hours until a cake tester shows the cornmeal is no longer wet in the interior. Cool, then chill.

To make the salsa, combine the raw kernels with the other ingredients.

Unmold the loaf and cut it into ½-inch slices. Broil, grill, or sauté until crusty on both sides. Top the slices with the corn-caviar salsa.

Hominy Primavera

SERVES 4 TO 6 AS A FIRST COURSE OR SIDE DISH

I know this is a hybrid title, but I also know that the name "pasta primavera" instantly conveys an appetizing image of pasta studded with all the reds and greens and yellows of garden vegetables. White hominy provides an even better backdrop to set off the vivid colors of spring's first fruits.

Served hot, it's a striking accompaniment to any kind of meat or bird. Served at room temperature, it makes a good salad to serve as a first course; if served cold, use olive oil instead of butter to help thicken the hominy liquid.

4 cups undrained canned hominy
1 sweet red pepper, seeded and diced
1 sweet green pepper, seeded and diced
6 stalks asparagus, chopped
8 snow peas, cut in half
2 ears fresh sweet corn, kernels cut off (to make 1 cup kernels)
2 slices thin prosciutto, shredded
4 tablespoons butter

Salt and freshly ground black pepper
¼ cup chopped Italian parsley

In a saucepan, mix the hominy and its liquid with the sweet peppers and bring to the simmer.

Add the remaining vegetables, in order, and finally the prosciutto and butter. Add salt and black pepper if wanted. Sprinkle with parsley and serve.

Good Grits

SERVES 6 TO 8

There are just hundreds of ways to cook grits good, but I find that when I've got a lot of family or company and need a tasty fodder to fill them up, I turn to grits in some combination like the one below. Sometimes I use sour cream, sometimes yogurt, sometimes plain milk, depending on my personal conscience relative to the diet-consciousness of my company. What cheese I add varies according to what I've got or can easily get. I don't know what it is about grits, but I've never had anyone not clean his plate.

Use instead of potatoes, rice, pasta, or other grain to accompany a big ham or turkey or fried chicken or grilled shrimp or sausages. You can make this ahead and reheat it easily in an oven or double boiler.

1　cup freshly ground white or yellow grits, coarse grind

3　cups chicken stock, boiling

1　poblano chili, roasted (see Note, page 5), seeded, and chopped

1　cup yogurt or sour cream

1　cup grated Monterey Jack cheese or other melting cheese such as sharp Cheddar, Fontina, Gruyère, etc.

¼　cup crumbled Gorgonzola cheese or other strong cheese such as Stilton, feta, etc.

3 or 4　tablespoons butter (optional)

Put the grits in the top of a double boiler and add the boiling stock. Stir until smooth. Place the top over the bottom of the boiler, filled with an inch or two of boiling water. If the grits are very coarse, you will want to steam them for at least twice as long as medium cornmeal. Put the lid on top and steam for 1½ to 3 hours, refilling the bottom of the boiler as needed.

After an hour stir in the chili pepper and yogurt, stir well and steam on. When the grits are thick and taste very creamy, add the cheese. If you want a richer grits, add butter.

Hominy and Broccoli Rabe

SERVES 4 AS A SIDE DISH

Just as thick pasta like penne goes well with that earthy bitter green broccoli rabe, so does the corn taste of hominy. This is a good way to use canned hominy because start to finish you can make this dish in under 15 minutes.

The dish goes well with grilled or barbecued meats, or fish. If you have leftover meat or chicken, dice it and add it to the hominy if you want a substantial main dish. But even without additions, the dish can stand alone as pasta does, bringing here a bright contrast of colors white and green and of tastes bland and bitter. This is also a fine dish cold as a salad, in which case omit the butter and at the last moment squeeze on a little fresh lemon juice.

1 bunch broccoli rabe
  (about 1 pound)
¼ cup olive oil
1 small onion, minced
2 to 3 cloves garlic, minced
1 16-ounce can hominy
  (not quite 2 cups), drained
  Salt and freshly ground black
  pepper
3 tablespoons butter

Chop the rabe in 1- to 2-inch pieces, keeping the stem pieces separate.

In a heavy skillet or wok, heat the oil over medium heat and add the stems. Cover and sauté 3 or 4 minutes. Turn up the heat, add the onion and garlic, and sauté until they are slightly browned. Add the chopped leaves and "blossoms" of the rabe and sauté quickly (2 or 3 minutes) until they turn bright green.

Add the drained hominy and toss it with the rabe. Taste for seasoning and adjust. Mix in the butter and serve.

Chicos and Bean Cakes

SERVES 4

Anciently, and that means from the time corn and bean seeds were planted together, corn and beans were also grown, harvested, dried, and cooked together. In summer fresh corn and beans were mashed together. In winter, corn flour (or *masa*) was mixed with bean flour and shaped into flat cakes or breads or dumplings. Or dried whole kernels and dried beans were reconstituted with water and cooked in similar ways.

Here I've pureed the beans and added a little *masa harina* to help shape the puree into cakes. I've also added whole dried sweet corn kernels (called "chicos" in the Southwest) for contrasting texture, but the corn could be pureed as well.

These cakes are very tasty cooked on a griddle over wood smoke and in any case they are excellent with wild game or farm-raised duck or squab. Also good for breakfast with fried eggs or for lunch with a green salad.

1 cup dried sweet corn kernels (chicos)

1 cup cooked (and well-seasoned) pinto or Anasazi beans

2 tablespoons *masa harina* or corn flour

½ teaspoon salt
Freshly ground black pepper

1 teaspoon pure ground chili, New Mexican type

1 tablespoon lard or vegetable oil

Soak the kernels in hot water to cover by at least a good inch at the top and let sit for 30 minutes to an hour until the kernels are soft. Drain them and reserve the kernels.

Puree the cooked beans with the *masa,* salt, pepper, and chili in a food processor until the mixture forms a soft dough.

Scrape the puree into the reserved corn kernels and mix well. Shape the mixture into small flat cakes about ⅓ inch thick and 2 inches round.

Heat the lard in a heavy cast-iron skillet to film the bottom, and when it is hot but not smoking add the cakes, frying a few at a time over high heat to pan-grill them, browning them on each side.

West Indian Fungie

SERVES 4 TO 6

I loved this dish at first bite, when I had it at a beachside restaurant in St. John's in the Virgin Islands. There "fungie" is not a dialect word for mushrooms, truffles, or molds, but means cornmeal mush with something added, usually okra. When I hear the word "fungie," suddenly the air turns wet and warm, a sea breeze stirs, palm leaves rustle, and children braid their hair with multicolored Day-Glo shoelaces.

Many Caribbean islanders trace the origin of the dish to Africa, where indigenous okra grew with corn brought to Africa by post-Columbian explorers. Okra, and the dish, came to Caribbean shores with the slave trade. In parts of Africa the same dish is called "frou-frou," in Barbados, "cou-cou." If we called it "polenta with okra," suddenly the silhouette of an Italian hilltown would profile against the sun and the air would be hot and dry. Names are as integral to a dish as any of its ingredients, so let's stick to "fungie" and think of the Caribbean, where cornmeal is whipped with butter and okra, then lightly shaped with the hands into a round green-flecked ball.

This is a good dish to eat with a very hot pepper sauce, along with grilled fish or meats. If you have any fungie left over, smooth the mush into a loaf pan and chill thoroughly. Then slice and broil or pan-grill it as you would polenta slices.

6	cups water
2 to 3	cups chopped fresh young okra
2	cups freshly ground yellow cornmeal, medium grind
2	teaspoons salt
6	tablespoons butter
½	small onion, minced

Bring the water to the boil in a heavy saucepan. Add the okra and cook until tender (about 5 minutes).

Meanwhile, prepare a double boiler with a couple inches of boiling water in the bottom. Put the cornmeal and salt in the top of the boiler and add the cooked okra and its liquid gradually, stirring until the meal is smooth. Place the top of the boiler over the bottom over medium heat.

In a separate pan melt the butter and sauté the onion for 5 to 8 minutes until very soft. Add the mixture to the cornmeal mush. Cover the pan with a lid and steam for 20 to 30 minutes until the mixture is very thick.

Serve as is or pour it into a buttered bowl, let it stand for 10 minutes, and invert it onto a platter.

Pennsylvania Scrapple

SERVES 6 TO 8

I grew up on scrapple in Southern California, far from the German immigrants who brought their cooking traditions to Pennsylvania, but not so far from the farming traditions that spelled out how to utilize every part of a slaughtered hog. Food historian William Woys Weaver has suggested that the name "scrapple" comes from a Lower Rhineland word, *schrapel*, meaning a scraping or scrap, such scraps as hog's innards—heart, liver, and lungs. The flavor of meat and fat melts through the cornmeal, which is molded into a loaf, chilled, then fried in slices, which should be soft inside and very crisp outside.

Originally buckwheat was a necessary part of the dish. If you have *polenta taragna* (a buckwheat and cornmeal mix), use that. If not, mix cornmeal and buckwheat half and half.

Scrapple and fried eggs are so good and so substantial that they make a meal for lunch or supper as well as breakfast.

1 pound pork scraps, plus pork bones
    or split pig's feet
2 teaspoons salt
1 large onion, halved
1 cup *polenta taragna* or ½ cup
    cornmeal plus ½ cup buckwheat
Freshly ground black pepper
Flour for dredging

Cover the meat and bones with cold water, add the salt and onion, and bring the water to the boil over low heat. Reduce heat, skim off the foam, cover the pot, and simmer over very low heat for about an hour, or until the meat is very tender.

Remove the meat and bones from the broth, discard the bones, and reserve the broth. Chop the meat rather fine, by hand or in a food processor, and set aside.

Reserve some of the fat for frying scrapple slices later.

Prepare a double boiler with an inch or two of boiling water in the bottom. Put the meal and buckwheat in the top pan of the boiler and gradually pour in 4 cups of the hot broth, stirring until smooth. Cover the top with a lid and steam the meal for 35 to 50 minutes. Add the pork meat and pepper and taste the mixture for salt.

Pack the mixture into an oiled 9 × 4 × 2½-inch loaf pan and chill until firm. To serve, unmold the loaf and cut it into ½-inch slices with a serrated knife. Heat the reserved pork fat (or use bacon fat) in a heavy skillet, just enough to film the bottom of the pan. Dredge each scrapple slice with flour and fry until the slices are very brown and crisp on each side.

Soups, Chowders
& Stews

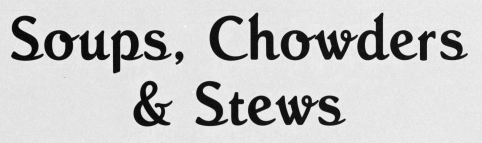

Vegetable Corn Stock

Corn and Fennel Broth

Sorrel and Sweet Corn Cream

Tart Berry and Sweet Corn Soup

Roasted Gazpacho

Creamy Chili Corn Soup

Corn Mushroom Cream
  (*Caldo de Huitlacoche*)

Sweet Corn and Scallop Soup

Green Meadow Farm Corn
  and Clam Chowder

Chinese Crab and Corn Velvet

Ecuadorian Vegetable Soup
  (*Locro de Zambo*)

Lobster Chili Chowder

Yucatán Lime and Chicken Soup
  (*Sopa de Lima*)

Golden Pepper and Toasted Popcorn Soup

Buttermilk Corn Bread Soup

Savoy Garlic and Spinach Soup
  (*Soupe aux Friquerons*)

Galician Salt Cod and Corn Soup
  (*Sopa de Maíz*)

Squatter's Corn Soup

Green Posole Soup-Stew
  (*Posole Verde*)

Mole Posole

They take the corn before it is ripe, boil it in a little water, allow it to dry
in the sun and preserve it for future use. Corn prepared this way is then boiled with meat, etc.
when it, as well as the soup in which it is boiled, is good to eat.

—*Peter Kalm,* Travels in North America *(English version, 1770)*

In soups, chowders, and stews, corn boasts a multiple life, for it appears fresh and dried, whole-kerneled, pureed, ground. Sometimes it's merely a garnish, sometimes a major ingredient, sometimes a thickener, sometimes a simple vegetable stock. Since with corn nothing goes to waste, corncobs, green husks, and leaves can flavor a broth even without the kernels. Corn's flexibility in both flavor and texture makes it an ideal ingredient for the soup pot and consequently we find it combined with local grains, vegetables, meats, and fish in the world's multiple cuisines.

Today we often use soups, and especially hearty ones like chowders and soup-stews, as a main course. But I've included such hearty main-course dishes in this section because there is a logical progression from a corn-flavored broth to a corn-thickened soup to a fish and corn chowder, to a meat and vegetable corn stew. Each culture creates its own uses: dried skinned corn in Mexican Green Posole Soup-Stew is a stomach filler; pureed sweet corn in Chinese Crab and Corn Velvet soup is a delicate background for crab.

Vegetable Corn Stock

MAKES ABOUT 6 CUPS

One way to exploit the thriftiness of the corn plant is to utilize the corncobs themselves, after you have stripped them of kernels, in a vegetable soup stock. You can increase the corn flavor by adding a few of the inner green layers of husk. You can add whatever vegetables you have on hand in your refrigerator, but the usual combination of carrot, onion, and celery makes for a solid base. You can use this instead of a chicken, fish, or meat stock and take it any place you wish.

Brendan Walsh, of the North Street Grill in Long Island, uses his corncob stock to create a remarkable grilled corn and shrimp soup, thickened with pureed fresh corn or *masa harina* and seasoned with red and green chili creams. For a simple vegetarian soup, try the Corn and Fennel Broth opposite.

½ cup chopped carrots
½ cup chopped celery
½ cup chopped leeks
¼ cup chopped onion
1 clove garlic
½ teaspoon dried thyme
1 bay leaf
A few sprigs of parsley or fresh cilantro
2 whole cloves
Salt and freshly ground black pepper
2 tablespoons vegetable oil
6 corncobs, plus a dozen green husks
2 quarts water

In a large soup pot, gently sauté the vegetables, herbs, and seasonings in the oil until they have softened. Add the corncobs, husks, and the water.

Cover and bring to the boil. Simmer for an hour or more. Remove the cobs and husks with a slotted spoon. Strain the liquid and press the vegetables in the strainer to extract all the juice.

If you want an intense vegetable flavor, return the liquid to the pan and reduce by a third.

Corn and Fennel Broth

SERVES 4 TO 6

Fennel has such a strong anise flavor that it can easily overwhelm an unwary companion, but where it is the star, as here, it is given a good backup with the vegetable stock of the previous recipe. Since you've got the flavor of leeks and onion already in the stock, the only other ingredients I'd add to the fennel, if you wanted a heartier soup than a broth, would be some diced potatoes and cubed white fish such as flounder or cod. But as a simple broth it is a wonderful restorative hot or chilled and makes an elegantly understated beginning to a rich meal.

6 cups Vegetable Corn Stock
   (opposite)
1 large fennel bulb, quartered
   Salt and freshly ground black
   pepper
2 tablespoons chopped fennel tops

In a large saucepan heat the vegetable stock.

In a food processor, slice the fennel quarters paper thin and add the slices to the stock. Season to taste. As soon as the liquid reaches the boiling point, remove and serve. Garnish the top of each soup bowl with some green fennel tops.

Sorrel and Sweet Corn Cream

SERVES 4

As some French gastronome said, the difference between a soup and a potage is a dozen eggs and a gallon of cream. No wonder I long ago fell in love with that pale green faintly tart cream soup that the French call Potage Germiny, based on an alarming quantity of egg yolks and heavy cream to smooth the sharp acidity of sorrel leaves. With or without the heavy stuff that evokes the lipoprotein jitters, I still find sorrel soup a blessed thing summer or winter, hot or cold.

Adding corn to sorrel balances sour with sweet and for those who have banished cream as wicked, the corn puree will thicken the broth as a cream substitute. For myself, I still want that supererogative creaminess that only a cow can give.

4　ears fresh sweet corn
　　　(to make 2 cups kernels)
3　cups chicken broth
¼　cup chopped onion
1　tablespoon olive oil
2　cups packed fresh sorrel leaves
¾　cup heavy cream (optional)
　　Chopped chives or other herbs
　　　for garnish

Preheat the oven to 400 degrees.

Roast the corn in the husk for 5 minutes. Remove husks and cut the kernels from the cob; scrape the milk from the cob into the kernels and put the mixture into a blender with the chicken broth. Puree until smooth.

In a skillet, sauté the onion in the oil for 4 or 5 minutes until the onion softens. Add the sorrel leaves and toss them in the oil for about 5 minutes until they have wilted. Add the mixture to the blender and puree again. Strain the mixture to make it perfectly smooth. Add cream if you wish.

To serve the soup hot, bring it quickly to the simmer. To serve it cold, chill it thoroughly in the refrigerator. Hot or cold, garnish with a few chopped chives or other fresh herbs.

Note: This also makes a lovely sauce for cold poached fish like salmon or sea bass. Just halve the amount of broth and enrich with a little sour cream, yogurt, or heavy cream.

Tart Berry and Sweet Corn Soup

SERVES 4

On the hottest of August days I long for the coldest of tart soups to appear like magic without labor or heat. My summer dream soup is also a magical color—dark red or deep purple. So naturally I dream of fruit soups, but most of them are too sweet and too thick for my taste. When I found I had both summer strawberries and white sweet corn on hand, I began to juggle the tartness of the berries with the sweetness of the corn. I bound them together with a soft fruity red wine like Zinfandel, low in acid and high in berry flavor, and deepened that berry taste with cinnamon and clove. The corn sweetens and thickens the mixture, but since the sweetness of corn, berry, and wine will vary, let your own taste guide you in adding honey for sweetness or a good balsamic vinegar for tartness. The color is a remarkable mauve, which you can accent with floating slices of strawberry.

2 pints strawberries
3 ears fresh white sweet corn
   (to make 1½ cups kernels)
   1-inch piece of cinnamon stick
3 whole cloves
   3 or 4 black peppercorns
3 cups fruity red wine
¼ cup fresh orange juice
1 to 2 teaspoons balsamic vinegar
   Honey if needed

Stem the strawberries. Reserve a few berries for garnish and puree the rest in a blender.

Husk the corn and cut the kernels from the ears, scraping the cobs to capture the milk. Add the corn to the blender and puree again.

Grind the cinnamon, cloves, and pepper in a spice grinder and add to the puree. Add the wine, orange juice, and half the vinegar, and puree until very smooth. Taste for sweetness and add the rest of the vinegar or add honey if needed.

Roasted Gazpacho

SERVES 4

I'm an impossible gazpacho snob. Among the myriad ways this soup is now served at home and abroad, I only want to eat it, like the Sinatra song, my way. I want the taste of all the vegetables intensified by roasting and I want the mixture thick and chunky, not with bread crumbs but with corn. I want the top garnished with black olives to contrast with yellow corn kernels and diced green cucumbers. And gazpacho my way is served very very cold.

2 large cloves garlic, skin on
4 large ripe tomatoes
2 sweet red onions
1 sweet red pepper
3 tablespoons olive oil
4 ears fresh sweet corn
    (to make 2 cups kernels)
1 Kirby cucumber, diced
2 tablespoons good sherry vinegar
¼ cup fresh basil leaves or fresh
    cilantro
  Salt and freshly ground black
    pepper
8 black Mediterranean-cured olives,
    pitted and diced

Preheat the oven to 450 degrees.

Put the vegetables in a roasting pan, dribble 2 tablespoons of the oil over them, and roast them in the oven for 25 to 30 minutes. Remove the garlic after 10 minutes (so it won't scorch) and when it is cool enough to handle, squeeze the pulp from the skins. Put all the vegetables in a blender.

Turn the oven setting to broil. Remove husks from the corn, put the ears in the roasting pan, and brush them with the remaining oil. Broil the corn for 2 or 3 minutes, turning the ears once. Remove, and when the ears are cool enough to handle, cut off the kernels.

Add 1 cup of the kernels to the blender, reserving the rest for garnish. Add half the cucumber and reserve the rest.

Add the vinegar, basil, and seasonings and puree the mixture until it is well mixed but still chunky. (If the mixture is too thick, dilute with a little tomato juice.)

Chill thoroughly. If you're in a hurry, you can put the mixture in the freezer for half an hour. When ready to serve, garnish the top of each bowl with corn kernels, cucumber, and black olives.

Creamy Chili Corn Soup

SERVES 4 TO 6

The young American chefs who have created Southwestern cuisine, whether it's served up in Washington, D.C., Long Island, or Seattle, all have versions of a creamy corn soup flavored with corn's natural complement, chili. The pairing is ancient in Mexico, cradle of both the corn and chili plants, and part of our pleasure in Southwestern cuisine is in discovering the rich culinary heritage of native America.

The combination appears in its essence in Ana de Benitez's *Cocina prehispánica* (1976) as "Sopa de Elote," meaning soup made from young (or "green") corn, garnished with post-Hispanic cheese. I prefer the rich velvet texture achieved by using post-Hispanic cream, since cream tempers chili's heat. I've used three chilies here, the fresh poblano for mild heat and green color, the dried chipotle for a smoky undertaste, and the dried almost-black ancho for color contrast.

1 chipotle chili

1 ancho chili

4 ears sweet corn (to make 2 cups kernels)

½ cup onion, chopped

2 cloves garlic, chopped

2 tablespoons olive oil

4 cups hot chicken broth

1 poblano chili, roasted (see Note, page 5), seeded, and chopped

⅓ cup crème fraîche or sour cream

1 cup heavy cream

Salt

Remove the stems and seeds of the chipotle and ancho chilies. Toast the chilies for a minute in a heavy cast-iron skillet (or for 4 to 5 minutes in a low oven), being careful not to scorch them. Remove and cover them with hot water. Let them sit for 10 minutes to soften. Drain, put the chipotle chili in a large saucepan and reserve the ancho.

Husk the corn and cut the kernels from the cobs. Heat the skillet very hot; dry roast the kernels 2 or 3 minutes to scorch them. Put them in a large saucepan.

Add the oil to the skillet, then brown the onions and garlic quickly and add them to the saucepan.

(continued)

Add the chicken broth and poblano chili to the saucepan and simmer the mixture 10 to 15 minutes.

Put the ancho chili in a blender with the crème fraîche. Puree until smooth, pour the cream into a bowl, and set aside for garnish. If the chili cream is too thick to drizzle from the end of a spoon, add a little chicken stock.

Pour the soup liquid into the blender and puree as smoothly as possible. Strain the liquid and return it to the saucepan.

Add the heavy cream, bring to the simmer, and cook until the soup thickens. Pour into soup bowls and swirl the ancho cream over the top of each bowl. The soup must be fairly thick in relation to the ancho cream to keep it from sinking.

Corn Mushroom Cream
(*Caldo de Huitlacoche*)

SERVES 4 TO 6

How to describe this unguently smooth sophisticated cream of corn mushroom soup in its art deco beige-greige color? Think of an aphrodisiac potion brewed by a benign witch to turn the object of your affection into a devoted slave and you're getting close. That's purple prose to describe a black-brown soup, but believe me when I say that this is one of the simplest and most gratifying ways to use the exotic corn mushroom.

This is best served hot and is a good prelude to a pork or beef roast or barbecued meats or an all-corn dinner.

2 tablespoons olive oil
1 small onion, chopped
2 cloves garlic, minced
2 poblano chilies, roasted, seeded, and chopped
½ cup chopped huitlacoche
2 teaspoons chopped fresh epazote
4 cups chicken broth
1 cup heavy cream
   Salt and freshly ground black pepper

Sauté in the oil the onion, garlic, and chili for 6 to 8 minutes until they have softened. Add the huitlacoche and epazote and simmer 5 minutes.

Scrape the vegetables into a blender, add 2 or 3 cups of the broth, and puree until very smooth. Add the remaining broth, the cream, and the seasonings. Pour into a saucepan, heat to the simmer, and serve hot.

Sweet Corn and Scallop Soup

SERVES 4

This is a most delicate white and light soup, floating tiny bay scallops in a puree of corn and leeks. For garnishing seafood soups, I like to use different kinds of dried seaweeds for their briny intensity, but if sea vegetables are not to your taste, a sprinkling of parsley, cilantro, chives, or a slice of lemon will do just fine.

The soup is excellent hot or cold, but if you want to serve it chilled, use olive oil instead of butter for sautéing the leeks and corn.

3 ears fresh white sweet corn
  (to make 1½ cups kernels)
½ cup finely chopped leeks
2 tablespoons butter
3 cups fish stock
¼ cup dry white wine
¼ cup half-and-half
  Salt and white pepper
1½ cups bay scallops (about ¾ pound)
  Lemon juice (optional)
  Wakame or other dried seaweed
    for garnish

Husk the corn, cut the kernels from the cobs over a bowl, and scrape the cobs with a knife to capture the milk.

Put the corn and the leeks into a large saucepan with the butter and sauté gently for 3 or 4 minutes over medium heat.

Scrape the mixture into a blender, add the fish stock, and puree until smooth.

Return the mixture to the pan, add the wine, the half-and-half, and the seasonings; bring the liquid to the boil.

Add the scallops and remove the pan immediately from the heat to avoid overcooking them. Taste again and add a few drops of lemon juice if wanted.

Garnish with a little wakame, or other dried seaweed such as nori, cut into tiny strips.

Green Meadow Farm Corn and Clam Chowder

SERVES 4 AS A FIRST COURSE

What I like about American cooking is the constant dialogue between other cultures and our own. I like our ability to absorb skilled chefs from Europe or Asia who apply their craft to American ingredients and continually regenerate our ever-changing, always hybrid cuisine. Philippe Chin, of Chanterelles in Philadelphia, is just such an American chef, who combines Asia, Europe, and America in himself. Chinese by heritage, but born and trained in Paris, he now presides with his American wife over a French-named restaurant within spitting distance of Independence Hall. That's the American way.

Just as American is Chin's chowder, with its summer combination of white sweet corn fresh from Pennsylvania's Green Meadow Farm, combined with littleneck clams in the shell, graced by a classically French herbed broth. This is light enough to serve as a first course.

2 tablespoons butter

1 tablespoon minced shallots

1 tablespoon minced onion

8 ounces (1 bottle) clam juice

4 ears fresh white sweet corn
 (to make 2 cups kernels)

1 bay leaf

1 tablespoon minced fresh parsley

1 sprig fresh thyme or a large pinch
 of dried thyme

2 dozen littleneck clams,
 thoroughly cleaned

Salt and freshly ground black
 pepper

In a large wide-bottomed saucepan, heat the butter. Add the shallots and onion and sauté for 2 or 3 minutes until softened. Add the clam juice, the corn kernels, bay leaf, parsley, and thyme and simmer about 5 minutes.

Add the clams in their shells, cover the pan with a lid, and simmer for 5 to 10 minutes, or until the clams have opened. Discard the bay leaf and any unopened clams. Taste for seasoning, and serve immediately in large soup bowls.

Chinese Crab and Corn Velvet

SERVES 4

The traditional crab or chicken "velvets" in Chinese-American cuisine usually contain canned cream-style corn to achieve the creamy texture of the soups they call *gunns* and we call bisques. Although field corn is an important part of the Chinese landscape, sweet corn is all but unknown. I like to imagine Chinese immigrants more than a century ago applying their treasured ingredients and spices to this new discovery, sweet corn in a can, and eventually marrying its velvety texture with raw ginger and soy. The marriage of Canton to Kansas by means of a can appeals to my imagination, but fresh corn appeals to my palate. Today when fresh sweet corn is so readily available, you can revivify this classic with a fresh corn puree that also eliminates the need for any cornstarch thickening.

This is a good first course for a Chinese- or Asian-based meal.

4	ears fresh sweet corn
	(to make 2 cups kernels)
2	tablespoons peanut oil
4	scallions, chopped fine
1	teaspoon minced fresh ginger
½	pound (or 2 cups) flaked crabmeat
1	tablespoon dry sherry or rice wine
3	cups fish stock
1	tablespoon light soy sauce
2	teaspoons sesame oil
1	egg, beaten
	White pepper

Husk the corn, cut the kernels from the cobs, and puree all but ½ cup of them in a blender. Reserve the whole kernels.

Heat the peanut oil in a wok, add the scallions and ginger, and stir for a few seconds. Add the crabmeat and sherry and stir again.

Add the corn puree and kernels to the wok with the fish stock and soy sauce, and bring to the simmer.

Stir until the soup begins to thicken, then add the sesame oil. Remove from the heat and dribble the egg over the top, stirring it with a fork to shred it. Season with pepper and serve.

Ecuadorian Vegetable Soup
(*Locro de Zambo*)

SERVES 4 TO 6

All through South America you will come upon different forms of the vegetable soup-stew called *locro*. This one is typical of the pastoral highlands of Ecuador, with green and yellow squashes (*zambo* and *zapallo*), potatoes, fresh corn (*choclos*), milk, and white salty cheese. I first savored *locro* in the candle-lit dining room of a seventeenth-century gem, Hacienda Cusin, near Ottavala, where if you visit the weavers you will find the rafters loaded with drying ears of corn as multicolored as the vegetable-dyed yarns on the looms below.

Essentially this is a vegetable soup thickened with cheese, served hot as a first course.

3   cups chicken stock
1   cup milk
1   medium potato, peeled and diced
1   medium yellow squash, diced fine
1   medium zucchini or other green
        squash, diced fine
½   red onion, diced fine
2   tablespoons olive oil
1   teaspoon *achiote* oil or paprika,
        for coloring (see Note, page 103)
2   ears fresh sweet corn
        (to make 1 cup kernels)
     White pepper
1   cup crumbled feta cheese

In a large saucepan, bring the stock and milk to the simmer. Add the potatoes, cover, and cook until the potatoes are tender. Puree in a blender and return the puree to the saucepan. Thin if needed with water or more stock.

In a skillet, sauté quickly the two squashes and onion in the olive oil and the *achiote* oil or paprika. Add to the puree.

Husk the corn and cut the kernels from the cobs, scraping them to capture the milk. Add the corn to the puree and taste for seasoning. Because of the feta cheese, you probably won't want salt.

Bring the soup to the simmer and cook, covered, for 5 minutes. Ladle into soup bowls and sprinkle with the cheese, which each diner can stir into the soup.

Lobster Chili Chowder

SERVES 4 TO 6

Lobster and corn are a classic pairing, from the native chowders of New England to posoles translated from New Mexico to New York. Wherever lobster is shipped, corn is a happy companion. I've had Jasper White's classical chowder in his eponymous restaurant in Boston and David Walzog's unusual lobster posole in Arizona 206 in Manhattan. Inspired by Walzog's exotically dark chili broth, I've started with a broth of charred tomatoes, flavored with chilies and some of the seasonings typical of a Mediterranean bouillabaisse, to bathe a mixture of lobster, clams, shrimp, and fresh corn.

This is a hefty dish to make a meal with, accompanied by good crusty bread and salad.

3 dried chilies (preferably a mixture
    of ancho, pasilla, chipotle)
2 ripe tomatoes, skin on
1 small onion, skin on
5 cups fish broth
    A piece of fresh or dried orange rind
    A few strands of saffron
1 teaspoon fennel seeds
    (or some chopped fennel leaves)
½ teaspoon dried thyme
½ pound raw shrimp in the shell
1 1½- to 2-pound lobster, cooked
8 Manila clams
3 ears fresh sweet corn
    (to make 1½ cups kernels)

Heat the oven to 250 degrees.

Remove the stems and seeds of the chilies and toast them for 4 or 5 minutes in the oven. Cover the chilies with hot water and let sit 10 minutes. Drain and put them in a blender.

Switch the oven setting to Broil and char the tomatoes and the onion until their skins are blackened. Discard the outer layers of onion skin and add the onion to the blender. Add the tomatoes, skin and all, to the blender. Add the fish broth and seasonings and puree. Pour the mixture into a large saucepan and bring it to the simmer.

Add the shrimp to the liquid and remove them with a slotted spoon after 1 minute. Remove the shells from the shrimp, reserve the meat, and add the shells to the broth.

Betty Fussell

Remove the lobster meat from its shell and reserve the meat. Add the shell, and any tomalley, coral, or interior juices, to the saucepan. Simmer, covered, for 15 to 20 minutes to extract flavor from the shells. Strain the liquid into another pan.

Husk the corn and cut the kernels from the cobs.

Bring the shellfish liquid to the simmer, add the corn and clams, cover and cook 2 or 3 minutes. Add the shrimp and the lobster meat, cover again, and cook until the clams open. Discard any unopened clams.

Serve immediately so as not to overcook the shellfish.

Yucatán Lime and Chicken Soup
(*Sopa de Lima*)

SERVES 4 TO 6

In Mexico there are sweet limes and sour limes and sweet-and-sour limes, but in the Yucatán they use the sour one, which is very like Florida's key lime, for this refreshing soup. The combination of chicken, tart citrus juice, and corn echoes the Greek lemon-chicken-rice soup called *avgolemono*. Often the Yucatán soup is served with leftover tortillas, cut into strips and fried until crisp. The soup is also a good way to use leftover chicken or turkey meat, although the flavors are wonderful even without the chicken.

Because of the meat, this is a good soup to make a meal of, served with some quesadillas or burritos.

2   tablespoons vegetable oil
4   corn tortillas, cut in strips
2   ripe tomatoes, seeded and chopped
1   small onion, chopped
1   clove garlic, minced
1   serrano or jalapeño chili
1   teaspoon dried oregano
½   teaspoon dried epazote (optional)
6   cups chicken broth
2   cups shredded cooked chicken
      breasts
3   ears fresh sweet corn
      (to make 1½ cups kernels)
⅓   cup chopped fresh cilantro
      Freshly ground black pepper
¼   cup fresh lime juice

Heat the oil in a heavy skillet and fry the tortilla strips until very crisp. Set them aside for garnish.

In the same skillet, sauté the tomatoes, onions, garlic, chili, oregano, and epazote about 5 minutes until the tomatoes have released their juice. Add 1 cup of the broth and ladle into a large saucepan.

Add the remaining broth, bring to the simmer, and add the chicken, corn, cilantro, and black pepper. Let the liquid simmer for 3 or 4 minutes. Add the lime juice to the broth and serve. Garnish the top of the soup bowls with the tortillas.

Golden Pepper and Toasted Popcorn Soup

SERVES 4

Like many other cooks, I like the challenge of making soup with whatever happens to be in my cupboard and fridge. But what would you do if the ingredients you found were 2 sweet yellow peppers, 1 jalapeño pepper, ½ jar of leftover clam juice, a still fresh carton of milk, and—a small bowl of leftover popcorn? You could use the popcorn as croutons, of course, but why not as a base? Popped corn, toasted and finely ground, provides an excellent medium for thickening and flavoring soups without the caloric penalties of butter or cream. Other vegetables and other liquids would no doubt blend with the nutty flavor of popcorn, but this soup was so simple and satisfying that I offer it as is.

This is a very light beautifully colored soup that can be served hot or cold, before any kind of main dish.

1 cup popped popcorn
2 sweet yellow peppers
1 jalapeño chili
2 cups vegetable, clam,
   or chicken broth
1 cup milk
   Salt and freshly ground black
      pepper only if you miss them

Preheat the oven to 200 degrees. In the oven, toast the popcorn in a pan for about 15 minutes. Put the corn in a blender and pulverize finely. Remove and set aside.

Roast the 3 peppers over a flame or under a broiler to char the skins. Remove the skins, stems, and seeds. Chop the peppers in pieces and put them in the blender.

Add the broth and milk to the blender and liquefy. Add the ground popcorn and liquefy again. Taste for seasoning and add salt and black pepper if desired.

Strain the liquid into a saucepan, bring it to the simmer, and simmer 3 to 5 minutes to blend flavors. Even if you're going to serve it cold, the soup will benefit from this brief simmering.

Buttermilk Corn Bread Soup

SERVES 6

O ne of the favorite ways of using leftover corn bread in the Deep South was to crumble it into hot or cold milk, cream, or buttermilk. The creamy texture of buttermilk countered by its slight tartness has made it one of my personal favorite foods and beverages since childhood, and it goes particularly well with the sweetness of corn. Crumbling corn bread into a buttermilk-based soup is just too down-home to get into cookbooks, but the dish is part of Dan Fearing's classy repertoire at the Mansion on Turtle Creek in Dallas. I've added a few collard greens here for color, flavor, and tradition, since collards, corn bread, and buttermilk are a kind of Deep South trinity. If you're starting from scratch, you could use any of the corn breads in the Breads section or make the small skillet bread below.

This is really a one-dish meal with a perfect balance of grain, protein, vitamins, and minerals.

FOR THE CORN BREAD:

- 1 teaspoon bacon fat or vegetable oil
- 1 cup freshly ground cornmeal, medium grind
- ½ teaspoon baking powder
- ½ teaspoon salt
- ¼ teaspoon baking soda
- 2 tablespoons butter, melted
- ½ cup buttermilk
- 1 egg

FOR THE SOUP:

- 4 cups crumbled corn bread
- 5 cups buttermilk
- 1 to 2 cups regular milk
- ½ small onion, chopped fine
- 1 cup finely shredded cooked collards or other greens

- ½ small hot red or green chili pepper, minced
- 1½ teaspoons bacon or ham fat or vegetable oil
- Salt and freshly ground black pepper

Preheat the oven to 450 degrees.

To make the bread, put the fat or oil in a 9-inch heavy cast-iron skillet (or baking dish) and place in the preheated oven.

Mix the dry ingredients. Beat the butter, buttermilk, and egg together and stir them into the dry mixture.

Scoop the batter into the hot skillet and bake for 10 to 15 minutes until browned.

For the soup, puree the bread and buttermilk together in two batches in a

food processor. Puree as smooth as possible. Pour the mixture into a saucepan and bring to the simmer. Remove from the stove and cover with a lid to keep it hot. (When ready to serve, you may need to add some regular milk to thin it, for the mixture will thicken as it stands.)

In a skillet sauté the onion, cooked collards, and chili in the fat for 4 to 5 minutes until well mixed.

Reheat the soup if needed, season with salt and pepper, ladle it into individual soup bowls, and garnish with the collard mixture.

Savoy Garlic and Spinach Soup
(*Soupe aux Friquerons*)

SERVES 4 TO 6

Both Mexico and Spain traditionally use cornmeal for thickening soups, but so too does the Savoy region of France. Through Madeleine Kamman, in *Savoie* (New York: Atheneum, 1989), we have learned that the Savoyards prefer this cornmeal-thickened soup lumpy rather than smooth. Since my memories of the Depression are too strong to allow me to cherish lumps in either mashed potatoes or mush, I disobey instructions and smooth out the lumps. The result is as soothing as childhood memory but as satisfyingly adult as garlic and cheese.

This is the kind of soup to serve for a simple Sunday supper among friends.

6 cups chicken broth
¾ cup freshly ground cornmeal, fine grind
Salt and freshly ground black pepper
4 cloves garlic, chopped fine
2 cups chopped spinach leaves
1 cup milk or half-and-half
¼ teaspoon freshly grated nutmeg
1 cup grated Gruyère, Tomme, or similar cheese

Bring the chicken stock to the boil and pour it gradually into the meal, stirring until smooth. Add salt and pepper, if needed, and cook the meal over medium heat for 15 to 20 minutes, until it starts to thicken. Add the garlic and mix. When the mush is thick as polenta, add the spinach.

Thin as desired with milk or half-and-half, sprinkle with nutmeg, and serve with a separate bowl of grated cheese.

Galician Salt Cod and Corn Soup
(*Sopa de Maíz*)

SERVES 4 TO 6

The hefty country cooking of Spain's Galicia has incorporated maize into its regional dishes ever since Columbus returned from his first voyage with a handful of New World seeds. Since the Spanish had already combined dried and salted cod with every possible vegetable and grain, this new grain must have provided a welcome new combination.

Definitely this cornmeal-thickened soup is a complete meal, incorporating grain, protein, and vegetable, especially good on a cold winter's night. The soup keeps well and even improves in reheating, though you may need to thin it with water or more stock.

1	pound boneless salt cod, soaked 24 hours in cold water and drained
1	cup freshly ground yellow cornmeal, medium grind
5	cups boiling fish stock
2	bay leaves
¼	cup olive oil
2	large onions, chopped medium fine
4 to 5	cloves garlic, chopped fine
½	teaspoon freshly grated nutmeg Freshly ground black pepper and cayenne
½	cup chopped fresh parsley
½	cup chopped fresh cilantro

Put the soaked cod in a saucepan, cover it with cold water, and bring to the simmer. Simmer very slowly until the fish flakes (about 15 minutes). Drain and set aside.

Put the cornmeal in the saucepan and gradually pour on the boiling fish stock, stirring until smooth. Add the bay leaves and bring to the simmer. Cover and cook over low heat 30 to 40 minutes, stirring occasionally, until the meal is cooked.

Heat the olive oil in a skillet. Sauté the onions for 10 to 15 minutes, then add the garlic and continue to sauté until browned. Season with the nutmeg and peppers.

Add the onions and garlic to the cornmeal, along with the salt cod. Discard the bay leaves. Thin the mixture as needed with additional stock, milk, or water.

Ladle into bowls and sprinkle with the fresh herbs.

Squatter's Corn Soup

SERVES 6

This should really be called Hunter's Corn Soup because it is made with "plenty of *fresh-killed,* fat, juicy venison," according to Miss Eliza Leslie in her *New Receipts for Cooking* of 1854. This is a soup backwoodsmen learned from the Indians with whom they squatted a couple of centuries earlier and it is a soup you can still eat today on Indian reservations where hospitality outlives change.

Miss Leslie's recipe insists on fresh venison to accompany "well-boiled green corn," which suggests hunting seasons were not as curtailed then as now. Today this is apt to be a midwinter soup of frozen venison and dried corn, but it's a good way to use the bony cuts of venison nobody else wants, and it's a wonderful way to use the dried fruits, berries, and vegetables that our hunting ancestors would have put into a winter soup or stew along with meats, fresh or dried. If venison is hard to come by, by all means use other game or beef.

Because of the unusual combination of flavors and because it is easy to make ahead, this soup-stew would make a good centerpiece for a large dinner party.

3 pounds venison with bone (shoulder, neck, shank)
¼ cup olive oil
2 cloves garlic, chopped
2 onions, chopped
6 cups beef stock
1 cup dried sweet corn kernels (chicos)
1 cup dried fruits, such as blueberries, cherries, cranberries, apples
¼ cup chopped dried tomatoes
2 teaspoons pure ground chili, New Mexican type
Salt and freshly ground black pepper

In a heavy skillet, brown the meat in the oil, then put the pieces in a stew pot.

Brown the garlic and onions for 8 to 10 minutes and add to the pot. Cover with the stock, bring to the boil, and simmer, covered, for 1½ hours. Strain the meat and reserve the stock. As soon as the meat is cool enough to handle, shred the meat and discard the bones.

Return the meat to the stock and add the dried corn, fruits, and tomatoes. Add the seasonings and bring to the simmer. Simmer for another hour or until everything is fork tender.

Green Posole Soup-Stew
(Posole Verde)

SERVES 6

There are as many kinds of posole, meaning a hearty corn soup-stew, as there are cooks to make them, but the word causes confusion. In Mexico and our own Southwest, posole names both the stew and the kind of processed corn on which it is based. The corn consists of dried whole kernels, of the same field varieties that are ground into meal, which have been boiled in lime water to remove their skins. The kernels are then dried to preserve them. Outside the Southwest, we call this corn "hominy" and we preserve the kernels in water in a can so that they are ready to eat without further boiling.

Of all the posoles I've tried, I like best this one called "green" for its sauce of pumpkin seeds, tomatillos, and green chilies. Green posole is a specialty, I learn from the Baylesses' *Authentic Mexican,* of the region of Guerrero, where Thursday is Green Posole Day. Pork and chicken are the traditional meats for most posoles because this is a dish for a festival and the pot should be brimming over with the rich fragrance of pork broth swelling the white earthy kernels of corn. Traditionally the garnishes should be plentiful: diced onion, diced avocado, sliced radishes, the crisp pork rinds called *chicharrones,* and crisp-fried slivers of tortillas.

Although posoles take both time and effort, the results are splendid and the flavor improves with any reheated leftovers. This dish is so filling that all you need are tortillas to scoop it up with and a little fresh salad on the side.

2 pounds pork with bone (neck, meaty spareribs, etc.)	1 teaspoon dried oregano
8 cups chicken broth	½ teaspoon dried epazote
4 chicken thighs	½ teaspoon fennel seeds
1 cup pumpkin seeds	1 tablespoon vegetable oil
1 poblano chili, roasted (see Note, p. 5), seeded, and chopped	5 tomatillos, husked and parboiled 5 minutes
1 small onion, chopped	Salt
2 cloves garlic	4 cups drained canned hominy (or precooked posole)

Put the pork in a large saucepan and cover with the broth. Bring to the simmer, skim, cover the pan, and simmer very slowly 1½ hours. Add the chicken thighs, again bring to the simmer, and cook another 45 minutes. Strain the liquid through a sieve, reserving the broth. When the meat is cool enough to handle, remove it from the bones and shred it.

In a heavy skillet over moderate heat, toast the pumpkin seeds lightly and put them in a blender. Add the chili to the blender.

In the same skillet, sauté the onion, garlic, and spices in the oil 4 or 5 minutes until softened and add to the blender with the tomatillos. Add a cup or more of the meat broth and puree. Add the puree to the remaining broth. Taste for seasoning before salting.

Add the hominy to the broth. Add the shredded meat and bring to the simmer. Taste again for seasoning. Simmer gently about 15 minutes to blend flavors, then serve in soup bowls. You don't really need garnishes, but if you have them, use them.

Mole Posole

SERVES 6 TO 8

Just as a Frenchman will judge a chef by the quality of his sauces, so a Mexican will judge one by the quality of his *moles*, meaning those thick, rich spicy sauces once ground with a pestle and mortar, a *molcajete*, and now happily pureed in a blender. While the town of Puebla south of Mexico City is regarded as the mother of these sauces and gives its name to *mole poblano* (meaning Puebla sauce, not poblano chili sauce), every region boasts its own combination of spices, aromatics, chilies, seeds, and nuts.

In Mexico you can buy beautiful *moles* in jars or cans so that you don't have to start each time from scratch, just as in the States we don't have to start with raw tomatoes each time we want to use ketchup. I happened to have a jar of *mole* on hand one night when I hungered for a posole, and since I also had on hand a can of hominy, I simply combined the two into a quick vegetarian soup-stew. If you have to start from scratch with either posole or *mole*, it will take you longer to prepare because *mole* demands so many ingredients, but the taste is worth every minute. I always make *mole* in sufficient quantity to put some in a jar and refrigerate for next time.

The *mole* here is a relatively simple one that can be used with tortillas, chicken, duck, or even as a sauce for fried eggs. With posole, it makes a very rich and filling soup-stew.

FOR THE *MOLE*:

- ⅓ cup unskinned almonds
- ¼ cup pumpkin seeds
- 2 tablespoons sesame seeds
- 6 dried chilies (preferably 3 ancho, 2 mulato, 1 pasilla), stems and seeds removed
- 2 whole cloves
- ½ inch piece of cinnamon stick
- 6 black peppercorns
- ¼ teaspoon aniseed
- 2 cloves garlic, skins on
- 1 small onion, chopped coarsely
- 2 tablespoons lard or vegetable oil
- 2 ripe tomatoes, chopped coarsely
- ½ cup raisins
- 1 cup chicken broth (or more as needed)

FOR THE POSOLE:

- 3 tablespoons vegetable oil
- 4 cloves garlic, minced
- 2 small onions, minced
- 2 cups chopped blanched green beans
- 2 ripe tomatoes, seeded and chopped
- 4 cups cooked posole or undrained hominy
- 1½ cups *mole*
- 2 to 3 cups hot chicken broth (optional)
- Salt and freshly ground black pepper

To prepare the *mole,* toast the almonds, pumpkin seeds, and sesame seeds in a heavy skillet, stirring to keep them from burning. Put them into a blender.

In the same skillet, toast the chilies and spices for a minute or two. Put the spices in a blender and soak the chilies in warm water to cover. When they are soft, drain and add them to the blender for pureeing, but save the water in case you need more liquid.

Over high heat char the garlic for 3 to 4 minutes until the skins are spotted. Remove pulp from skins and add pulp to blender.

Char the chopped onion and add to the blender.

Add the lard to the skillet and sauté the tomato over high heat. Add to the blender. Add the raisins and chicken broth and puree as smooth as possible. Makes about 3 cups sauce.

To prepare the soup-stew, heat the oil in the skillet and sauté the garlic and onions for 2 or 3 minutes until softened. Add the beans, tomato, and posole (if using hominy, add the liquid in the can). Stir in the *mole*. Thin with chili liquid or chicken broth if you want more of a soup than a stew. Taste for seasoning before adding any salt or pepper.

Main Dishes

Angel-Hair with Avocado Corn Cream

West African Shrimp Curry

Corn Flour Pasta with Summer Vegetables

Michael Roberts's Corn "Risotto"

Corn-Mushroom Torte
   (*Budín de Huitlacoche*)

Skillet-Grilled Lobster and Corn

Cod, Leeks, and Corn

Blue Corn Crusted Bluefish

Sole Smoked in Silks and Husks

Oyster Skillet Roast with Low Country Grits

Shrimp-Corn Quiche in a Corn Crust

Chicken in Yogurt and Lemon Corn Cream

Blue Corn Fried-Chicken Salad

Brazilian Couscous
   (*Cuscuz de Galinha*)

Latin American Boiled Dinner
   (*Sancocho*)

Rabbit with Red Masa

Polenta with Portobellos

Scallops and Polenta with Corn Mushrooms
   (*Huitlacoche*)

Quail with Truffled Polenta
   (*Quaglie e Polenta Tartufata*)

Savoyard Polenta Pilaf
   (*Polenta en Pilaf*)

Moldavian Cheese Pie

When the cracked corn was mixed with minced meat and boiled again . . . it was called **pahofa.**
When mixed with grape juice and syrup the dish was called **walusha.** *When cracked and*
parched and mixed with sugar and ground hickory or walnuts to make a thick dough, it was
bahar. *And when cooked corn was beaten into a dough and mixed with cooked beans, then*
wrapped in corn shucks and boiled, it was **abunaha.**

—*John R. Swanton,* Source Material for the Social and Ceremonial Life
of the Choctaw Indians, *1931*

Aglance at the ceremonial dishes of the Choctaw Indians indicates how hard it is to slot corn, even today, into menu categories. What's bread and what's dessert, what's a main dish and what's fringe, depend largely on the eater. Since a hefty serving of Polenta with Portobellos is as satisfying as meat and potatoes, I've included it among the Main Dishes, although you might well want to serve it as a side dish with meat or game. However a dish is used, my main concern throughout has been to select dishes where corn is not simply a garnish but an essential part of the dish.

Once again, there's a world of corn to choose from. Sometimes corn on the cob, cut in chunks, enlivens an Ecuadorian beef stew. Sometimes a fresh corn puree smooths an African coconut curry. Sometimes blue cornmeal crusts a fish or a chicken. In a Brazilian dish, cornmeal is treated like couscous and steamed with vegetables and fruits. In a French dish, cornmeal is treated as a rice pilaf and sautéed with onions and dried pears. In a California dish, fresh corn kernels become a kind of "risotto." And in the midst of all this globe-trotting, there are plenty of helpings of down-home grits.

Angel-Hair with Avocado Corn Cream

SERVES 4

The avocado is another of the New World's gifts to the Old, cradled in Mexico along with corn. Like fresh corn, avocado is a natural thickener for a sauce, and when you put the two together, you get a heavenly golden-green cream that is beyond compare. I've used tomatillos in this sauce for tartness, to balance the rich oil of avocado and the sweetness of corn. If you can't get tomatillos, use a little more lemon juice or add some lime juice. Because the sauce is delicate, I use it with capelli d'angelo (angel-hair, or capellini), in itself a delicate pasta that drinks up a lot of sauce.

A sliced tomato salad makes a good color contrast to the green and you might end with fresh blueberries. That would keep the whole meal as simple as this sauce.

2 to 3 cups chicken stock, boiling
2 ears fresh sweet corn
   (to make 1 cup kernels)
1 ripe avocado
2 tablespoons chopped garlic chives
1 teaspoon lemon juice
4 tomatillos, parboiled
1 jalapeño chili, seeded and chopped
1 tablespoon olive oil
   Salt and freshly ground black
      pepper to taste
1 pound angel-hair pasta,
   cooked *al dente*
½ cup freshly grated Parmesan cheese

Put all the ingredients except the pasta and cheese in a blender, beginning with 2 cups of chicken stock and adding more stock as needed. Taste for seasoning and adjust. Pour the sauce into a pan and bring to the simmer, stirring frequently. Pour the sauce over the cooked pasta, toss and serve with a bowl of the Parmesan cheese passed separately.

West African Shrimp Curry

SERVES 4

It was Portuguese sailors who first brought corn from the Americas to Africa 400 years ago, and Portuguese slavers who shortly after brought peanuts. While both corn and peanuts fed the miserable slave trade that followed, they also married the destinies of continents East and West in more fruitful ways. From Cameroon comes a wedding of fresh corn with local shrimp in a curried sauce of peanuts and coconut milk. Cameroon, which provides West Africa with some of its best shrimp and prawns, gave the Portuguese their name for prawns, *camarões*.

This curried peanut sauce is excellent with chicken as well as fish. It's also good for jazzing up leftover meats and vegetables. Most health-food stores carry unsweetened coconut meat (grated and dried), and many supermarkets now carry cans of unsweetened coconut milk, which saves time and trouble.

3 cups unsweetened coconut milk

1 pound medium shrimp, in the shell

1 tablespoon sesame seeds

1 teaspoon cumin seeds

½ teaspoon cardamom seeds

2 tablespoons vegetable oil

½ cup finely chopped onions

2 cloves garlic, minced

2 serrano or other fresh chili peppers, roasted (see Note, page 5), seeded, and chopped

1 teaspoon salt

2 tablespoons grated fresh gingeroot

½ cup roasted peanuts

4 ears fresh sweet corn (to make 2 cups kernels)

½ cup shredded unsweetened coconut meat

4 cups boiled white rice

Bring the milk to the simmer in a saucepan, and add the shrimp. Cover the pan with a lid, remove from the heat, and set aside.

In a heavy skillet, toast the sesame, cumin, and cardamom seeds for 2 or 3 minutes, then put them in a blender.

Add the oil to the skillet and over medium high heat sauté the onions and garlic until they begin to brown, about 5 minutes. Add the onions, garlic, chili peppers, salt, ginger, peanuts, and corn kernels to the blender.

Strain the coconut milk from the shrimp into the blender and puree to make

a thick crunchy sauce. If the mixture is too thick, thin with a little water. Pour the sauce into the skillet and bring to a simmer over low heat.

Shell and devein the shrimp and add them, with the shredded coconut, to the sauce. Cook until the shrimp are just heated through.

Pour the shrimp mixture over the hot rice and serve.

Corn Flour Pasta with Summer Vegetables

SERVES 4 TO 6

If I had my druthers, I would never again make pasta at home because I am lazy. But this is a delicate egg pasta that I can't buy in a store because it is made with *masa harina*. Instead of using a pasta machine, you simply roll the dough very thin with a rolling pin and then cut it in fairly wide strips.

I once tasted an extraordinary dish of this pasta at the hands of Brendan Walsh, in which he combined smoked duck, chilies, and asparagus with a richly fruited *mole*. You might use as a sauce for this pasta the *mole* on page 52 (see Mole Posole), or you might make a quick and easy sauce from whatever fresh vegetables are in your garden or green market.

FOR THE PASTA:

    2⅔ cups all-purpose flour
    1½ cups *masa harina*
    4 eggs
    1 tablespoon olive oil

FOR THE SAUCE:

    4 ears fresh sweet corn
      (to make 2 cups kernels)
    1 cup fresh beans (fava, limas,
      chopped green beans), parboiled

    1 sweet red pepper, diced
    3 green onions, chopped
    ½ cup sugar snap peas, cut in thirds
    ¼ cup chopped Italian parsley
    Salt and freshly ground black
      pepper
    1 tablespoon olive oil
    ¼ cup chicken stock
    ½ cup heavy cream
    ⅛ pound Parmesan cheese, in one piece

To make the pasta, combine wheat and corn flours in a food processor and pulse to mix.

Beat the eggs with the olive oil and add to the processor. Pulse a few times to mix the ingredients, then pulse in longer intervals (2 or 3 seconds each pulse) until the dough forms a ball (no more than 1 minute). Turn it onto a cutting board and knead with the palm of your hand until smooth and elastic.

Divide the dough in quarters and roll out each portion evenly ⅛ inch thick. Let the pasta dry for 5 to 10 minutes, then cut with a sharp knife into strips about ½ inch wide.

Bring a large kettle of salted water to boil while preparing the vegetables for the sauce.

In a large bowl toss all the vegetables together with the parsley, seasonings, and olive oil. In a wok or large sauté pan, heat the stock and cream together and bring to the simmer. Add the vegetables, mix well, and cook for 2 or 3 minutes.

Add the pasta to the boiling water in the kettle and cook over high heat for 2 or 3 minutes, until just tender. Drain well and toss the pasta gently with the sauce. Shave slices of Parmesan cheese over the top.

Michael Roberts's Corn "Risotto"

SERVES 4

When Michael Roberts was chef at Trumps restaurant in Los Angeles, this dish typ-ified his imaginative improvisations on classical themes. Treating corn kernels as if they were rice may at first seem perverse, but Roberts said that the texture of fresh corn in cream reminded him of a risotto he had eaten in Cremona. It's the creaminess that makes the connection. Since we build our personal food chains by just such associations, corn's ability to vary its taste and texture makes corn a central building block.

The dish is wonderfully rich in all the things I love, like corn, butter, cream, cheese, mushrooms. Roberts calls also for okra but I've used peas here, for color and sweetness.

8 tablespoons (1 stick) unsalted
   butter
6 ears fresh sweet corn
   (to make 3 cups kernels)
2 tablespoons minced scallions
   or shallots
1 cup chicken broth
1 cup heavy cream
½ cup freshly grated Parmesan cheese
12 porcini or shiitake mushroom caps,
   sliced
½ cup fresh peas
½ teaspoon salt
   Freshly ground black pepper

Preheat the oven to 200 degrees.

Melt half the butter in a pan, add the corn and scallions and cook 1 minute. Add half the broth, turn heat high, and reduce the liquid quickly until mixture thickens. Add the cream and reduce again until thick (5 to 7 minutes). Remove from heat and stir in the cheese.

Scoop the mixture into a food proces-sor and pulse to chop the corn without pureeing it smooth. Put the mixture in an ovenproof serving bowl and keep it warm in a low oven.

Heat the remaining butter in a skillet over high heat and brown the mushrooms. Lower heat, add the peas and the remaining stock, and reduce the liquid for 3 to 5 min-utes until it thickens. Add the seasonings. Fold the mixture into the corn and serve.

Corn-Mushroom Torte
(*Budín de Huitlacoche*)

SERVES 8 TO 12

Those familiar with Mexico City know that layered tortes, or *budíns,* are one of its grand traditions, whether the layering is separated by cornmeal mush, corn tortillas, or corn crepes. Corn mushrooms, or huitlacoche, make a traditional savory filling between layers, as wild mushrooms might. I first tasted this beautiful torte when Josefina Howard astonished us with an all-huitlacoche dinner at the James Beard House in Manhattan.

There are many versions of this torte and in this one I've layered sautéed huitlacoche with grated cheese, then cloaked the whole in a creamy green poblano sauce. If you use tortillas that are a standard 5½-inch round, you can make four stacks in a large baking pan (12 × 9½ × 1½ inches). The dish is filling and needs no more than a mango and papaya salad to complete the meal.

4 to 6 tablespoons olive oil

2 medium onions, chopped fine

2 cloves garlic, minced

3 tomatoes, peeled, seeded, and chopped (to make 2 cups pulp)

2 jalapeño chilies, roasted (see Note, page 5), seeded, and chopped

2 cups chopped huitlacoche (drained if frozen)

1 tablespoon dried epazote

1 teaspoon dried thyme

1 teaspoon salt

½ teaspoon freshly ground black pepper

16 corn tortillas, about 5½ inches around

¾ pound manchego cheese, grated (to make 2½ cups)

FOR THE SAUCE:

4 poblano chilies, roasted (see Note, page 5), seeded, and chopped

2 cups sour cream

Preheat the oven to 325 degrees and lightly oil a large baking pan.

Heat the olive oil in a heavy skillet and sauté the onions and garlic for 4 to 6 minutes until softened. Add the tomatoes, jalapeños, huitlacoche, and seasonings and simmer for 10 minutes or so until the liquid has evaporated.

Put four of the tortillas in the bottom of the baking pan and spread them with half of the huitlacoche mixture. Sprinkle on a third of the grated cheese. Repeat with four more of the tortillas, the remaining

huitlacoche, and another third of the cheese. Top with the remaining tortillas and sprinkle on the remaining cheese.

To prepare the sauce, puree the poblano chilies with the sour cream in a blender until perfectly smooth. Pour half the sauce over the stacked tortillas. Cover the pan tightly with foil and bake for 10 to 15 minutes.

Remove the foil and cut each stack in half or quarters. Place a portion on each plate, and pour the remaining sauce over the top of each, as you might with enchiladas.

Skillet-Grilled Lobster and Corn

SERVES 4

Cooks like me, who live in a city apartment sans terrace, are always looking for ways to get a good grilled taste without that smoking grill. From Jasper White, whose grilled lobster is one of the most asked-for dishes at his Boston restaurant, I picked up the trick of combining broiler and skillet to cook the lobster indoors. To the grilling skillet, I've added fresh sweet corn, appropriate to a lobster that's going to be flamed in corn liquor.

To serve the dish, I save some of the green corn husks to make a decorative platter on which to reassemble the lobster, cloaked in a corn and butter sauce. Good with boiled new potatoes, sliced tomatoes, and garden lettuces for a summer feast.

4 lobsters (1½ pounds each)
2 tablespoons corn oil
4 ears fresh sweet corn (to make 2 cups kernels), plus husks
½ cup bourbon
½ cup dry white wine
8 tablespoons (1 stick) butter
1 tablespoon chopped fresh tarragon leaves
1 tablespoon chopped chives
Salt and freshly ground black pepper

Have ready a medium saucepan of boiling salted water. Place each lobster on a chopping board and with a cleaver or heavy sharp knife, chop off the front end of the body, marked on top of the shell by a cross-mark. Break off the two big arms and claws attached to this part of the body and discard the body's "head."

Put the arms and claws in the pot of boiling water and let them simmer for 3 minutes. Drain and cool. Break open the claws and remove the meat in one piece. Set aside.

Sever the body from the tail where the two join, and split each part lengthwise. Remove and discard the gut. You will now have four pieces in the shell for each lobster.

Preheat the broiler and preheat a large heavy cast-iron skillet until very hot. Add the oil to the skillet and grill the corn kernels until slightly charred. Remove the kernels and set aside. Put the lobster pieces shell side down in the same skillet and cook for 1 minute. Then turn each piece over (shell side up) and put the skillet under the broiler to char the shells, 1 to 2 minutes.

Return the skillet to the stove on high heat, lay the claw meat on top of the shells, and add the bourbon. Ignite the bourbon and when the flames die down, add the wine. Shake the pan for 1 minute to distribute the liquid.

On each serving plate arrange a few large green corn husks. Reassemble a lobster for each plate on top of the husks.

Melt the butter in the skillet, add the herbs and seasonings and mix well. Add the reserved corn and pour the corn mixture over the lobsters.

Cod, Leeks, and Corn

SERVES 4

This is a trio as natural to New England as a summer clambake, and it wears summer colors of white, yellow, and green. Cod happens to be a favorite of mine, but of course other fish, such as salmon or swordfish, take to the same simple treatment. If you serve this hot, accompany the fish with little new potatoes baked with herbs, or perhaps with a hot spicy corn bread. The dish is particularly good cold because the natural gelatin in the fish helps thicken the garlic-cream sauce.

4 tablespoons olive oil
  Salt and freshly ground black
    pepper
4 cod steaks, 1½ inches thick
    (about 2 pounds)
2 large leeks, sliced crosswise with
    part of the green
2 tablespoons finely chopped fresh
    basil
1 cup fish stock
½ cup dry white wine
2 cloves garlic, minced
⅓ cup heavy cream
3 ears fresh sweet corn
    (to make 1½ cups kernels)

Preheat oven to 375 degrees.

Heat the oil in a heavy skillet that you can put in the oven. Season the cod steaks and sear them quickly on both sides. Remove and reserve the steaks.

Add the leeks to the pan and sauté for 5 to 8 minutes until soft. Add the basil, fish stock, and white wine; bring to the simmer. Put the cod on top of the leeks, cover the skillet tightly with foil and bake for 10 to 12 minutes, until the fish is fork tender. Remove the steaks to a serving platter and keep warm.

While the fish is baking, simmer the garlic in the cream for 10 minutes. Then add the cream to the fish stock and reduce the liquid by half. Add the corn kernels and simmer 2 or 3 minutes, then pour the mixture over the cod.

Blue Corn Crusted Bluefish

SERVES 4

Using cornmeal to crust fish for frying is an American cooking tradition that transcends regions, although Southerners still like to claim primogenital rights to this territory. But since every cornmeal has its own taste and texture, it's worth experimenting with meals other than the standard commercial yellow. Popcorn, toasted and ground fine, makes a sweet and nutty flour for coating foods. So blue cornmeal lends its own color and flavor. When the meal is finely ground, it's particularly good with an oily fish like bluefish because the meal will absorb the oil. Remember that with blue corn, you always need to add a pinch or more of baking soda to keep the blue blue. With both popcorn flour and blue cornmeal, you need to restrict heat to medium to avoid overbrowning the crust.

These fillets go very well with a chili mayonnaise or a fresh corn and tomato salsa. Although they'll taste best hot, they will also keep well in their crust if you want to serve them at room temperature or chilled.

4   bluefish fillets (about 2 pounds)
1   cup buttermilk
1   cup freshly ground blue cornmeal,
       fine grind
½   teaspoon salt
¼   teaspoon freshly ground black
       pepper
1   teaspoon ground cumin seeds
¼   teaspoon baking soda
2   tablespoons corn oil

Dip the fillets in the buttermilk.

Mix the meal with the salt, pepper, cumin, and baking soda.

Heat the oil in a heavy skillet over medium heat. Lay in the fillets and crisp them on both sides. If the skillet is too hot, the meal will burn, so keep the heat moderate. The fillets should cook through in 5 to 7 minutes, depending on their thickness.

Sole Smoked in Silks and Husks

SERVES 4

Since the fireplace in my city apartment does not work, I've learned to improvise ways to smoke fish and other foods, as city dwellers have done for centuries. I use a Chinese wok for smoking and when I experimented with using corn husks and corn silk as fuel, both for flavor and thrift, I learned that such fuel is as old as corn itself. The husks and silks give off their own flavor just as different woods do.

Try this method for other fillets or small fish, such as trout, snapper, fresh sardines, and even shellfish like scallops or shrimp. I find smoked fish best served at room temperature and for fish as delicate as sole, you might serve it with the corn kernels made into a raw corn salad or a corn and goat cheese flan.

4 ears fresh sweet corn
4 fillets of sole or flounder
   (1½ to 2 pounds)
   Salt and freshly ground black
   pepper

Strip the husks and silks from the corn; save the kernels for another purpose. Soak the husks and silks in cold water for 5 minutes. Shake off the excess water and lay half the husks in the bottom of a wok. Spread half the silks on top of the husks. Place a metal rack on top of the silks. Cover the wok with a tightly fitting lid and turn the heat high for 5 minutes to get the smoke started.

Season the fillets on both sides with salt and pepper. Remove the lid, lay two of the fillets on the rack, with space between. Cover them with the lid and smoke them on high heat for 5 minutes (the husks and silks will smoke but not flame because they are green and wet). Remove the wok from the heat and if the fillets are thicker than ⅓ inch, leave them in the wok with the lid on for an additional 5 minutes. They are done when the flesh is opaque and fork tender.

Repeat the smoking procedure with the remaining husks and silks and the remaining two fillets. Whatever fish you use, don't crowd them on the rack or they will not cook or smoke evenly.

Oyster Skillet Roast with Low Country Grits

SERVES 4

Way down in low country, on Edisto Island in South Carolina, Philip Bardin specializes in grits and what goes with them in The Old Post Office, now a restaurant. He orders speckled grits (ground with the black nib on, which makes the speckles) coarsely ground from a local mill and has the grits steaming in cream and butter on the back burner all day long. What goes with them depends on what you've got, and on Edisto he's got plenty of fresh shrimp and oysters. The oysters he flavors with a garlic-parsley butter to make Low Country Escargot.

This is a savory supper dish to serve with some collard greens and a fresh peach or berry pie.

FOR THE GRITS:

- 1 cup freshly ground speckled heart grits, coarse grind
- 3 cups water or chicken or fish stock, boiling
- 1 cup half-and-half
- 4 tablespoons butter

FOR THE SAUCE:

- 2 tablespoons butter
- 1 teaspoon olive oil
- 2 cloves garlic, minced
- 2 shallots or scallions, minced
- 1 tablespoon minced fresh parsley
- 2 dozen oysters, freshly shucked, with their juice
- Salt and freshly ground black pepper
- 1 to 2 tablespoons lemon juice

Start the grits 3 hours before serving time. Put the grits in the top of a double boiler and gradually add the boiling water or stock, stirring until smooth. Place the top over the bottom of the boiler, filled with an inch or two of boiling water. Put the lid on top and steam for an hour. Add the half-and-half, cover again, and steam until the grits are creamy and thoroughly cooked. Depending on the coarseness of the grind, this may take 1 or 2 hours longer. When they are done, stir in the butter and keep them warm over the double boiler.

For the sauce, heat the butter and oil in a heavy cast-iron skillet and sauté the garlic, shallots, and parsley for a minute or two to mix them. Add the oysters and their juice, and season with salt and pepper. Cook the oysters just until their edges begin to curl. Add a little lemon juice and taste. Add more if wanted.

Dish up the grits into soup bowls and put the oysters on top. If the oysters have given up a lot of juice, reduce the juice quickly in the skillet before pouring it over the oysters and grits.

Shrimp-Corn Quiche in a Corn Crust

SERVES 4 TO 6

Making a piecrust of grated fresh corn is a Southern tradition as old as the recipes collected in Blanche Rhett's *200 Years of Charleston Cooking* or in Sarah Rutledge's *The Carolina Housewife,* or beyond that to Native American traditions of green corn cooking. The combination of shrimp and corn is native to wherever these two live together, as in the Shrimp Rim of Mexico, the Caribbean, Louisiana, and along our Southern coasts.

You can make one 8- or 9-inch pie with this crust or four individual ramekins (4 inches in diameter). You get a double shot of corn here, since the crust is filled with a shrimp-corn custard, thickened with cheese. Serve for lunch, as you might a quiche, with a big platter of asparagus or a salad of green beans.

FOR THE CRUST:

- 4 ears fresh sweet corn
  (to make 2 cups kernels)
- 4 tablespoons butter, melted
- 2 egg yolks
- 1 teaspoon salt
- ¼ teaspoon white pepper
- 1 cup freshly ground corn flour,
  yellow or white

FOR THE FILLING:

- 1 tablespoon olive oil
- 1 pound raw shrimp in the shell,
  medium size
- 4 ears fresh sweet corn
  (to make 2 cups kernels)
- 3 scallions, chopped, including some
  of the green
- 1 teaspoon salt
- ½ teaspoon freshly ground black
  pepper
- 1 cup grated Gruyère cheese
- 1 egg, beaten
- 1 cup heavy cream
- ¼ teaspoon mace

Preheat the oven to 375 degrees.

To make the crust, process the corn kernels and the butter in a food processor. Add one of the egg yolks, the salt and pepper, and pulse until well mixed. Add the corn flour and pulse again until barely mixed. Press the mixture into a greased 8- or 9-inch pie plate or four greased ramekins to make a thin shell. Beat the remaining egg yolk with a fork and brush it on the crust to keep it from going soggy once it is filled. Prebake the crust for 20 minutes, or until it looks firm and set; remove it, and lower oven to 350 degrees.

Heat a skillet over high heat, add the oil, and sauté the shrimp in their shells until the shells turn pink (1 or 2 minutes), turning them frequently. Remove the shrimp and when they are cool enough to handle, remove the shells, devein, and chop the shrimp meat.

Sauté the corn kernels with the scallions and seasonings in the same skillet for 1 or 2 minutes. Add the corn mixture to the chopped shrimp. Add the grated cheese.

Beat the egg with the heavy cream and mace and add to the corn and shrimp. Pour the mixture into the piecrust and bake for 20 to 25 minutes (15 to 20 for ramekins) until the mixture is set.

Chicken in Yogurt and Lemon Corn Cream

SERVES 4

Marinating chicken in yogurt both tenderizes and flavors it and is a good way to cook it fat-free. The sauce of sweet corn puree thickens as well as sweetens the baked chicken and yogurt juices, and a little fresh lemon acts as a fulcrum between sweet and sour. You end with a soothingly creamy sauce that is as fine cold for a hot summer's evening as it is hot for a cold wintry one.

If served hot, accompany it with a platter of basmati rice and hot pita bread. If cold, accompany it with tabbouleh or well-spiced couscous.

¾ cup yogurt

1 to 2 large cloves garlic, minced

½ small onion, chopped fine

2 teaspoons grated fresh ginger

½ teaspoon powdered green chili or
    1 jalapeño chili, roasted
    (see Note, page 5), seeded,
    and chopped

½ teaspoon salt

¼ teaspoon freshly ground cumin

¼ teaspoon freshly ground white
    pepper

1 tablespoon chopped fresh cilantro

2 pounds chicken parts (4 thighs with
    drumsticks attached, preferably)

3 ears fresh sweet corn
    (to make 1½ cups kernels)

1 teaspoon lemon juice
    Grated rind of 1 lemon
    Sprigs of cilantro for garnish

Make a marinade by combining the yogurt with the garlic, onion, ginger, green chili, salt, cumin, pepper, and cilantro. Put the chicken pieces in a plastic bag (or bowl) and cover them thoroughly with the marinade. Refrigerate for at least 2 hours.

Preheat the oven to 450 degrees. Put the chicken, skin side down, in the marinade in a baking dish and bake on the top shelf of the oven for 15 minutes. Turn the chicken pieces skin side up and bake about 30 minutes more until the skin is slightly browned.

Remove the chicken pieces with a slotted spoon to a serving platter. Pour ½ cup of the cooking juices into a blender. Add the corn kernels and the lemon juice and puree. Pour the sauce over the chicken and garnish with grated lemon rind and cilantro sprigs.

Blue Corn Fried-Chicken Salad

At the Mesa Grill in Manhattan, Bobby Flay has been a constant innovator with chilies and corns. In this hefty salad, which I've simplified somewhat, he piles roasted vegetables on chicken thighs crusted in blue cornmeal and adds a buttermilk dressing hot with cayenne. So hot, in fact, that I've added olive oil to cool and smooth it.

The blue corn crust retains but a footnote of blue in the browning, so yellow cornmeal would do as well here. There's plenty of color in the red and yellow sweet peppers and in the salad greens. You may prefer a plain vinaigrette for dressing, enlivened perhaps with fresh lime juice and a little mild chili pepper instead of potent cayenne.

2 eggs, beaten
1 tablespoon Worcestershire sauce
1 tablespoon Tabasco
1 cup freshly ground blue cornmeal, medium grind
   Salt and freshly ground black pepper
4 chicken thighs, skinned and boned
   Oil for deep frying
2 red bell peppers
2 yellow bell peppers
4 cups mesclun or mixed salad greens

BUTTERMILK-CAYENNE DRESSING:

2 tablespoons sour cream
½ cup buttermilk
1 teaspoon minced garlic
1 teaspoon minced red onion
1 tablespoon fresh lime juice
1 teaspoon cayenne
½ teaspoon salt
   Pinch of freshly ground black pepper
2 tablespoons olive oil

Mix the eggs, Worcestershire, and Tabasco sauce in a bowl. Put the cornmeal in a shallow bowl or plate. Season the cornmeal with salt and pepper. Dip the chicken thighs first in the egg mixture and then in the cornmeal.

Heat oil in a wok or heavy skillet to 375 degrees for deep frying. Fry the chicken until brown on all sides. Drain well and set aside.

Char the peppers on all sides over the flame of a gas burner (or grill under a broiler), remove charred skins and inner seeds, and cut the flesh into strips. Reserve.

Arrange the mesclun on four plates and surround the greens with the roasted peppers. Slice the chicken thighs lengthwise to arrange each in a fan shape placed on top of the greens.

To make the dressing, combine all the ingredients except for the olive oil. Slowly whisk the oil into the buttermilk mixture and pour over the chicken and greens.

Brazilian Couscous
(*Cuscuz de Galinha*)

SERVES 8 TO 10

In a fascinating adaptation of local materials to traditional dishes originating elsewhere, Brazil treats cornmeal here as if it were the hard semolina wheat processed into tiny pellets that makes the splendid couscous of the Berbers of North Africa. North Africans transplanted to the New World, according to Barbara Karoff in her book *South American Cooking,* substituted corn for wheat and steamed it with fowl, meats, or fish in a steamer Brazilians call a *cuscuzeiro.* You can of course substitute for a traditional couscousière any sort of steamer basket inserted within a large kettle or use Chinese bamboo steamers.

Clearly this is a party dish because it is worth making only in quantity, but I have found cornmeal much easier to cook with than couscous. The pleasure of the dish is in the combined flavors of a lemony chicken, ham, chilies, and toasted cornmeal, not to mention the decorative possibilities of a mound covered with slices of hard-cooked eggs and olives, tomatoes, and peas.

FOR THE CHICKEN AND SAUCE:

- 1 lemon
- 1 medium onion, chopped fine
- 2 cloves garlic, mashed
  Salt and freshly ground black pepper
- 1 teaspoon freshly ground coriander seeds
- 2 tablespoons vegetable oil
- ¼ cup wine vinegar
- ½ cup tomato sauce
- ½ cup chicken stock
- 1 frying chicken, cut up, or 2 pounds chicken pieces

FOR THE CORNMEAL COUSCOUS:

- 4 cups freshly ground white cornmeal, medium grind
- ½ pound (2 sticks) butter
- 1 cup salted water, boiling

FOR THE STEAMING:

- 1 cup cubed cooked chicken meat
- 1½ cups sauce (see above)
- 1 cup cubed cooked ham
- 3 serrano or jalapeño chilies, seeded and minced
- 8 tablespoons (1 stick) butter, melted
- ¼ cup chopped fresh cilantro
  The prepared cornmeal couscous (see above)
- 6 cherry tomatoes, halved
- 2 cups cooked green peas
- 3 hard-cooked eggs, sliced
- 12 pimiento-stuffed olives
  Fresh orange slices for garnish

Grate the lemon peel and squeeze the lemon's juice into a large saucepan. Add the remaining ingredients for the sauce and bring the mixture to the simmer. Add the chicken, cover tightly, and simmer for 1 hour, or until the meat is fork tender. Remove the chicken and reserve the sauce. When the chicken is cool enough to handle, separate the meat from the skin and bones and cut the meat into large cubes. Reserve.

To prepare the couscous, toast the cornmeal in a heavy skillet over low to medium heat, stirring frequently to avoid burning. When it begins to brown (about 5 minutes), remove it from the heat. Add the butter and stir until it melts. Add the boiling water and return the skillet to medium heat. Cook for 2 minutes, stirring, to mix well. Set aside.

For the steaming, heat the chicken meat in 1½ cups of its sauce in a large saucepan. Add the ham, chilies, butter, and cilantro and mix well. Remove from the heat and stir in the cornmeal.

Brush a 3-quart colander well with oil. Line the colander with the tomatoes, peas, eggs, and olives, holding them in place with a layer of the cornmeal mixture. Fill the colander with the remaining mixture.

Cover the colander with a folded napkin or towel and steam inside a large lidded kettle for about 1 hour. Remove the colander from the pot and let it stand 5 minutes before unmolding it onto a platter. Garnish with slices of orange around the edge of the mold.

Latin American Boiled Dinner
(*Sancocho*)

When Irishmen think of boiled beef and cabbage, Frenchmen think of *pot au feu* and South Americans of *sancocho*. Essentially all of these are hearty meat and vegetable soup-stews where ingredients are simmered together in the same pot (*sancochar* means to parboil). From Puerto Rico to Peru *sancocho* is a constant, made with a variety of meats and such tropical rooty vegetables and tubers as plantains, yuca, taro, chayote, yam, and always ears of corn cut in chunks crosswise. This is a good way to explore tropical vegetables that you may not be familiar with but now see everywhere in American cities that have a large Hispanic population.

Because of the bright colors and crisp textures of the vegetables, this makes a bright, light stew, freshened with lime juice and lovely to look at. Since the number of ingredients is large, *sancocho,* like other boiled dinners, is best made for a group and especially a group that wants to share the earth's bounty in a communal feast.

5 pounds beef brisket

2 tablespoons salt

2 jalapeño chilies

2 sprigs of fresh rosemary

8 sprigs of fresh thyme

6 sprigs of fresh oregano

2 cloves garlic, mashed

6 quarts beef stock or water

THE VEGETABLES:

1 pound yuca (cassava), peeled and cubed

6 very small onions

1 pound yams, peeled and cubed

1 pound calabaza (or pumpkin), peeled and cubed

3 plantains, peeled and cut in 2-inch lengths

3 chayotes, peeled, seeded, and quartered

3 to 4 ears fresh sweet corn, cut in thirds crosswise

Salt and freshly ground pepper to taste

¼ cup chopped fresh cilantro

2 or 3 limes, quartered

Put the brisket in a large stockpot with the seasonings, herbs, and garlic. Cover with the stock or water and bring to the simmer over low heat, skimming off the scum that rises to the surface. Cover the pan and lower the heat even more, to keep the stock just barely simmering. Cook for about 3 hours or until meat is tender.

Add the yuca and cook 15 minutes. Add the onions, yams, calabazas, and plantains and cook 15 minutes more. Add the chayotes and corn and cook 3 to 5 minutes more. Taste the stock for seasoning and adjust if necessary.

Fork out the meat, trim off any excess fat, and cut the meat in slices. Arrange the slices on a large platter surrounded by the vegetables. Sprinkle the whole with cilantro. Pour the broth into a tureen and serve each guest a large soup bowl or plate with a quarter of lime. Pass the platter of meat and vegetables so that each guest may choose what he wants, then pass the tureen so that he may ladle in some broth and squeeze in some lime.

Rabbit with Red Masa

SERVES 4

Both Mexico and Guatemala, heart of the Mayan empire, use *masa harina* to thicken sauces for various meats, just as colonists from the Old World used wheat flour to thicken theirs. The sauce may be thick as a soft polenta or thin as a gravy. Because the *masa* has been precooked (with the slaked lime) and ground very fine, it can act as an instant thickener without long cooking.

The *masa* I used for this dish, however, was not ground fine but was very coarse. The reason was simple: I wanted to use a magnificent red corn posole, from corn grown by Elizabeth Berry of Gallina Canyon Ranch north of Santa Fe, a corn that retains its color through the slaked-lime processing. At the moment, she had no red *masa* ground from this corn to send me, so I made my own by grinding the posole first in a food processor and then in a blender. The result was a pleasantly chunky meal with a very aromatic smell and taste and a nutty crunch. It was also colored a beautiful pale sandy red.

As we know, color is not essential to flavor but red *masa* or blue *masa*, for that matter, perks our attention and makes a good background not only for rabbit, but for any white meat or fish or reddish shellfish. You can always color a white *masa* (or grits or polenta) red with tomato or sweet red peppers. With red corn *masa* you help maintain the color with an acid (in this recipe with white wine), as you maintain blue with an alkali (usually baking soda). With finely ground *masa*, cooking time depends solely on whether you want a barely thickened sauce or a thick mush.

1 **2- to 2½-pound rabbit, cut in 4 serving pieces**	1 **tablespoon fresh rosemary leaves**
½ **teaspoon salt**	1 **cup dry white wine**
¼ **teaspoon freshly ground black pepper**	5 to 6 **cups boiling chicken stock**
4 **tablespoons olive oil**	1 **cup red *masa harina* (see Note)**
2 **carrots, sliced thick**	
1 **bulb fennel, sliced crosswise**	
½ **cup chopped fennel tops**	
1 **small onion, sliced**	
3 **cloves garlic, chopped**	

Season the rabbit pieces with salt and pepper. Heat the oil in a heavy skillet over high heat and sear the pieces well on both sides for 8 to 10 minutes until lightly browned. Remove them and reserve.

In the same skillet, pan-roast the carrots, fennel slices, fennel tops, onion, garlic, and rosemary for 8 to 10 minutes until they are slightly browned. Return the rabbit to the pan, add the wine and 1 cup of the stock, and bring the liquid to the simmer. Cover with a lid and cook over very low heat 45 to 60 minutes, or until the rabbit is fork tender.

Preheat the oven to very low (200 degrees). With a slotted spoon, remove the rabbit and vegetables, cover them, and keep warm in the preheated oven.

Add the *masa* to the skillet and mix it with the pan juices. Slowly pour 4 cups of the remaining chicken stock into the *masa* and stir until well mixed. Cover the skillet and cook for 20 to 30 minutes, stirring occasionally and adding more stock if needed. Ladle the *masa* onto one end of a warmed serving platter and place the rabbit and vegetables at the other end.

Note: If you use regular white *masa harina,* for liquid use half stock and half tomato juice. If you use blue *masa,* add a large pinch of baking soda to retain the blue color.

Polenta with Portobellos

SERVES 4

If you like wild mushrooms, and who does not, polenta makes a fine edible "platter" on which to display their beauty. Fortunately, in addition to the large-capped portobellos, many kinds of wild mushrooms such as shiitake, porcini, cremini, etc., appear now on the produce counters of supermarkets across the country, so add whatever wild beauty excites your interest and imagination. They're costly but worth it.

For me the mushrooms are as good as a steak, so this is a meat-and-potatoes dish in itself. But it would also complement a good beefsteak or veal chop or lamb roast.

FOR THE POLENTA:

- 1 cup freshly ground yellow cornmeal, medium grind
- 4 cups boiling water
- 2 teaspoons salt
- 2 tablespoons butter
- ½ cup freshly grated Parmesan cheese

FOR THE TOPPING:

- 1 small onion, chopped fine
- 2 cloves garlic, minced
- 3 tablespoons olive oil
- 1½ pounds portobellos (and/or other wild mushrooms)
- ½ teaspoon salt
  Freshly ground black pepper
- 1 tablespoon dried oregano
- 2 tablespoons chopped Italian parsley

Put the cornmeal in the top of a double boiler, pour in the boiling water, and stir until thoroughly mixed. Add the salt. Fit the top into the bottom of the boiler, filled with an inch or two of boiling water, put a lid on the top, and steam the polenta for 30 to 45 minutes. Stir occasionally. When the mush is thick, stir in the butter and cheese.

In a heavy skillet, sauté the onion and garlic in the olive oil over high heat, add the mushrooms (whole caps or thickly sliced), and sauté quickly 5 to 8 minutes, turning them to brown on both sides. Lower the heat, add the seasonings and herbs, and mix well. Cook until the mushrooms are just tender (5 to 7 minutes).

Pour the polenta onto a large serving platter and cover it with the mushrooms.

Scallops and Polenta with Corn Mushrooms
(*Huitlacoche*)

SERVES 4

Polenta is now restaurant lingo for cornmeal mush no matter what the context. When I asked Josefina Howard "What's new?" at her restaurant Rosa Mexicano, she described in mouthwatering detail this dish of pan-grilled polenta rounds, covered with pan-grilled scallops, the white circles laid on yellow islands floating on a dark huitlacoche puree.

If you don't have huitlacoche in your freezer, substitute an eggplant roasted in its skin, then pureed and seasoned similarly with onion and garlic. Serve with a guacamole salad.

Salt, freshly ground black pepper, and cayenne
1 cup *masa harina*
1½ pounds sea scallops (about an inch round)
2 cups cooked polenta, spread ½ inch thick in a sheet pan and chilled
⅓ cup diced salt pork
½ small onion, minced
1 clove garlic, minced
1 small sweet red pepper, diced
1 cup chopped huitlacoche (drain thoroughly if frozen)
Fresh cilantro for garnish

Mix the seasonings (salt lightly because of the salt pork) into the *masa harina* in a flat dish. Dip the tops and bottoms of the scallops in the *masa harina* and set aside.

Cut the polenta into 4- to 5-inch circles with a flan ring or by laying on a saucer and cutting around it. Set aside.

In a heavy skillet, sauté the salt pork for about 5 minutes until the cubes are crisp. Remove cubes with a slotted spoon.

Preheat oven to low.

In the pork fat, brown the polenta rounds on both sides for 8 to 10 minutes until crisp, remove them with a spatula, and keep warm in the preheated oven. Sear the scallops quickly on both sides (no more than 3 to 4 minutes), remove and keep warm with the polenta.

In the same skillet, sauté the onion, garlic, and red pepper for 3 to 4 minutes until slightly softened. Add the huitlacoche, season to taste, and sauté, stirring, for 3 to 4 minutes more. Put half the mixture into a food processor and puree.

Mix the puree with the rest of the huitlacoche and spread it on a platter. Put the polenta circles on top and cover them with scallops. Garnish each polenta round with fresh cilantro.

Quail with Truffled Polenta
(*Quaglie e Polenta Tartufata*)

SERVES 4 AS A MAIN DISH

Italians know the joys of little game birds in ways that most of us who fancy little birds on the bone can only dream of because we can't get the woodcocks, thrushes, doves, ptarmigans, grouse, etc., of yesteryear. But we can get quail, and quail with polenta is as Italian as black truffles from Urbino, hidden like black gold in a creamy cheese-rifted mountain of polenta. An especially good kind of polenta to use here is the one that mixes cornmeal with buckwheat, *polenta taragna*. Grilled endive makes a fine accompaniment.

FOR THE POLENTA:

- 1½ cups *polenta taragna,* or plain cornmeal, medium grind
- 1 teaspoon salt
- 6 cups chicken stock, boiling
- 4 tablespoons butter
- ½ cup diced young sheep cheese, such as Pecorino Toscano
- ⅓ cup freshly grated Parmesan cheese
- 1 black truffle, whatever size you can afford, sliced thin

FOR THE QUAIL:

- 8 small quail, butterflied
  Salt and freshly ground black pepper
- 2 tablespoons olive oil
- 2 cloves garlic, minced
- 2 ounces pancetta, minced
- 1 tablespoon juniper berries
- 3 tablespoons chopped fresh herbs such as marjoram, rosemary, and thyme
- ½ to 1 cup chicken stock, boiling

To prepare the polenta, put the cornmeal and salt in the top of a double boiler, pour the boiling stock into it, and stir until smooth. Place the top of the pan over the bottom of the boiler, filled with 1 or 2 inches of boiling water. Cover the pan with a lid and steam for 35 to 40 minutes, stirring occasionally.

When the mush is thick, stir in the butter and cheese, cover and keep warm over the double boiler.

To prepare the quail, pat the quail dry with paper towels, then season on both sides with salt and pepper.

In a large heavy skillet, heat the olive oil over medium heat, add the garlic and pancetta, and sauté 1 or 2 minutes. Remove them with a slotted spoon and set aside.

Turn the heat to high. Add half the quail and sear them quickly on both sides (about 2 minutes a side). Repeat with the other half.

Turn the heat back to medium, put all the quail in the skillet, sprinkle with the garlic, pancetta, juniper, and herbs. Pour the chicken stock on top and cook for 3 minutes, scraping the bottom of the skillet to get all the juices.

Quickly ladle half the polenta onto a serving platter, spread the layer with slices of truffle, and cover with the remaining polenta. Heap the quail and their juices on a separate platter. Serve immediately.

Savoyard Polenta Pilaf
(Polenta en Pilaf)

SERVES 4 TO 6

In the French Savoy they sometimes treat cornmeal as if it were rice, sautéing it with onion and butter, and then steaming it like a Turkish pilaf or pilau. Madeleine Kamman in her book *Savoie* mentions four different ways to serve it: with dried pears and smoky bacon, with snails in a mustard cream sauce, with Italian sausages, or with stewed and thickened cherries. I'm especially fond of dried fruits, so I've used a mixed compote here, flavored with bacon. I found the texture of the cornmeal very delicious, nutty in flavor, and hearty in a way that would complement roast pork, country ham, or rich game such as quail, moulard, venison.

FOR THE PILAF:

- 1½ cups freshly ground cornmeal, coarse grind
- 4 tablespoons butter
- 1 large onion, chopped fine
- 5 cups chicken stock, boiling
  Salt and freshly ground black pepper

FOR THE COMPOTE:

- 2 cups cut-up mixed dried fruit (pears, apples, prunes, apricots, cherries, etc.)
- 2 cups chicken stock, boiling
- ½ cup diced smoked bacon
- 3 tablespoons coarsely chopped hazelnuts
  Lemon juice to taste

In a heavy skillet, toast the cornmeal over medium heat until it is lightly browned, stirring frequently. Add half the butter and all the onions and sauté, stirring, until the onions have softened, 3 to 5 minutes.

Scoop the mixture into the top of a double boiler and gradually add the boiling stock to it, stirring until the cornmeal is smooth. Season to taste. Set the top into the bottom of the double boiler covered with 1 to 2 inches of boiling water. Cover the pan tightly and steam for 30 to 40 minutes.

Meanwhile, put the dried fruit for the compote in a small pan with the 2 cups chicken stock. Cover the pan and simmer the fruit 20 to 30 minutes, or until it is nicely plumped. Remove the fruit with a

slotted spoon and reserve. Use the stock for another purpose, such as soup.

In a skillet, fry the bacon until crisp and discard the fat. Add the hazelnuts and toast them for 3 or 4 minutes until they begin to brown. Add the fruit to the skillet and sauté quickly for a minute or two to mix flavors. Squeeze on a little lemon juice to counteract the sweetness.

Add the remaining butter to the cooked pilaf, fluff it with a fork, and heap it on a platter. Pour the fruit and bacon mixture over the top of the pilaf.

Moldavian Cheese Pie

SERVES 4 TO 6

The ubiquity of cornmeal dishes in the Balkan states today reminds us that corn was as important to this region as it was to northern Italy for peasant survival. A Moldavian dish I like particularly in Vladimir Mirodan's *The Balkan Cookbook* combines polenta with cheese in a manner that might be Italian but for an egg custard poured over the top and for the sour cream sauce with wild mushrooms served with it. I've used ricotta cheese in my version, with a Gruyère for grating.

This makes a good lunch or a light supper dish, like a layered pasta, to be served with green vegetables or a leafy salad.

2¼ cups milk
½ cup freshly ground cornmeal, medium grind
½ teaspoon salt
4 ounces Gruyère cheese, grated (about 1 cup)
4 tablespoons butter
4 ounces ricotta cheese
¼ teaspoon freshly ground black pepper
2 large eggs

FOR THE SAUCE:

2 tablespoons olive oil
½ small onion, chopped fine
2 cups sliced wild mushrooms (porcini, shiitake, etc.)
1 cup sour cream
Salt and freshly ground black pepper

(continued)

Bring 2 cups of the milk to the simmer and pour it over the cornmeal in the top of a double boiler. Stir until mixture is smooth, add salt, then put the top of the boiler over the bottom filled with an inch or two of boiling water. Put a lid on the pan and steam the polenta for 20 to 30 minutes until thickened.

Preheat the oven to 350 degrees.

Butter a square 9 × 9-inch baking dish and put one third of the polenta on the bottom of the dish. Cover it with all but $\frac{1}{4}$ cup of the grated cheese, dot with half the butter, and cover with half the remaining polenta.

Add a layer of ricotta, sprinkle with pepper, and cover with the final layer of polenta. Dot with the remaining butter.

Beat the eggs with the remaining $\frac{1}{4}$ cup milk and pour the mixture over the pie. Sprinkle the top with the remaining grated cheese.

Bake for 30 to 45 minutes, until the top is well browned.

Meanwhile make the sauce by heating the olive oil in a heavy skillet. Add the onions and sauté over high heat 2 or 3 minutes. Add the mushrooms and sauté quickly 4 or 5 minutes until browned. Pour in the sour cream and remove immediately from the heat. Season to taste.

Cut the baked pie in squares and serve with the sauce.

Breads

NATIVE AMERICAN BREADS

- ■ To Make Tortillas
- Quesadillas with Wild Mushrooms
- Tostados
  (*Totopos*)
- Avocado Tomatillo Tacos
- Gorditas with Chilis and Cheese
  (*Gorditas de Chili con Queso*)
- Tortilla-Cheese Casserole
  (*Chilaquiles con Queso*)
- ■ To Make Tamales
- Classic Chili-Orange Pork Tamales
- Peruvian Fresh Corn Tamales
  (*Tamales d'Elotes*)
- Pumpkin or Squash Tamales
  (*Tamales de Oaxaca*)
- Black Tamales
  (*Tamales Negros*)
- Puerto Rican Coconut Tamales
  (*Guanimes de Maíz*)
- Fresh Strawberry Tamales
  (*Tamales de Primeras Comuniones*)

PANCAKES AND CREPES

- Charleston Corn Batter Cakes
- Sweet Corn Flapjacks
- Pagataw Oyster Pancakes
- Whitecap Flint Jonnycakes
- Pumpkin Corn Pancakes
- Hominy Waffles
- Savoy Corn Crepes
  (*Matafans de Maïs*)

QUICK BREADS

- Crackling Cornpone
- Corn Dodgers
- Venezuelan *Arepas*
- Hot and Smoky Peppered Corn Bread
- Espetanga Corn Bread
- All-in-One Thanksgiving Turkey Stuffing
- Toasted Corn Sticks
- Hot Tomato Muffins
- Santa Fe Blue Corn Muffins
- Blueberry Blue Corn Muffins
- Sweet Corn Chili Muffins
- Sweet Potato Corn Muffins
- Hominy Bread
- Moldavian Feta Cheese Corn Bread
- Brendan Walsh's Buttercup Spoon Bread
- Roasted Garlic and Goat Cheese
  Spoon Bread
- Punjabi Corn Griddle Bread
  (*Makki Ki Roti*)
- Classic Boston Brown Raisin Bread
- Peruvian Corn Bread
  (*Pastel de Choclo*)

YEAST BREADS

- Cornmeal Pizza with Corn Topping
- Herbed Corn Focaccia
- Lemon Pepper Oregano Bread
- Sun-Dried Corn and Tomato Bread
- Black and White Braided Bread
  (*Huitlacoche* Bread)
- Sourdough Three-Grain Bread
- Sourdough Bread with Masa Yeast
- Sweet Corn Sourdough Bread

They have not learned how to make flour that can be kneaded like wheat flour, and when they do make it as one makes wheat bread, it is good for nothing.

—*Friar Diego de Landa,* Yucatán Before and After the Conquest, *1566*

The proof of corn is not in the pudding but in the bread. Bread everywhere is the true sustainer of life and corn is called *Zea mays,* the seed of life, because it is the native bread of the Americas. That fact caused our colonial forebears to despair, because this savage grain did not behave like wheat. Since corn has no gluten, yeast did it no good at all. Where a yeasted wheat dough would rise on the bake stone or griddle, corn remained flat as a pancake.

When it comes to making any kind of baked bread or griddle cake with cornmeals, the one thing to remember is that corn is not wheat. Let's repeat that loud and clear: *corn is not wheat.* Cornmeal, coarse or fine, behaves according to its own character and temperament. You can leaven corn in various ways, with eggs or with chemical powders like baking soda or baking powder, which were originally derived from powdered wood ash, but for baker's yeast to affect corn you must mix corn with wheat.

While corn's proteins lack the power to form sheets of gluten, they do have an extraordinary power to absorb liquid. And because different varieties of corn and different methods of milling them will affect the amount of liquid any specific meal can absorb, the ratio of liquid to grain will vary. You can't standardize the formulas the way you can with wheat. On the other hand, you can enjoy corn's individuality and take comfort in the fact that airy lightness is not what corn breads are about. They are about flavor and crunchy texture, whether it's a flat cornpone or an aerated spoon bread.

The native breads were all flat breads, but Native Americans had hundreds of ways to lighten and flavor them, including mixing the meal with powdered minerals and herbs or with ashes from different kinds of wood. The Pueblos of the Southwest favored the ash of chamisa, a desert plant known as the "four-winged saltbush." The Northeast favored ash from hickory and chestnut. In Mexico they used and still use tequesquite, an alkaline salt from the lake beds.

Native Americans also fermented cornmeal to exploit wild yeasts for brewing and bread making, both for taste and nutrition. Corn is a good yeast starter because it has such a high percentage of sugar, so fermentation takes place faster than with wheat, barley, potatoes, or other starches traditionally used for making yeast from scratch. I experimented wildly with corn sourdough breads, fermenting everything from *masa* to grits, and I became passionate about the particular sourdough taste that fermented cornmeal brings. Mixing fermented cornmeal with wheat flour gives you the best of both worlds, the flavor of corn and the leavening power of wheat. I offer a sampling of my experiments here in the hope that others will carry on the exploration of corn sourdoughs.

Native American Breads

American bread making began where corn began, in Middle America, and reached its apotheosis in the baroque elaboration of prehistoric cornpone in the royal court of Moctezuma. What is a tortilla or a tamale but a highly refined version of that quintessential pone? Refined is the operative word, because a tortilla or tamale is to ordinary pone what a French baguette is to an oat bannock. But just as native Gauls had several thousand years in which to develop the art of turning their native grains into breads, so did the natives of Mesoamerica. In both of these cultures, the process of turning coarse grain into a fine, mouth-delighting delicacy was complex and skilled. Yet our wheat-culture prejudice is such that we tend to think of all corn breads, and particularly those south of the border, as primitive. Earthy yes. Primitive no.

The bread making art of Mesoamerica spread north and south of the Yucatán and Tehuacán, where corn began, and evolved in the centers of Olmec and Mayan civilizations. But the art reached astonishing heights during the Aztec empire in the valley of Mexico. Moctezuma was offered daily for his noontime feast some 2,000 dishes, most of them based on corn dough shaped into the thin grilled cake called *tlaxcalli,* which the Spaniards renamed tortilla, or the fatter steamed cake called *tamal.*

The Spanish chroniclers detailed tortillas thin and thick, stretched and folded, with turkey eggs, honey, amaranth, squash, winged ants, tuna cactus, dried duck, yellow chili, tomatoes, sorrel, avocado, lobster, locusts, plums. They listed tamales tasty

with fish, tadpole, rabbit, quail, bees, maize flowers, insect eggs, fish eggs, garden cress, squash flowers, tomatillos, sapotas, sweet potatoes, cherries. The wonder is that even today in Mexico and Guatemala you can find a similar variety of shape, texture, and flavorings in the tortillas and tamales of different regions, each with specific names and traditions.

The best way to explore the basic corn dough and discover how to turn it into bread is to experiment in the privacy of your own kitchen. Of course nowadays you can buy packaged precooked tortillas of varying quality all over America, but so can you buy French baguettes. I recall the months, years, I spent in the 1960s perfecting the quintessential French loaf à la Julia Child; so when I get impatient at my fumblings with tortillas or tamales à la Diana Kennedy or Rick Bayless, I remind myself that Tenochtit-lán (now Mexico City) was not built in a day.

You don't need any special equipment for your experiment, but you do need the right dough. This is a problem, because the art of making hominy in this country is close to a lost art. As Americans moved from the country to the city, they left their big cast-iron hominy pots back at the farm. These were the pots in which they cooked dried field-corn kernels in water with wood ash (which made potash or lye, potassium hydroxide) to soften the hulls, which they could then rub off with their fingertips. South of the border they more commonly used limestone instead of wood, which they powdered and mixed with water to make a similar alkali, slaked lime (calcium hydroxide). What we call hominy Mexicans call by a Nahuatl word, *nixtamal*. When we grind up whole hominy, sometimes we call it hominy and sometimes grits. Mexicans call it *masa*, and that *masa* is the basic dough for both the tortilla that is patted thin and grilled and for the tamale that is enriched and steamed like a dumpling.

In Mexico you can buy in the market a variety of dried white field corn prized for the quality of its starch, *maíz cacahuazincle*. With it you can buy a hunk of the limestone (*cal*) to slake with water and then boil with the corn to soften the hulls. If you're making *masa* for tortillas, soak the corn in the lime water for 1 or 2 days until the skins, which have now turned yellow, rub off easily and the corn is soft and very white. Then grind it as fine and smooth as you can in a plate-style corn mill or take it to the mill of a tortilla factory, thankful that you no longer have to grind it by hand with a grinding stone (*mano*) on a stone metate.

If you are making *masa* for tamales, soak the corn a shorter time, just overnight, so that the corn will not be as soft and the dough will be coarser and more textured, which results in a lighter, spongier dough. An additional leavening is often used to "fluff" the dough, achieved by an infusion that combines acid and alkali the way our commercial baking powder does. In Mexico they combine tequesquite (alkaline salts harvested anciently, as today, from the lake beds around Mexico City) with the acid of tomatillo husks. I'm heavily indebted to Beatriz Ramírez, whose family produce Tamales Especiales in Mexico City, for all tamale information, and also to Diana Kennedy (*The Art of Mexican Cooking*) and Rick and Deann Bayless (*Authentic Mexican*). Their books can give you detailed instructions on how to make your own *masa* from scratch.

But, thank God, there are simpler alternatives. You can begin with the dried corn flour called *masa harina,* available now in some supermarkets and most Hispanic markets in the United States. (A good brand is Maseca, put out by the Azteca Milling Co. in Texas and California.) This processed corn flour is made industrially by drying and then powdering the fresh corn dough. Because it has been cooked and dried, it keeps well (in an airtight jar) and does not have to be refrigerated. In working with *masa harina*, it's useful to know that it will instantly absorb much more liquid than uncooked corn flour or meal: 1 cup *masa harina* to ⅔ or ¾ cup liquid will make a soft dough for tortillas; 1 cup *masa harina* to 2 cups liquid will make a good batter for pancakes.

The classic tamale of Mesoamerica today is a product of the Columbian Exchange, or rather of the Cortés-Moctezuma Exchange, for the native corn dough is both leavened and enriched with pork lard. As we've seen, there was no shortage of flavorings and enrichments for native dough, but tamales, since the earliest time of Olmec and Mayan, were the sacred bread, the communal wafer, the bread symbolic of man's kinship with the gods. After the introduction of Spanish pigs, the new ingredient of pork fat, deliciously flavorful and more unctuous than cacao butter, would have seemed as heaven-sent as the conquistadores with their white-winged sails and sun-glittering helmets.

When most of us today think of tamales, however, we think first of the wrapper, whether it is a green or dried corn husk, a green or dried banana leaf, a plantain or maguey leaf, or the *bijao* leaf of the Amazon. Next we think of whether the dough is made with fresh corn or dried, with white or sweet potatoes, with quinoa or rice, with

plantains or yucca. Then we wonder if something delicious has been stuffed inside the dough.

The pleasure of a tamale for the eater is in unwrapping a hidden treasure, not unlike the initial pleasure of unwrapping husks to find rows of nestled kernels, the more precious for being hidden. And with a filled tamale the pleasure is doubled by discovering a second sweet or savory treasure hidden within the dough. The pleasure for the cook is the more practical one of flexibility, so that he or she can make portions large or small, communal or individual, and can cook them in quantity by baking, steaming, or boiling. More than the tortilla, the tamale is the universal cornpone of Hispanic America.

TO MAKE TORTILLAS

First the dough: If you can't get fresh *masa*, mix a flour and water dough from *masa harina*, in proportions about 2 to 1: 2 cups flour to 1¼ to 1⅓ cups of hot water. Knead together with your fingers. The dough should be soft, malleable, and plastic (like Play-Doh, says Bayless), neither crumbly nor sticky. If the dough is the right consistency, everything else is easy. Remember that you can work and rework a corn-flour-and-water paste vigorously without its getting gummy, the way a wheat-flour-and-water paste might.

One really easy dough to make is from canned hominy. First drain the kernels thoroughly and pat them dry on paper towels before putting them in a food processor to puree as finely as you can. Hominy usually comes packed in brine, which to the horror of a tortilla purist gives a salt flavor to the dough. Traditionally tortillas are without salt for two reasons: the alkali process gives a distinct taste, or seasoning, to the corn; this corn taste is the base note for the melodies and harmonies of highly seasoned sauces. Personally, I like the salt taste of the hominy dough and find the dough very easy to work because it is coarser and wetter. But you'd still have to call it a Yankee cousin twice removed of the *pura* Mexican tortilla.

Whatever dough you use, you need to work with it quickly because it will dry out.

For shaping, it's easier to start with smaller cakes, say 3 inches round rather than 5 inches. Tear off a small piece of dough (keep the rest covered with a damp towel or plastic wrap), shape it into a little ball, and put it in the center of a square of heavy plastic (cut open a freezer bag and cut the bag in two). Put a second square of plastic on top. Take a small heavy skillet, or anything flat and heavy, and press down hard and evenly on top of the ball to make a thin round (no more than 1/16 inch thick).

A tortilla press will guarantee even pressure, but unless you decide to make tortillas often and in quantity, you don't need it. The press is a mere 400 years old, introduced by the Spanish as a laborsaving device when they ran short of slaves.

Once the dough has been flattened, carefully remove the top sheet of plastic from the tortilla. Invert the tortilla onto the fingers of your right hand and carefully peel the plastic from the dough. If it sticks, the dough is too wet; if it breaks, the dough is too dry. Then place the tortilla on a hot griddle or heavy cast-iron skillet that will retain an even heat. In Mexico you would cook your tortilla on a large round griddle called a *comal*.

Remember that the flour in this dough has already been cooked once and that you are now cooking it a second time to give it a particular shape and texture. You want the tortilla to cook fast, less than 2 minutes total time. Cook it first on one side just long enough to firm the dough but not dry it (15 to 20 seconds), then loosen the tortilla with a spatula and invert it to cook the underside (it should be flecked with brown in 20 to 30 seconds). Finally, flip the tortilla again to finish browning the first side (15 to 30 seconds). If all goes well (the dough is the right wetness and the griddle the right heat), the tortilla will puff up as the moisture trapped between the two cooked surfaces, or "skins," expands, and evaporates. You can help it to puff by pressing the top surface lightly with your fingertips. Mexican women call this "tickling the tortilla." If the tortilla doesn't puff, it will still taste good, so worry not, because the little puffed ball is going to deflate anyway the moment it's off the griddle. Just go after the next one.

As you finish each tortilla, stack them up inside a large napkin and cover them completely to keep them warm and soft. Fresh tortillas should be whisked straight to the table to be eaten immediately, while they are still soft, pliable, and moist. I love to eat them with butter and a sprinkling of salt, authentic to my California childhood if to nothing else. But I was pleased to hear from a friend at San Juan Pueblo in New Mexico that his favorite food as a child was tortillas spread with fresh pork lard and salt and over that lots of powdered chili caribe. "That's *really* good," he said.

A leftover tortilla, as you know, never goes to waste. You can reheat them in foil in the oven to soften them or cut them in tiny strips to fry as a garnish for soups or as a kind of "pasta" in casserole dishes like *chilaquiles*. Or you can fry them whole to make *tostados* (or *totopos*), or cut them in quarters to make *tostaditos*, which we call corn chips. Or you can grind them to form a version of the thick fried cakes called *gordas* or *gorditas*, and on it goes. Tortillas form the base for hundreds of dishes, only a few of which are household names in the States— names like tacos, nachos, enchiladas, quesadillas, flautas. But there are literally hundreds of others—*molotes, chalupas, papadzules, sopitos, cazuelitas, polkanes, panuchos*—tortilla dough shaped like miniature boats, pots, snakes' heads, weavers' bobbins, canoes, filled or sauced in myriad ways. If only we had a Larousse Gastronómico of Mexico we would begin to see what it is to be a *novicio* in the kitchens of Moctezuma.

Quesadillas with Wild Mushrooms

MAKES 8 QUESADILLAS, OR 24 SMALL PIECES

In Mexico, quesadillas are usually made of corn tortillas, shaped like turnovers to contain fillings that range from fresh cheese (which gives the little turnover its name—*quesa*) to cactus leaves (*nopales*) to squash blossoms (*flores de calabaza*) to corn mushrooms (*huitlacoche*). Here I've used wild mushrooms for a filling.

Plain corn tortillas are hard to fold to make turnovers, so it's wise to mix a little wheat flour and shortening into the dough to make a more flexible wrapper. For bite-size appetizers, cut each in thirds.

FOR THE FILLING:

- ½ cup finely chopped onion
- 2 cloves garlic, minced
- 1 jalapeño chili, roasted (see Note, page 5), seeded, and chopped
- 1 teaspoon dried oregano (or epazote)
- 1 tablespoon olive oil
- 1½ cups chopped wild mushrooms, including stems
  Salt and freshly ground black pepper

FOR THE TORTILLA DOUGH:

- 1 cup *masa harina*
- ½ cup all-purpose flour
- ½ teaspoon salt
- ½ teaspoon baking powder
- ¼ cup vegetable shortening, chilled
- 1 cup warm water
  Vegetable oil for frying

To make the filling, sauté the onion, garlic, jalapeño, and oregano in the oil over medium heat for 3 or 4 minutes, until the onion and garlic are softened. Turn the heat high, add the mushrooms, salt, and pepper, and sauté for 4 to 5 minutes until the mushrooms are browned.

To make the dough, mix the *masa harina* with the flour, salt, and baking powder. Cut in the shortening, then mix in the water to make a soft dough. Shape the dough into 8 balls. Cut wax paper into 16 squares (8" x 8"). Roll each ball flat between two squares of paper to make a tortilla 4 to 5 inches in diameter. Peel off the top square from each and put a spoonful of filling in the middle. Fold the tortilla in half and pinch the edges together, like a turnover.

Fill a heavy skillet with about ½ inch of oil and heat over a medium flame until the oil is 375 degrees. Fry the turnovers 1 or 2 at a time, until golden brown on both sides (about 5 minutes). Drain well.

Tostados
(*Totopos*)

Here leftover tortillas do better than fresh ones because you want them dry to begin with. A standard-size tortilla makes a tostado; a tortilla cut in quarters or small pieces makes *tostaditos,* or corn chips.

I find it easiest to use a wok for deep frying, and a wok will hold a single tortilla nicely. Just pour an inch or two of vegetable oil in the bottom, heat the oil to 380 degrees, and fry the tortillas one at a time, using tongs to flip them once to brown on both sides (about 30 seconds a side). Drain on paper towels.

The tostado now serves as the base for an open-faced sandwich or salad: layer it with what you wish, like a sprinkling of chopped lettuce topped by black-bean puree (*frijoles refritos*), slices of grilled chicken or smoked fish, avocado slices, thin-sliced Bermuda onion, ripe tomatoes, a crumbly white cheese, topped by sour cream or crème fraîche. This is a good way to use leftover grilled meats and vegetables.

Avocado Tomatillo Tacos

MAKES 8 TACOS

For those dyspeptic from one too many beef tacos from Taco Bell, try this vegetarian delight of diced avocado and tomatillo held together in a good fresh farmer's cheese, enlivened with onion and garlic, and seasoned with fresh cilantro and lime.

FOR THE FILLING:

1 ripe avocado, diced

4 tomatillos, peeled and chopped

1 cup fresh farmer's cheese

1 serrano chili, roasted (see Note, page 5), seeded, and chopped

2 tablespoons finely chopped onion

1 tablespoon chopped fresh cilantro

1 teaspoon fresh lime juice

Salt and freshly ground black pepper

Vegetable oil for frying

8 cooked corn tortillas

½ cup sour cream (optional)

Mix the avocado and tomatillo into the cheese, along with the chili, onion, cilantro, lime, and seasonings.

Pour about ¼ inch of oil in the bottom of a wok or heavy skillet. Heat the oil until hot but not smoking. Soften the tortillas by dipping them quickly in the oil; then drain them on paper towels.

Put 2 large spoonfuls of the filling in the middle of each tortilla, fold the tortilla in half, and secure it with one or more toothpicks. Add the tortillas to the hot oil 1 or 2 at a time, turning them once to make them crisp on both sides. Drain well and serve hot.

Gorditas with Chilies and Cheese
(*Gorditas de Chili con Queso*)

MAKES 10 TO 12 SMALL *GORDITAS*

Since the word *gorditas* means "little fat cakes," these are made slightly thicker than ordinary tortillas, with dough leavened by baking powder and wheat flour. They are deep-fried and split open to be filled with any number of good things from shredded cabbage to chorizos. The mixed dough and the chili-cheese filling of this one, which the Baylesses give as a classic of Sonora, suggest how arbitrary is the border between Sonora and Arizona or between corn cakes North and South.

FOR THE FILLING:

1 large tomato, roasted

4 poblano chilies, roasted (see Note, page 5), seeded, and chopped

1 cup chicken broth

8 ounces fresh farmer cheese (or *queso fresco* if you can get it)

Salt and freshly ground black pepper

FOR THE DOUGH:

½ teaspoon salt

¼ cup all-purpose flour

1 teaspoon baking powder

2 tablespoons lard

2 cups tortilla dough (fresh *masa* or made from *masa harina*)

Oil for frying

To make the filling, puree the tomato, skin and all, in a blender, then strain into a saucepan. Add the chilies and the broth and simmer until the liquid is reduced almost to a glaze. Remove from the heat and stir in the cheese. Season to taste and set aside.

To make the *gordita* dough, mix together the salt, flour, and baking powder. Cut in the lard with your fingertips, then work in the tortilla dough.

Preheat a griddle over medium heat. Shape and press the dough into rounds, as in making tortillas, only make these slightly thicker (⅛ inch) and 3 to 4 inches in diameter. Cook each *gordita* on the griddle, turning it frequently to brown on both sides, for a total of 3 to 5 minutes.

In a wok or heavy skillet, heat an inch of oil to 375 degrees. Add no more than two *gorditas* at a time and cook, turning frequently, for 1 to 2 minutes, until they puff and begin to pull apart. Drain them well on paper towels.

If they haven't split open, slit them with a knife about a third of the way around and fill them with the prepared filling.

Tortilla-Cheese Casserole
(*Chilaquiles con Queso*)

SERVES 4 TO 6

*C*hilaquiles is a dish Americans should get to know better because it is thrifty, easy, and as soothingly convenient as tamale pie. You can use leftover tortillas or store-bought ones because you are going to cut them in strips and fry them until crisp. With cheese, shredded chicken (or any meat you like), and a tomatillo sauce, you have a quick and delicious combination of layers and textures that the word "casserole" does not convey, but "*chilaquiles*" does.

Mexicans often eat *chilaquiles* for breakfast, but they are a small, quick one-dish meal for any time of day or night.

Oil for frying
6 precooked tortillas (page 93)
1½ cups shredded cooked chicken
2 cups grated Monterey Jack cheese
1 small onion, chopped
2 cloves garlic, chopped
1 jalapeño or serrano chili, roasted
   (see Note, page 5), seeded,
   and chopped
2 tablespoons vegetable oil
¼ cup chopped fresh cilantro
6 tomatillos, husked and parboiled
   5 minutes
2 cups sour cream
   Salt and freshly ground black
   pepper

Preheat the oven to 325 degrees. Heat an inch or two of oil in a wok or heavy skillet to 350 degrees.

Cut the tortillas in half and then into ¼-inch strips at right angles to the cut. Fry the strips a few at a time for 1 or 2 minutes until very crisp. Remove with a skimmer and drain on paper towels.

Combine the strips with the chicken and cheese in a buttered 13 × 9-inch baking pan.

Sauté the onion, garlic, and chili in the 2 tablespoons oil for 3 to 5 minutes until the vegetables are softened. Put them in a blender with the cilantro, tomatillos, and sour cream and puree until smooth. Taste for seasoning. Pour the sauce over the top of the casserole, cover with foil or a lid, and bake about 20 minutes until the flavors are blended and the cheese melted.

TO MAKE TAMALES

FOR THE DOUGH:

Ideally the fresh *masa* for tamales should be ground more coarsely than for tortillas to give a textured dough. I experimented with chopping canned hominy in a food processor, but found the result wet and heavy even when mixed with *masa harina* to lighten it. The best formula I've found for the initial *masa* is that of the Baylesses in mixing *masa harina* with quick-cooking grits (not instant, but quick) in the proportion of nearly 1 to 1. Into that *masa* first beat lard, then chicken (or meat or vegetable) broth, then baking powder to make a spongy batter so light that a little ball of it will float in a glass of cold water. A spoonful of lard will float best, so the higher the proportion of lard to dough, the lighter the texture and the more melting the flavor.

Some purists add no baking powder, but there is lots of precedent for an additional leavening. The anthropologist Frank Cushing, who described in detail the culinary methods of Zuni Pueblo in the late nineteenth century in his *Zuni Breadstuff,* spoke of their frequent use of "lime yeast." This was made by fermenting cornmeal or flour that had been processed with wood ash or lime, and that was then used as a

leavening as we would use baking powder or soda today. Fermented *masa* was a constant in Aztec breadstuffs and even today many Mexicans prefer to use *masa* that is soured, or *agria.* I've found in my own experiments that fermented dough gives a wonderfully rich flavor to any tortilla, tamale, or sourdough yeast bread.

TO PREPARE TAMALE MASA

⅔ cup quick-cooking grits
¾ cup *masa harina*
1¼ cups boiling water

Grind the grits as fine as possible in a blender and mix them with the *masa harina.* Add the boiling water, stir until smooth, and let cool to room temperature. This makes two cups *masa.*

TO COMPLETE TAMALE DOUGH

½ cup good lard
½ to ⅔ cup chicken stock,
       at room temperature
1 teaspoon baking powder
½ to 1 teaspoon salt (depending on
       saltiness of the stock)

Beat the lard in an electric mixer (a food processor won't allow the lard and dough to incorporate as much air as a

mixer will). Beat until it is light and fluffy, about 2 to 3 minutes. Beat in half the prepared grits mixture until well blended. Beat in the rest of the mixture in small bits alternately with the stock until the dough makes a slapping noise and has the texture of a butter-cream frosting.

Add the baking powder and salt and beat 2 or 3 minutes more until a small piece of the dough will float in a glass of water. If it doesn't float, don't worry; you'll still have a good-tasting tamale dough even if it's not of ideal lightness. This dough will keep well, wrapped and refrigerated, until you are ready to use it.

TO WRAP THE DOUGH

A word of caution before we begin: the flavor of an organic leaf is part of the dish, so you should think twice or thrice about substituting aluminum foil for corn husks or banana leaves. Beyond that, much of the pleasure of individually wrapped tamales is in their presentation as little gifts to untie, which again foil contradicts. If you want a tamale taste but have no wrappings, use the dough and its fillings as a layered and baked tamale pie.

If you have the wrappings but don't want to indulge in the intensive labor that individually wrapped tamales demands, make a communal tamale by lining a baking dish with leaves, layering in the dough and filling, then covering the layers with more leaves, and finally baking the dish in the oven. Unwrapping the top leaves at the dining table to reveal the treasure within can provoke communally the same kind of happy response provoked by individually wrapped gifts.

The wrappers most easily available in the States are dried corn husks. Soak them in boiling water to cover for at least 30 minutes, maybe longer, until they become pliable. Then pat them dry. Unfortunately, these prepackaged corn husks are cut short, above the broad cupped base, which makes wrapping with them more difficult. But there are many ways to wrap. One easy and safe way is to make little square packages by putting the wide ends of two corn husks together, overlapping the husks where they join, and laying in a smaller husk to cover the seam. Spread 3 to 4 tablespoons of dough in a rough square in the middle of this inside husk, then lay a tablespoon of filling down the center of the square. Cover the filling with another layer of dough to enclose it. Bring the bottom edge of the husk up over the dough and bring the top edge down to overlap. Fold in both extended ends to overlap each other and tie the package with a thin strip of corn husk.

If you're using fresh green corn husks (they give the best flavor), an easy way is to make an open-ended wrapping by spreading a wide strip of dough near the bottom edge

of the wide cupped base. Then lay on the fill-ing and bring up the two sides of the husks to enclose the filling within the dough. Overlap the sides and fold up the tapered end of the husk to overlap the wide end. Tie with a strip of husk around the middle and set the packages so that the open end remains upright in the steamer (you can prop them against an inverted metal funnel or a pyramid of crushed aluminum foil).

Banana leaves are also good flavorers. The ones we get in the States are usually imported from the Philippines and they come frozen, cut in large squares 14 × 15 inches. After thawing them, wipe them gently, then pass them quickly through an open flame or put them under a broiler for a few seconds to increase their pliability. Spread about ½ cup of the dough in a 8 × 4-inch rectangle, 2 or 3 inches from the lower edge of the leaf. Put the filling on the top half of the dough. Fold up the bottom edge of the leaf so that the dough encloses the filling. Fold down the top of the leaf over the bottom and fold in the sides, to make a square package. Tie with string around the middle.

To Cook Tamales

Any kind of steaming arrangement will do, but Chinese bamboo steamers are ideal, as are traditional metal steamer pots. If you don't have a steamer, you can improvise by putting in a large kettle a round cake rack set on balls of foil or tin cans or inverted Pyrex cups or even corncobs, if you're using fresh corn. It's good if you have extra husks or leaves to lay the tamales on and to cover them with, to help absorb moisture and increase flavor. If you lack husks, use a folded towel on top for absorption. You need a tight-fitting lid to keep the steam in. Put at least an inch of boiling water in the bottom of the pot, bring it to the boil, clap on the lid, lower the heat, and steam for 1 to 1½ hours, depending on how closely packed your tamales are. Check during the steaming to make sure the pot has not run out of water.

Note: In the recipes that follow, the first one uses the tamale *masa* turned into the classic tamale dough above. Others may use the basic tamale *masa* but complete the tamale dough differently.

Classic Chili-Orange Pork Tamales

MAKES ABOUT A DOZEN TAMALES

The combination of pork flavored with cumin, chili, currants, orange peel, and sour orange juice will alert any lover of Mexico that good things are in hand. Alas, we are not yet importing Spanish America's excellently flavored sour oranges, so it is still necessary to substitute lemon or lime juice to get the right sharpness.

FOR THE FILLING:

- 2 cloves garlic, minced
- 2 tablespoons *achiote* oil (see Note)
- 1 tablespoon ground cumin seeds
- 1 tablespoon pure ground chili, New Mexican type
- ½ teaspoon freshly ground black pepper
- 1½ cups shredded or diced cooked pork
- ¼ cup currants
- 1 tablespoon grated orange peel
- 1 tablespoon sour orange juice or a mixture of orange and lemon juices
- ¼ cup pork or chicken broth
- 2 cups basic tamale dough (page 100)

Sauté the garlic in the oil over low heat, with the cumin, chili, and black pepper. Add the pork and sauté another 2 or 3 minutes. Add the remaining filling ingredients and simmer for 3 or 4 minutes until the liquid has evaporated.

Spread the dough on wrappers, as instructed above, and spoon filling on the dough. Fold and tie the wrappers and steam, as above.

Note: To make *achiote* oil, pulverize 1 tablespoon annatto (*achiote*) seeds in a spice grinder. Heat the ground annatto with 2 tablespoons of olive oil long enough to color the oil a bright yellow-orange. Pass it through a strainer to remove the seeds. If you have no *achiote*, color the oil with a little paprika. If you have some *achiote* paste (*recado rojo*), mix 1 teaspoon of it into the oil.

Peruvian Fresh Corn Tamales
(*Tamales d'Elotes*)

MAKES ABOUT A DOZEN TAMALES

The sweet corn we get in the States doesn't by itself have the body needed for a tamale dough, but it's easy to puree the kernels and mix the puree with tamale dough. A friend from Lima told me that her favorite breakfast treat was a tamale made of fresh corn, ground coarsely in a blender. She filled that dough with diced sweet red pepper, some peanuts, black olives, and a square of soft pork rind. My recipe is an improvisation on her breakfast tamale, this time using butter with a little lard in the dough.

FOR THE DOUGH:

3 ears fresh sweet corn (to make 1½ cups kernels), with husks

1 Bermuda onion, chopped fine

2 cloves garlic, minced

2 tablespoons pure ground chili, New Mexican type

Salt and freshly ground black pepper

1 tablespoon oil

6 tablespoons butter

2 tablespoons lard

2 cups basic tamale *masa* (page 100)

1 teaspoon baking powder

FOR THE FILLING:

1 sweet red pepper, chopped fine

⅓ cup peanuts

1 cup shredded cooked pork or chicken

2 jalapeño chilies, roasted (see Note, page 5), seeded, and minced

½ cup pitted and chopped black olives

2 tablespoons chopped fresh cilantro

Remove husks and silks from the corn and reserve the husks. Cut kernels from the cobs and puree the kernels in a food processor. Sauté the onion, garlic, and seasonings for 3 to 5 minutes in the oil until they have softened. Add them to the processor and puree with the corn. Sauté the puree until thick and shiny.

Beat the butter and lard in an electric mixer until fluffy. Add alternately portions of the corn puree and the basic tamale *masa*

and beat until the dough is very light and spongy. Add baking powder and beat again.

Mix together all the ingredients of the filling.

Spread the dough on the largest of the reserved corn husks as outlined above. Add a spoonful of filling and enclose it in the dough. Fold and tie the husks and stack them in a steamer. Steam for 45 minutes to an hour, depending on how closely packed the tamales are (see Note).

Note: This is a good dish to turn into a tamale pie, instead of individually wrapped tamales. Bake the dish at 350 degrees for 45 to 60 minutes, depending on the thickness of the pie. To serve, unwrap the top husks and spoon out the cooked corn.

Pumpkin or Squash Tamales
(*Tamales de Oaxaca*)

MAKES ABOUT A DOZEN TAMALES

Pumpkin or squash puree beaten into the tamale dough gives these tamales a glowing golden color. Prized especially in the Oaxacan region of Mexico, and in Bolivia, the tamales are flavored with typical hot and sweet spices and filled with chopped almonds, raisins, and dried apricots.

FOR THE DOUGH:

    2 cups basic tamale dough (page 100)
    1¼ cups pureed cooked pumpkin
        or winter squash
    1 teaspoon fresh ground chili,
        New Mexican type
    1 teaspoon ground cinnamon
    ½ teaspoon freshly ground black
        pepper

FOR THE FILLING:

    ⅓ cup chopped toasted almonds
    ⅓ cup raisins
    ½ cup slivered dried apricots

Prepare dough by beating into the basic tamale dough the cooked pumpkin and spices.

Prepare the filling by mixing the ingredients together.

Proceed as directed for wrapping and steaming.

Black Tamales
(*Tamales Negros*)

MAKES A DOZEN TAMALES

I saw these first, with some astonishment, in the market of Quezaltenango in the high-lands of Guatemala. The dark color comes from that incomparably rich sauce, *mole,* which uses grated bitter chocolate for body and flavor—and color. Blackness is intensified by using dark chilies such as chili mulato and, in this version, black prunes in the filling.

FOR THE SAUCE:

- 2 tablespoons pumpkin seeds
- 2 tablespoons sesame seeds
- 1 teaspoon ground cinnamon
- 1 mulato chili and 1 pasilla chili
- 2 pounds ripe tomatoes, roasted with skins on
- 2 ounces bitter chocolate, grated

FOR THE DOUGH:

- ½ cup lard
- 2 cups basic tamale *masa* (page 100)
- ½ cup sauce (see above)
- 1 teaspoon baking powder
- ½ teaspoon salt

FOR THE FILLING:

- ½ cup diced cooked chicken or pork
- 6 pitted prunes, chopped
- ⅓ cup raisins
- 6 large green pitted olives, chopped
- ½ cup sauce (see above)

First prepare the sauce, some of which you'll mix into the dough and the rest into the filling. Lightly toast the pumpkin and sesame seeds in a skillet over medium heat (about 5 minutes), sprinkle them with the cinnamon and toast a minute more. Scrape them into a blender and return the skillet to the heat.

Lightly toast the chilies for a minute or two, then remove their stems, shake out their seeds and discard them. Tear the chilies into pieces and put them in the blender.

Add the tomatoes to the blender with the grated chocolate and puree. Turn the sauce into a saucepan and stir over low heat for 3 to 4 minutes until it is thick and shiny. Measure out ½ cup of sauce and let it cool.

For the dough, beat the lard in an electric mixer until very light and fluffy. Beat half the basic *masa* into the lard, then add gradually the rest of the *masa* alternately with the sauce. Sprinkle on baking powder and salt and beat some more.

Mix the ingredients of the filling with the remaining sauce.

Spread the dough on wrappers as instructed above. Spoon the filling on the dough, fold up the wrappers and steam.

Puerto Rican Coconut Tamales
(*Guanimes de Maíz*)

MAKES A DOZEN TAMALES

This version, suggested by Carmen Valldejuli's *Puerto Rican Cookery,* is made with a dough of plain yellow cornmeal, instead of the special tamale dough. Adding thick creamy coconut milk to the dough, however, does what lard does in a traditional tamale dough. Traditionally they are wrapped in banana or plantain leaves. Flavored with molasses and aniseed these tamales taste like wrapped taffies. So simple. So delicious.

1 **cup freshly ground yellow cornmeal, medium grind**
½ **teaspoon aniseed**
½ **teaspoon salt**
2 **cups unsweetened coconut milk**
¼ **cup molasses**

Mix the cornmeal with the aniseed and salt. Then mix in the coconut milk and molasses and beat together. Spread the dough with a spoon in long cigar shapes in banana or plantain leaves. Fold, tie, and steam (see "To Make Tamales," pages 100–102)

Fresh Strawberry Tamales
(*Tamales de Primeras Comuniones*)

MAKES ABOUT A DOZEN TAMALES

First Communion tamales are made three ways, *de chile, de dulce, y de manteca,* "the chili kind, the sweet kind, the buttery kind." Children prefer the sweet and their parents the chili kind. The sweet kind is usually made of fresh fruit, either strawberry or pineapple, and colored pink or yellow with a little food coloring.

The family secret for these tamales, Beatriz Ramírez says, is to "make them happy, make them with love and make them with calm." If you don't, the tamales will never cook and you'll have to dance and pray in front of the *baño maría,* the steam kettle.

1½ **cups fresh sweet corn kernels**
     (to make ¾ cup kernels)
1 **cup fresh strawberries**
1 **teaspoon vanilla**
½ **cup sugar**
     A few drops red food dye (optional)
8 **tablespoons (1 stick) butter**
3 **cups basic tamale *masa* (page 100)**
     Pinch of salt
2 **teaspoons baking powder**
½ **cup chopped toasted almonds**
½ **cup raisins**

Puree the corn kernels, strawberries, and vanilla in a food processor. Add the sugar and food dye (if used), and process again.

In an electric mixer, beat the butter until light. Beat in half the basic tamale *masa,* then alternate the corn-strawberry puree with the *masa.* Add the salt and baking powder and beat again.

Fold the almonds and raisins into the dough.

Spread the dough on wrappers to make a cylindrical tamale. Fold and tie, then steam as directed above (see "To Make Tamales," pages 100–102). Because the strawberries give juice, this dough even after it's steamed will be very moist.

Pancakes and Crepes

Charleston Corn Batter Cakes

MAKES 12 TO 18 CAKES

New England and the Deep South are still the twinned hearts of traditional corn-cake cooking, whether the batter goes into pancakes, muffins, or breads, but none better than this classic pancake included in Blanche Rhett's *200 Years of Charleston Cooking*. The recipe was supplied by Mrs. Rhett's butler, which might suggest something from *Gone With the Wind*, but the butler was named William Deas and he liked to serve these cakes with batter-fried chicken and cream gravy.

If possible, don't omit the lard; the quantity is very small and it does its own wonderful thing to flavor and texture. This is a batter you can make the night before and keep in the refrigerator ready for breakfast (add a little more milk, as needed). To the batter you can add any number of delicious things like chopped pecans or fresh corn kernels and blueberries (they're wonderful together). If you want the cakes sweetened, add maple syrup, honey, or rum. If you want to use them as a savory to accompany fried chicken or sausage patties or a shrimp sauté, add fresh herbs or chilies or minced onion.

2 cups freshly ground cornmeal, medium grind

½ cup all-purpose flour

2 teaspoons baking powder

½ teaspoon salt

1 tablespoon butter, melted

1 tablespoon lard, melted

1 egg

1¼ to 1¾ cups milk

Preheat a heavy griddle or cast-iron skillet.

Sift the dry ingredients together into a large bowl. Beat together the butter, lard, egg, and milk and mix into the cornmeal mixture.

Lightly grease the griddle and ladle on small dollops of batter to make cakes 2 to 3 inches in diameter. Brown the cakes for a few minutes on both sides.

Sweet Corn Flapjacks

MAKES 2 DOZEN CAKES

Flapjacks or slapjacks is good old American slang for pancakes, and particularly appropriate for cakes made with Native American corn, as in Amelia Simmons's 1796 recipe in *American Cookery* for "Indian Slapjack." But I like the explanation of the word "flapjack" in *The Pocumtuc Housewife* of 1805, where the authors describe a too energetic cook who once, to turn her griddle cakes, tossed them so high that they "flapped up through the wide kitchen chimney and came down outside." "This," the authors caution, "should be avoided."

A batter of fresh corn puree makes not only a delicious-tasting flapjack but helps the batter stick together when you flip or flap or slap it on the griddle. This is the kind of basic batter you can turn sweet or savory, by adding a teaspoon of honey or maple sugar or a few blueberries, or by adding ground pecans or bacon bits or curried minced onions or chopped chicken livers or any chili mixture—you name it.

½ cup freshly ground cornmeal, medium grind

1 to 1¼ cups buttermilk

4 ears fresh sweet corn (to make 2 cups kernels)

2 eggs

2 tablespoons butter, melted

½ cup all-purpose flour

1 teaspoon baking powder

¼ teaspoon baking soda

½ teaspoon salt

½ teaspoon ground cardamom (optional)

Preheat a griddle or heavy cast-iron skillet and grease it lightly just before you are ready to fry the cakes.

Mix the cornmeal with 1 cup of the buttermilk and set aside.

Puree the corn kernels in a food processor, add the eggs and butter, and then the cornmeal mixture.

Sift together the flour, baking powder, baking soda, salt, and cardamom.

Combine the dry ingredients with the corn puree and adjust thinness or thickness of the batter by adding more buttermilk as wanted. Ladle out a large soupspoonful of batter onto the skillet, to make 2- to 3-inch rounds. When browned on one side (2 to 3 minutes), flip the cake over to brown the other side.

Pagataw Oyster Pancakes

MAKES 18 TO 24 CAKES

H. Stuart Ripley, when cooking at The Green Lake Grill in Seattle, sent me a recipe for these tasty pancakes made with fresh corn and chopped oysters. He got the idea for them, he said, from an old New England cookbook he found in Groton, Massachusetts, that described a native dish: "They bake bread of Indian corn, which they call pagataw: with this and austres [oysters], a kind of snail, they make a dish which is widely used."

It's odd to think of oysters as a kind of sea snail, but it was not odd for natives to put corn and oysters together, since both were abundant. Ripley says that when oysters are scarce, he uses smoked salmon. I often use clams. I've adapted his recipe to make it simpler and heartier, using basically the batter for Sweet Corn Flapjacks (opposite), with the addition of oysters and herbs.

These make a fine Sunday brunch or supper dish and, if you make the cakes small, a tasty hors d'oeuvre.

½ cup freshly ground cornmeal,
   medium grind
½ cup all-purpose flour
1 teaspoon baking powder
¼ teaspoon baking soda
1 teaspoon salt
½ teaspoon freshly ground black
   pepper
2 tablespoons butter, melted
1 cup buttermilk
½ teaspoon lemon juice
2 eggs, beaten
4 ears fresh sweet corn
   (to make 2 cups kernels)
2 tablespoons finely diced sweet
   red pepper
1 tablespoon minced chives

1 tablespoon finely chopped fresh
   cilantro
2 cups chopped shucked oysters

GARNISH:

½ cup heavy cream, whipped
1 jalapeño chili, roasted (see Note,
   page 5), seeded, and minced
⅓ cup salmon roe

Preheat a griddle or heavy cast-iron pan and grease it lightly.

In a large bowl, mix together the cornmeal, flour, baking powder, baking soda, and seasonings.

Mix together the melted butter, buttermilk, lemon juice, and eggs and stir into the dry ingredients.

(continued)

Fold in the corn kernels, red pepper, chives, cilantro, and oysters.

Spoon the batter onto the griddle to make cakes 2 to 3 inches in diameter. Turn to brown them a few minutes on both sides.

For the garnish, mix cream and jalapeño chili together. Top each pancake with a dollop of the mixture and a dab of salmon roe.

I wants a piece o' hoecake, I wants a piece o' bread,

An' I wants a piece o' Johnnycake as big as my ole head.

—*Old Charleston folk rhyme*

Whitecap Flint Jonnycakes

Amelia Simmons, whose *American Cookery* in 1796 gave us our first official cookbook, was the first to print a recipe for "Johnny Cake or Hoe Cake," but in fact it was simply a cornpone baked before the fire. The name johnnycake persisted throughout the Colonies, but it was Rhode Island that declared the pone a state dish and decreed by legislative act that it must be spelled "jonnycake" and must be made of meal ground from Rhode Island Whitecap flint corn. Rhode Islanders were thus the first to elevate a cornpone to the controlled appellation of a Bordeaux estate wine.

Having agreed on the essential ingredient, Rhode Islanders agree on nothing else. Newport County dictates a thin batter to make an elegantly crisp lacy wafer. South County decrees a thick cake like a sausage patty. Some add sugar or molasses for sweetness and butter or shortening for texture. I find melted butter works wonders, but thin or thick, the taste is in the corn and in the grinding, and fortunately there are several small mills in Rhode Island that can supply you with Whitecap flint (see A Source List, page 223).

Rhode Islanders serve jonnycakes with everything from roast turkey to beefsteak. Because they're not sweetened, they also make a good hors d'oeuvre, topped with a little deviled crab or a tapenade or a square of smoked salmon.

Thin Jonnycakes

MAKES 20 TO 25 CAKES

1½ cups cold milk
 1 cup freshly ground flint meal,
     fine grind
 ½ teaspoon salt
 4 tablespoons butter, melted

Preheat a heavy griddle and grease it well.

Stir the milk gradually into the meal, add the salt and butter, and mix well. Drop the batter from a tablespoon onto the hot griddle to make cakes about 3 inches round. Little holes will appear in the batter but they'll gradually fill in. Cook the cakes 4 to 5 minutes on each side until brown and crusty. (Turn carefully with a spatula; these cakes stick to the griddle.)

Thick Jonnycakes

MAKES 12 CAKES

 1 cup boiling water
 1 cup freshly ground flint meal,
     fine grind
 ½ teaspoon salt
 4 tablespoons butter, melted

Stir the water gradually into the meal, add the salt and butter, mix well and let the batter sit 5 minutes. Shape into small cakes, 2½ inches round, and fry on a hot griddle or lightly greased skillet 5 to 8 minutes until browned on both sides.

Pumpkin Corn Pancakes

MAKES 10 TO 12 CAKES

The pairing of pumpkin and cornmeal was convenient and natural to American colonists and their descendants. Lydia Child, in *The Frugal Housewife* (1829), describes an "Indian cake, or bannock" (a British term for a griddle or hearthstone bread) made with meal, molasses, and "a little stewed pumpkin." I'm partial to molasses but if you prefer a lighter sweet, try this lovely harvest pancake with maple syrup or honey.

For breakfast, top these with butter and sprinkle them with powdered sugar and cinnamon. Spiced with lots of black pepper, they're also good with chicken, turkey, duck, or game.

1 cup freshly ground yellow
    cornmeal, medium grind
½ cup all-purpose flour
½ teaspoon salt
2 teaspoons baking powder
½ teaspoon baking soda
½ teaspoon ground cinnamon
¼ teaspoon ground allspice
½ cup pumpkin puree
1 cup buttermilk
2 eggs, beaten
2 tablespoons molasses
1 tablespoon butter, melted
1 tablespoon grated fresh ginger

Preheat a griddle or heavy cast-iron skillet.

Sift together the dry ingredients into a large bowl.

In a separate bowl, beat together the pumpkin, buttermilk, eggs, molasses, butter, and ginger. Add the pumpkin mixture to the cornmeal and mix well (add more buttermilk if needed).

Grease the griddle lightly, drop batter onto the griddle in small dollops, and brown the pancakes for 3 to 4 minutes on each side.

Hominy Waffles

MAKES 4 TO 6 WAFFLES

Southern cookbooks of the nineteenth century abound in recipes for waffles made with cooked hominy at a time when hominy was a kitchen staple. These are light and crisp on the outside, yet moist within. Mary Leize Simons (who contributed this recipe to *200 Years of Charleston Cooking* [1930]) claims that they are as thrifty as they are delicious, "for one of these waffles is as satisfying as two of the usual ones."

As with other unsweetened corn cakes, these are good at any meal, not just breakfast. I like to serve them instead of bread with a hearty soup or chef's salad.

1 cup drained hominy
2 cups buttermilk
2 eggs
2 tablespoons butter, melted
1 cup all-purpose flour
1 teaspoon salt
½ teaspoon baking soda

Preheat a waffle iron and lightly grease it when ready to pour in the batter.

Puree the hominy in a food processor, mix in the buttermilk, eggs, and butter and process again.

Sift the flour with the salt and soda and blend with the hominy mixture.

Pour in the hot waffle iron and bake 4 or 5 minutes, or until crisp.

Savoy Corn Crepes
(Matafans de Maïs)

MAKES 4 LARGE CREPES (10 OR 12 INCHES)

The *matafan,* Madeleine Kamman explains in her book *Savoie,* is the region's "rustic semi-pancake, semi-crepe," made since the first Stone Age settlers spread a thin gruel of native grains on a hot stone to bake in the fire. Since the eighteenth century they have made *matafans* with two immigrants from the New World, corn and potatoes. Typical of the French, however, they transform an American cornpone into a light and airy crepe with a quantity of eggs.

The toppings Kamman suggests may help broaden the horizon of American pancake eaters. Traditionally they are rolled with honey and butter, which seems familiar enough, but they are also topped with creamed mushrooms and zucchini or most deliciously with Bosc pears sautéed with bacon.

FOR THE CREPES:

- ½ cup freshly ground corn flour
- ½ cup all-purpose flour
- ½ teaspoon salt
- 6 eggs, separated
- ¾ to 1 cup buttermilk (or sweet milk)
- 4 tablespoons butter, melted

FOR THE PEAR AND BACON FILLING:

- ½ lemon
- 3 Bosc pears, peeled and sliced
  Freshly ground black pepper
- 6 slices bacon, cut in small pieces

Preheat a crepe pan (or griddle) and just before adding the batter grease the pan generously with a little extra butter.

Mix the cornmeal and flour with the salt. Beat in the egg yolks one by one, and finally the buttermilk and butter.

In a separate bowl, beat the egg whites until they form soft peaks. Fold them lightly into the batter.

Pour enough batter into the crepe pan to make a ¼-inch layer overall. Cook for 2 or 3 minutes until the top appears dry, then invert it on a plate, and slip it back onto the pan to brown the other side.

To prepare the filling, squeeze juice of ½ lemon over the sliced pears and sprinkle them with pepper.

In a sauté pan, render the fat from the bacon, remove the meat with a slotted spoon, and pour off all fat but a thin film.

Brown the pear slices over high heat in the fat and mix with the bacon.

Put a spoonful on each crepe and roll.

QUICK BREADS

Two cups Indian, one cup wheat,

One cup sour milk, one cup sweet,

One good egg that well you beat.

Half cup molasses, too;

Half cup sugar add thereto,

With one spoon of butter new.

Salt and soda each a teaspoon;

Mix up quick and bake it soon.

Then you'll have corn bread complete,

Best of all corn bread you meet.

"A Poem to Make Corn Bread By"
(from Charles J. Murphy's American Indian Corn, *1917)*

Crackling Cornpone

SERVES 4 TO 6

Pone (from an Algonquian word "to roast or bake") is as simple and as rustic as it sounds. Originally it was a generic name, like tortilla, for cornmeal and water shaped into a thin cake and baked over an open fire or in the ashes. By the time of nineteenth-century ladies' cookbooks, this ash cake or pone was fancied up with lard or butter and eggs and milk. Even plain pone, however, was still in favor in the South in 1885, when Mary Stuart Smith wrote in her *Virginia Cookery Book,* "A bit of hot ash cake, sent up with a glass of buttermilk fresh from the dairy, is often served to the most delicate ladies, and not only relished, but thought to be particularly strengthening."

(continued)

While there is something to be said for a cake of meal, water, and salt, a plain pone—unlike the tortilla with its highly refined corn flour—is apt to be coarse and dry. Pone needs a lubricant like pork cracklings for flavor and texture. A good pone displays a beautifully crisp crust, achieved by pouring the batter into a very hot skillet heated with fat.

If you can't get fresh fatback for cracklings, you can usually get salted fatback, which you can dice fine and fry to render out the fat, but remember not to add any salt to the recipe. Or you can always make mouth-melting chicken or duck or even beef cracklings.

Pone is also made delicious by using pureed hominy instead of cornmeal to make a hominy pone, or by using chopped freshly shucked oysters or clams instead of cracklings to make an oyster or clam pone. Served with a salad you need nothing more to make a meal.

1 cup cracklings
2 tablespoons melted fat
    (pork, chicken, etc.)
    or corn oil
1¼ to 1½ cups water
2 cups freshly ground white
    cornmeal, medium grind
1 teaspoon salt

Preheat the oven to 450 degrees.

Heat cracklings until very crisp in a heavy cast-iron skillet. Remove them with a slotted spoon and set aside. If they have rendered less than 2 tablespoons of fat, add enough melted fat or oil to cover the surface of the skillet. Place the skillet in the oven to heat.

Bring the water to the boil and gradually stir in the cornmeal, beating vigorously until smooth. Add the salt (unless you're using salted fatback) and mix well. Stir in the cracklings.

Remove the hot skillet (use oven gloves) from the oven, scrape the batter into the sizzling fat, and return it to the oven. Bake for 10 to 15 minutes, until lightly browned on top. Invert the pone onto a plate so that the bottom crust is on top.

Corn Dodgers

Corn Dodgers are made of plain pone, shaped into ovals about 5 inches long and 1 inch in diameter, and baked on a hot griddle greased with lard. Like Hush Puppies, the real origin of the name Dodgers is lost in the legends of folk-say, but both names suggest that day-old corn cakes, baked or fried, could be useful missiles. Dodgers, nonetheless, had advocates as sophisticated as that bon vivant of the 1930s George Rector, who opined, "Corn dodgers is to ordinary corn breads what brandy is to wine."

Venezuelan Arepas

MAKES 8 TO 10 CAKES

The national corn bread of Venezuela is a bread grilled over a wood fire, then split open, the doughy insides pulled out and the interior filled with a local fresh runny cream cheese. The cheese is something like crème fraîche, but I find mascarpone a better substitute. The best substitute for cooking these cakes over a wood fire or a charcoal grill is to first toast them in a cast-iron griddle or skillet and then bake them in an oven. The point is to get a crust on the outside since you can remove any uncooked dough on the inside.

2 cups *masa harina*
1 teaspoon salt
2 cups water
2 cups mascarpone

Preheat the oven to 350 degrees and lightly grease a baking sheet.

Mix the flour with the salt and water in a bowl to make a stiff but moist dough. Cover bowl with plastic wrap and let sit for 5 minutes.

Form the dough into eight or ten balls and flatten them into 3-inch rounds, about ½ inch thick.

Heat a cast-iron griddle, grease it lightly, and cook the cakes over moderate heat for 5 minutes on each side. Put the cakes onto the baking sheet and bake for 25 to 35 minutes, turning them twice to brown evenly. When done, they should sound hollow when tapped.

Split them open, pull out any wet dough, and spoon the cheese inside. Eat immediately.

Hot and Smoky Peppered Corn Bread

MAKES 9 TO 12 SQUARES

With cornmeal it is better to add than to subtract because the meal will bind and blend the most diverse flavorings and ingredients. I made this bread once to hand out at the Greenmarket at Union Square in Manhattan, where I was demonstrating the beauties of sweet corn. I worried that the combination of fresh corn kernels, roasted sweet peppers, smoked chili peppers, roasted onions, and sweet raisins might be too exotic for mainstream Greenmarket shoppers until I realized I was simply adding a tamale mixture to gringo corn bread. Sure enough, the samples disappeared before I'd properly started, and not just because they were free.

1 cup freshly ground cornmeal, medium grind
¾ cup all-purpose flour
1 tablespoon baking powder
1 teaspoon salt
¼ teaspoon baking soda
1 tablespoon sugar
2 ears fresh sweet corn
    (to make 1 cup kernels)
½ cup diced roasted sweet red pepper
    (see Note, page 5)
2 tablespoons finely ground chipotle
    (or other smoked) chili
½ cup minced roasted onion
½ cup raisins
4 tablespoons butter, melted
2 eggs, beaten
¾ cup buttermilk
¼ cup sour cream

Preheat the oven to 425 degrees. Prepare a 9 × 9-inch baking tin by greasing it well.

Sift the dry ingredients together.

Add the corn, sweet peppers, chili pepper, onions, and raisins and mix well.

Beat together the butter, eggs, buttermilk, and sour cream. Add liquids to the other mixture and stir until barely blended.

Scoop batter into the pan and bake 20 to 30 minutes, or until a tester comes out clean. Cut bread into squares.

Espetanga Corn Bread

SERVES 6 TO 8

This is the intriguing name Sarah Rutledge gave to a sweet potato corn bread in 1847 in *The Carolina Housewife,* which was included with dozens of other corn recipes that Célestine Eustis reprinted in 1917 in *Fifty Valuable and Delicious Recipes Made with Corn Meal for 50 Cents.* The price of ingredients may have gone up slightly from the time Miss Eustis recommended these "pour les pauvres," and it may no longer be convenient to bake this bread in a covered skillet "placed on hot coals," but the combination of sweet potato and cornmeal is as delicious now as a century or a century and a half ago. I've found that toasted cornmeal gives a wonderfully nutty flavor and crunch to the sweet potato, and I've made it hot with ginger and black pepper to live up to an exotic name like Espetanga, the origin of which is unknown to me.

This is a bread that stands up well to spiced dishes like chili beans or barbecued meats.

1 to 2   cooked sweet potatoes
(to make 2 cups of chunks)
4   tablespoons butter, melted
1   egg, beaten
½   cup milk
3   tablespoons brown sugar
1½   cups freshly ground cornmeal, medium grind
1   tablespoon baking powder
1   tablespoon ground ginger
1   teaspoon ground cinnamon
1   teaspoon salt
½   teaspoon freshly ground black pepper

Preheat the oven to 350 degrees.

Toast the cornmeal in a shallow baking pan for about 10 minutes in the preheated oven, stirring occasionally. Remove and set aside.

Raise the heat to 400 degrees. Grease well a heavy cast-iron skillet with butter or shortening and heat it in the oven about 5 minutes before you add the batter.

Peel the cooked sweet potatoes, cut them in chunks, and put them in a food processor with the butter, egg, and milk. Puree until smooth.

Sift together the dry ingredients and add them into the sweet potato mixture. Pulse until well mixed.

Scoop the mixture into the heated skillet, cover with a lid (or foil), and bake for 15 minutes. Remove the lid and cook until the top is slightly browned, 10 to 15 minutes more.

All-in-One Thanksgiving Turkey Stuffing

MAKES ABOUT 6 CUPS

The only bad part about preparing the big bird for the big meal is that hurried last-minute preparation of the stuffing, combining the wet things with the dry breadstuffs. To save time, labor, and have it ready the night before, I decided to bake all my favorite stuffing ingredients into the corn bread itself. Into the batter went the traditional sausage meat, onions, celery, parsley, sage, rosemary, and thyme, plus some roasted jalapeños and dried fruits like cranberries, blueberries, and cherries. I baked it in a large shallow pan to get the bread good and crusty to soak up roasting turkey juices the way dried bread cubes do. Fixing the bird was never so easy and the stuffing was never so good. Why didn't I think of this before?

½   pound well-spiced sausage meat
1   cup chopped onions
½   cup chopped celery
1   tablespoon mixed dried rosemary, sage, and thyme
    Salt and freshly ground black pepper
3   jalapeño chilies, roasted (see Note, page 5), peeled, and chopped
¾   cup mixed dried cranberries, blueberries, and cherries
⅓   cup finely chopped fresh parsley
2   cups freshly ground cornmeal, medium grind
1   cup all-purpose flour
4   teaspoons baking powder
¼   teaspoon baking soda
1½ teaspoons salt
2   eggs, beaten
1¼ cups buttermilk
⅓   cup corn oil or melted butter

Preheat the oven to 400 degrees and butter or oil an 8½ × 11-inch baking pan.

Sauté the sausage meat in a heavy skillet until it has begun to lose its pinkness (don't overcook). In the same pan (add oil if necessary), sauté the onions, celery, and seasonings for 5 to 8 minutes until the vegetables are slightly softened.

Add the jalapeños, fruit, and parsley and sauté 2 or 3 minutes to mix them well together. Remove from the fire and set aside.

In a large bowl, mix together the dry ingredients of cornmeal, flour, baking powder, baking soda, and salt. In a small bowl, beat together the eggs, buttermilk, and oil.

Add the liquid mixture to the dry mixture and stir lightly. Fold in the sausage mixture and turn the batter into the baking pan.

Bake for 20 to 25 minutes until the bread is crusty and lightly browned. When ready to roast the turkey, break the corn bread in small pieces and stuff the neck and belly of the bird.

Toasted Corn Sticks

MAKES A DOZEN CORN STICKS

For the benefit of the world's bakers, America was the first to contribute the cast-iron baking molds that made muffins round. America also contributed the cast-iron pan indented not with round cups but with molds shaped like ears of corn to make what became known as "corn sticks." Too often these were made sweeter than muffins, but I prefer them savory with cheese and hot pepper sauce to eat as a bread with anything from soup to salad to entree. Any corn breads or muffins should be eaten hot from the oven. If you make them ahead, wrap them in foil and reheat or cut them in two and toast them in a toaster oven. Any corn breads will freeze well if you wrap them tightly.

1   cup freshly ground yellow
    cornmeal, medium grind
1   cup all-purpose flour
1   tablespoon baking powder
1   teaspoon salt
¼   cup corn oil
1¼ cups milk
¾   cup freshly grated Parmesan cheese
    Tabasco
4   tablespoons butter, melted, for
    brushing the molds

Preheat the oven to 350 degrees.

Toast the cornmeal in a shallow baking pan for about 10 minutes in the preheated oven, stirring occasionally. Remove and set aside.

Increase the oven heat to 400 degrees and place a cast-iron corn stick pan in the oven to heat it.

Combine the cornmeal, flour, baking powder, and salt and mix well. Stir in the oil, milk, cheese, and a few drops of Tabasco and mix until batter barely holds together.

Remove the pan from the oven, brush butter into each corn mold, and fill each about two-thirds full.

Bake for 15 to 20 minutes, until tops are nicely crusty.

Hot Tomato Muffins

MAKES A DOZEN MUFFINS

This is one of hundreds of variations on the theme of what I call CORN MUFFINS PLUS, the plus meaning anything you find in the cupboard of refrigerator that excites your imagination at muffin-making time. For the basic corn muffin batter, I usually use half cornmeal and half wheat flour to balance corn crunch with wheat lightness. You can shift the balance of grains either way to make the muffin crunchier or lighter. For 2 cups of mixed grains, I usually use 1 tablespoon of baking powder (½ teaspoon more than for wheat flour alone), 2 eggs, and at least 1 cup of liquid. When that liquid is sour or acidic, like the sour cream here, I add a small amount of baking soda to neutralize it. This is the way corn muffins have been made, more or less, for a century.

What is relatively new is the variety of the PLUSes we incorporate into that batter. The muffin recipes that follow give a brief glimpse of what corn can absorb. For this one, I happened to have some Bloody Mary mix on hand, but I could have used any kind of tomato or V-8 juice. I added more Tabasco and a little cinnamon, along with raisins and walnuts. The result is a muffin that is moist, balanced, crunchy, and gutsy.

1 cup freshly ground cornmeal
    medium grind
1 cup all-purpose flour
1 tablespoon baking powder
¼ teaspoon baking soda
2 tablespoons sugar
½ teaspoon salt
½ teaspoon ground cinnamon
1 cup raisins
½ cup coarsely chopped walnuts
¼ cup corn oil
2 eggs, beaten
½ cup sour cream
½ cup Bloody Mary mix
    (or Tabasco-spiked tomato juice)
	Preheat the oven to 350 degrees.
	Prepare muffin tins by greasing cups or lining them with paper inserts.
	    Toast the cornmeal in a shallow baking pan in the oven for about 10 minutes, stirring once or twice. Remove and set aside. Raise oven heat to 400 degrees.
	    Sift together all the dry ingredients, including cornmeal. Mix in the raisins and walnuts to coat them with flour.
	    Beat together the oil, eggs, sour cream, and Bloody Mary mix. Add the liquids to the dry mixture and stir until barely blended.
	    Scoop into the muffin pans and bake for 20 to 25 minutes, until tops are crusty and lightly browned.

Santa Fe Blue Corn Muffins

MAKES A DOZEN MUFFINS

I like to pack muffins with goodies, balancing the heat of chilies with the sweetness of fruit and increasing crunch with nuts and seeds. In other words, I like a muffin to be a meal in itself. Blue corn, sweet and fragrant, takes well to these additions, adding another layer of taste to muffins that are moist without being heavy and are variously textured. The mixture of oil and butter gives them a nice crumb. A half dozen of these, with a canteen of water, would take you from Santa Fe to Gallisteo on foot, but as always they are best eaten hot from the oven.

1¼ cups freshly ground blue cornmeal, medium grind
1 cup all-purpose flour
1 tablespoon baking powder
½ teaspoon salt
¼ teaspoon baking soda
2 tablespoons sugar
⅓ cup seeded and diced roasted sweet red pepper
2 jalapeño chilies, roasted (see Note, page 5), seeded, and minced
½ cup toasted sunflower seeds
½ cup sultana raisins
¼ cup piñon nuts or pumpkin seeds
¼ cup vegetable shortening, melted
4 tablespoons butter, melted
1 cup buttermilk
2 eggs, beaten

Preheat the oven to 375 degrees. Prepare muffin tins by greasing the cups thoroughly or using paper inserts.

Sift the dry ingredients together in a large bowl. Mix in the prepared sweet pepper, jalapeño peppers, sunflower seeds, raisins, and piñon nuts.

In a separate bowl, mix together the melted shortening, butter, buttermilk, and beaten eggs. Pour the liquid into the dry ingredients and stir lightly until barely mixed.

Spoon batter quickly into each of the cups and bake for 20 to 25 minutes, until tops are crusty and lightly browned.

Blueberry Blue Corn Muffins

MAKES A DOZEN MUFFINS

Blueberries intensify both the blueness and perfume of blue cornmeal. These are good not only in summer, when blueberries are ripe on the bushes, but also in winter when you can get blueberries dried. You can also use dried cherries or other dried fruits to good effect. I like muffins with more tang than sweetness, but you can always increase the amount of sugar or other sweetening to suit yourself. Sour cream helps keep the muffins moist.

These are good breakfast muffins to eat hot or toasted or to freeze for future use.

1 cup freshly ground blue cornmeal,
   medium grind
1 cup all-purpose flour
1 tablespoon baking powder
½ teaspoon salt
¼ teaspoon baking soda
1 tablespoon sugar
2 cups fresh blueberries or
   1 cup dried
4 tablespoons butter, melted
2 eggs, beaten
1 cup sour cream

Preheat the oven to 400 degrees. Prepare muffin tins with cup liners or by greasing the cups.

Sift the dry ingredients together. Stir in the blueberries.

Mix together the melted butter, eggs, and sour cream. Pour the liquid into the dry ingredients and stir until barely mixed.

Spoon batter quickly into the cups and bake for 15 to 20 minutes until crusty and lightly browned, or until a tester comes out clean.

Sweet Corn Chili Muffins

MAKES A DOZEN MUFFINS

The addition of sweet corn kernels, fresh or dried, provides a little explosion of sweetness that counters the distinct flavor, aroma, and heat of different kinds of chilies. This recipe makes use of three or four chilies common to New Mexico, and if for your cornmeal you can obtain some of the red corn grown at Gallina Canyon Ranch, you're in for a triple treat. Eat the muffins hot or freeze them for future use.

1 cup freshly ground red, yellow, or white cornmeal, medium grind
1 cup all-purpose flour
1 tablespoon baking powder
3 tablespoons finely ground mild chili powder (like Chimayo)
1 cup milk
6 tablespoons butter, melted
2 tablespoons dark molasses
2 eggs, beaten
1 tablespoon minced orange or lemon zest
1 tablespoon dried oregano
1 cup fresh or dried sweet corn kernels
1 poblano chili, roasted (see Note, page 5), seeded, and chopped fine
1 Anaheim chili (or 2 jalapeños), roasted, seeded, and chopped fine

Preheat the oven to 400 degrees and grease the cups of a muffin pan or insert paper liners into the cups.

Sift together the dry ingredients into a large bowl. Beat together the milk, butter, molasses, and eggs and add to the flour mixture.

Fold in the orange zest, oregano, corn kernels, and chilies and scoop the batter into the muffin cups. Bake for 12 to 15 minutes, until crusty and lightly browned.

Sweet Potato Corn Muffins

MAKES A DOZEN MUFFINS

The sweetness of corn has an affinity for the sweetness of sweet potatoes, and since they are both natives of the New World we should put them together more often. Certainly our ancestors did, and I have often made a sweet potato pie with a cornmeal crust or whipped a sweet potato puree into polenta.

This batter is simply a variant on the simpler one that makes Espetanga Corn Bread (page 121). Here I've balanced the sweetness of raisins and molasses with yogurt and orange juice. I like using yogurt in muffins as part of the "liquid" because it supplies a flavor and richness. Eat them hot or freeze for future use.

1 cup freshly ground yellow or white cornmeal, medium grind
1 cup all-purpose flour
1 tablespoon baking powder
½ teaspoon salt
1 cup raisins
2 eggs, beaten
¼ cup vegetable oil
¼ cup blackstrap molasses
½ cup yogurt
1 cup fresh orange juice
1 cup cooked sweet potatoes, pureed

Preheat the oven to 400 degrees and prepare muffin pans by greasing or putting paper inserts in the cups.

Sift the dry ingredients together. Mix in the raisins.

Beat together the eggs, oil, molasses, yogurt, orange juice, and sweet potato puree. Add the liquid to the dry ingredients and stir until barely mixed.

Scoop batter into the muffin pans and bake for 15 to 20 minutes, until crusty and lightly browned.

Hominy Bread

SERVES 4 TO 6

According to anthropologist A. C. Parker, the Iroquois would first boil dried corn with lye to remove the hulls, then pulverize the corn in a mortar and pestle, then sift it finely. This meal they mixed with water, shaped into a cake, and baked in hot ashes. Because it was portable and durable, this was "the approved form for hunting and war parties."

Our early colonists called this corn "hominy" by Anglicizing Algonquian words like *rock-ahominie* or *tackhummin*. They also Anglicized native methods by using hominy for griddle cakes and hearth-baked loaves and spoon breads. Sarah Rutledge offers many "Hommony Breads" in her *Carolina Housewife* (1847), often enriching them with butter and eggs, sometimes mixing them with grits, cornmeal, rice, or wheat flour. The bread below is very moist and textured, more like a white corn pudding than a corn bread. I use canned hominy, well drained, and here I've added some flavorful herbs for the flecked green color as well as for taste. Hominy takes well to greens of all kinds.

This makes a flat bread because of the density of hominy, mixed with corn flour instead of wheat flour. I cut it in small squares or wedges and use it as one might a focaccia or other flavorful herbed bread.

2 cups drained hominy
1 cup *masa harina*
1 teaspoon salt
¼ teaspoon white pepper
4 tablespoons butter, melted
2 cups milk
4 eggs
½ cup chopped fresh cilantro or parsley
¼ cup chopped chives

Preheat the oven to 375 degrees and butter well a 9 × 9-inch baking pan or a 1-quart soufflé dish.

Chop the hominy in a food processor. Mix the *masa harina* with the salt and pepper and add to the hominy. Add the remaining ingredients and pulse until the batter is well mixed and the herbs are chopped fine, but don't make a smooth puree.

Pour the batter into the baking pan and bake for 30 to 40 minutes, until lightly browned on top.

Moldavian Feta Cheese Corn Bread

SERVES 6 TO 8

Four centuries ago Moldavia, as the eastern region of Romania, was a breadbasket of wheat and corn for the Ottoman Empire. The wheat went to the emperors, the corn to the subject races who served them. Thank God for class differences, for otherwise Moldavians might never have devised this earthy peasant meal in the shape of a loaf of corn bread flecked with pockets of creamy white cheese. I've adapted this recipe from Anya von Bremzen's and John C. Welchman's *Please to the Table,* 1990.

Because of the cheese and eggs, this is a very rich bread to accompany something light like grilled fish or vegetables.

3 cups crumbled feta cheese

½ cup sour cream

2 large eggs, beaten

2 cups milk

6 tablespoons butter, melted

2 cups freshly ground yellow cornmeal, medium grind

¾ cup all-purpose flour

2 teaspoons baking powder

½ teaspoon baking soda

½ teaspoon sugar

Preheat the oven to 375 degrees and butter a 13 × 9-inch baking dish.

Mix cheese with the sour cream, eggs, milk, and butter in a bowl.

Sift together the dry ingredients and stir them into the cheese mixture. Blend well, cover the bowl with a lid or plastic wrap, and let sit for 15 minutes.

Scoop the batter into the baking dish and bake for 35 to 40 minutes, or until golden brown on top.

Brendan Walsh's Buttercup Spoon Bread

SERVES 10 TO 12

S poon bread is really a type of cornmeal soufflé leavened by eggs, in which yolks and whites are sometimes beaten together and sometimes separately. I like spoon breads with a lot of texture, so I favor those in which yolks and whites are beaten together. This golden spoon bread, colored by buttercup squash, has an extra creamy texture to make it "an all-American favorite" of Chef Walsh. Walsh suggests serving this one with roasts or grilled game.

1 buttercup or other winter squash
   (1 to 2 pounds to make
   2 cups puree)
6 tablespoons butter
⅛ teaspoon ground cloves
3½ teaspoons salt
½ teaspoon freshly ground black
   pepper
5 eggs, beaten
1 cup heavy cream
¼ cup honey
4 cups milk
2 cups freshly ground yellow
   cornmeal, medium grind
1 teaspoon baking powder

Preheat the oven to 400 degrees.

Halve the squash and remove its seeds. Put the halves cut side up in a baking pan, rub the cut surface of the squash with 1 tablespoon of the butter, and bake for 20 to 30 minutes, or until fork tender.

When it is cool enough to handle, peel and discard the skin. Puree the pulp in a food processor or food mill with the ground cloves and season with ½ teaspoon salt and ¼ teaspoon pepper. Add the eggs, cream, and honey and process again. Set aside.

Lower the oven heat to 375 degrees and butter a 12 × 12 × 2-inch baking dish or a 2-quart soufflé dish, to hold the spoon bread.

Bring the milk to a simmer, add the remaining salt and pepper, and stir in all but 1 tablespoon of the remaining butter (reserve 1 tablespoon to dribble over the top later).

Put the cornmeal in a large saucepan and gradually stir in the hot milk. Cook the meal over low heat, stirring constantly for 10 to 15 minutes, until it thickens. Remove the pan from the heat and beat in the squash puree and the baking powder.

Scoop the mixture into the baking dish and bake for 25 to 30 minutes, or until the top is golden brown. Drizzle the remaining butter over the top and serve the spoon bread hot or warm.

Roasted Garlic and Goat Cheese Spoon Bread

SERVES 6 TO 8

I've used freshly ground white grits for this spoon bread because of their interesting texture and I've leavened them with egg whites beaten separately. Of course you can use other grinds of cornmeal from coarse to fine and if you want a denser spoon bread, you can beat the yolks and whites together.

This is a good way to use up leftover grits, hominy, or mush, combining the corn with whatever flavors you choose to make a taste-full "bread" that can serve as a one-dish meal rather than as an accompaniment.

2 cups boiling water
1 cup freshly ground white grits, medium grind
1 cup sour cream
6 ounces fresh goat's cheese (chèvre)
1 teaspoon salt
1 teaspoon freshly ground black pepper
2 sprigs of fresh rosemary, stems removed (to make 2 tablespoons)
8 cloves garlic
1 cup milk
4 extra-large eggs, separated

Pour the boiling water into the grits in the top of a double boiler. Add the sour cream, cheese, seasonings, and rosemary and mix thoroughly. Cover the pan, put the top over the bottom of the double boiler, filled with an inch or two of boiling water, and steam 20 to 30 minutes, until the grits are thick and creamy.

Preheat the oven to 375 degrees and butter a 12 × 10 × 2-inch baking dish or a 2-quart soufflé dish. If you use a soufflé dish, you may need to tie a buttered collar of parchment paper or foil around the top so that the spoon bread can rise.

When the oven is hot, roast the garlic cloves in foil for about 15 minutes. When the cloves are cool enough to handle, squeeze the cloves from their husks and put the cloves in a food processor. Add the milk and puree until smooth. Add the cooked grits to the processor and puree again.

With the machine running, add the egg yolks one at a time through the opening in the lid. Scoop the mixture into a large bowl.

Beat the egg whites separately until they form soft peaks. Fold them lightly into the grits and scoop the mixture into the baking pan or dish. Bake at 375 degrees until the top is lightly browned and puffed, about 20 to 25 minutes.

Punjabi Corn Griddle Bread
(Makki ki Roti)

MAKES 8 SMALL ROUND BREADS

We don't often think of corn greening the valleys of India's Himachel Pradesh, but in the late summer and fall the air is redolent with roasting ears of corn, grilled over charcoal fires and eaten with salt and fresh lime. The corn is a type of field corn, so it has plenty of character, and when dried and ground into meal, it makes a griddle bread that is like a tortilla fried in butter. This bread is especially popular among the Punjabi when it is heaped with grated radish and fresh ginger and eaten with a bowl of bitter greens, such as spinach or mustard.

1 cup *masa harina*
1 teaspoon salt
⅔ cup boiling water
4 tablespoons butter
1 cup grated daikon radish
¼ cup grated fresh ginger root

Mix the flour with the salt and add the water gradually until you have a pliant but stiff dough, as in tortilla dough. Divide the dough into 8 balls, cover them with plastic wrap, and set aside.

Cut 16 squares (8 x 8 inches) of wax paper. Flatten each ball of dough between 2 of the squares to make a 4-inch round about ⅛-inch thick.

Heat a griddle (or heavy cast-iron skillet) until hot but not smoking. Peel off the top layer of paper and invert the round onto the skillet, then peel off the remaining paper.

Cook about 3 minutes, until the underside is lightly flecked with brown. Turn and cook the other side another 2 or 3 minutes. Finish by frying the round in 1½ teaspoons butter until crisply golden brown. Repeat with the remaining rounds.

To serve, pile radish and a little ginger on each bread.

Classic Boston Brown Raisin Bread

MAKES 2 LOAVES

To the colonists of New England, "white" bread meant wheat flour, "brown" meant rye meal stretched with Indian (corn) meal. Because neither rye nor corn had enough gluten to react to yeast, the dough was better made into a kind of grain pudding that you could steam rather than bake. As Maria Parloa said in her *Appledore Cook Book* of 1872, "I will say here that you cannot steam brown bread too much." Raisins are a later but most welcome addition and I've packed this dough with them. Proportions varied, with whole-wheat or white flour sometimes added, but molasses in varying quantities was a constant.

Traditionally, Boston brown bread accompanied Boston baked beans, but it's also excellent with chili beans, roasted or barbecued pork, fried or roasted chicken.

1 cup freshly ground yellow
   cornmeal, medium grind
1 cup rye flour
1 cup whole-wheat flour
1 tablespoon baking powder
1 teaspoon salt
½ teaspoon baking soda
2 cups raisins
2 cups buttermilk
¾ cup blackstrap molasses
2 tablespoons lard or vegetable
   shortening, melted

Grease well two 1-pound cans (coffee cans are good) or a large pudding mold, and put a kettle of water on to boil.

Sift dry ingredients together in a large bowl. Mix in the raisins.

Mix together the buttermilk, molasses, and shortening, and add to the flour mixture. Stir until just mixed.

Spoon batter into the cans, filling them two-thirds full. Cover each with aluminum foil and fasten tightly with string or rubber bands. Put the cans in a steamer or on a rack in a large pan. Pour boiling water halfway up the sides of the cans. Cover tightly with a lid and simmer about 2 hours until firm and compact, replacing the boiling water as necessary.

Remove the cans from the steamer, take off the foil lids, let the cans cool for 5 minutes, then invert them on a rack. Cut thick slices with a string or a very sharp slicing knife and serve the bread hot.

Peruvian Corn Bread
(*Pastel de Choclo*)

SERVES 6 TO 8

Late this very light, rich, and buttery soufflé bread, served in rectangles about 4 inches high, in a restaurant in Arequipa—Peru's most staggeringly beautiful colonial city, carved entirely of white stone. Although the bread was very sweet and very moist, it complemented finely my bowl of fiery meat stew. I begged my translator-companion, Hilda Linares, to get me the recipe and of course there are many versions, but this is one.

The bread's sweetness balances any chili-hot dish, but it can also be served on its own as a kind of hearty dessert because it is quite sweet with its raisins, coconut, and liqueur. It's best eaten hot, but it can be made ahead and reheated when ready to serve.

8   tablespoons (1 stick) butter
8   ears fresh sweet corn
       (to make 4 cups kernels)
1   12-ounce can evaporated milk
¾ to 1   cup sugar
¼   cup *anisette*
5   eggs
½   cup corn flour (or *masa harina*)
1   cup raisins
½   cup grated coconut

Preheat the oven to 350 degrees and butter well a 9 × 9-inch baking pan or 1-quart soufflé dish.

Melt the butter and let it cool slightly.

Remove the kernels from the cobs and puree in a food processor or blender, with the milk, sugar, and anisette. With the machine on, add the eggs one by one through the lid opening. Process until the mixture is light.

Mix the corn flour with the raisins and coconut. Pour the corn puree into the flour and mix well.

Scoop the batter into the baking dish and bake for 35 to 45 minutes, until the top is lightly browned and the mixture is firm.

YEAST BREADS

Although most Americans nowadays associate cornmeal with quick breads, our ancestors, who lived at a tempo more conducive to the slow fermentation of yeast breads, often used corn with wheat and other grains. What they once did by necessity, to stretch the wheat flour that was rarer and more costly, we now often do by choice. Cornmeal lends texture as well as flavor to commercially grown and ground wheat flour, which pays the cost of its standardized super-refinement by being boringly uniform and bland. I've called for all-purpose flour throughout, but if you can get bread flour, use it because its extra glutenous power will help elevate the nonglutenous corn. What corn supplies is character, whenever you want a hearty full-bodied loaf rather than a loaf of genteel refinement.

Cornmeal Pizza with Corn Topping

MAKES 1 LARGE OR 4 SMALL PIZZAS

In our current craze for pizza, cornmeal furnishes a welcome variation to the standard all-wheat dough by providing a nice crust and a slight crunch. As with any pizza, there is no end to the toppings, but a corn crust makes a good base for a beautiful display of vegetables, held in place with a layer of cheese. Other thinly sliced vegetables, such as eggplant, zucchini, and fennel, are also fine but I like the sunburst colors of red, yellow, and orange in this particular display.

FOR THE DOUGH:

- 1 tablespoon dry yeast
- 1 cup very warm water
    (110 to 115 degrees)

- 2 cups all-purpose flour
- 1 cup freshly ground cornmeal,
    medium grind
- 1 teaspoon salt
- 2 tablespoons olive oil

For the topping:

- 1 tablespoon olive oil
- 1 cup grated mozzarella
- 1 Bermuda onion, sliced paper thin
- 2 small red tomatoes, sliced thin
- 2 small yellow tomatoes, sliced thin
- 1 orange sweet pepper, sliced thin
- 2 ears fresh sweet corn, kernels cut off (to make 1 cup kernels)
    Salt and freshly ground black pepper to taste
- ¼ cup pesto sauce (or basil and olive oil puree)

To make the pizza dough, dissolve the yeast in the water, then add the flour, cornmeal, salt, and oil, stirring until well mixed. Knead by hand or in a machine until the dough is smooth and elastic, adding more flour if necessary.

Put the dough in a bowl, cover with plastic wrap, and let it rise for 30 minutes. Punch the dough down, roll it into a ball, wrap it in the plastic wrap, and chill in the refrigerator for an hour before shaping (in order to relax the gluten). Let the dough return to room temperature before shaping and baking.

Preheat the oven to 500 degrees and prepare a 14- to 15-inch pizza pan by sprinkling cornmeal over it (or insert a pizza stone in the oven to heat).

Roll or pat the dough out to form one large thin circle about ⅛ inch thick, or divide dough into quarters to make smaller individual pizzas (7 to 8 inches around). Place the dough on the baking pan (or wooden peel if using a stone) and cover it with the topping.

For the topping, brush olive oil over the dough, then sprinkle with the cheese. Add in layers the onions, tomatoes, sweet pepper, and corn kernels. Sprinkle with salt and pepper.

Bake the pizza (see Note) for 12 to 15 minutes until the crust is golden brown. Remove and make a design of wavy lines with the pesto sauce over the top.

Note: Rather than bake, you can pan-grill the pizza dough on a griddle or skillet (about 5 to 8 minutes a side), then lay on the topping and run the pizza under a broiler to roast the vegetables and melt the cheese.

Herbed Corn Focaccia

MAKES 1 LARGE THIN ROUND

Italian breads made with cornmeal are typical of Lombardy and I've turned this one into a focaccia because the taste and texture of cornmeal lend themselves to the supremely Italianate combination of olive oil, garlic, rosemary, and Parmesan cheese.

The bread is best served hot or warm and if you make it ahead, reheat it quickly before serving. The bread will keep well frozen.

- 1 tablespoon dry yeast
- 1 cup very warm water (110 to 115 degrees)
- 2 cups all-purpose flour
- ¾ cup freshly ground cornmeal, medium grind
- 1 tablespoon sea salt
- ⅓ cup olive oil
- ½ cup dry white vermouth
- ¼ cup finely chopped garlic
- ¼ cup chopped fresh rosemary leaves
- ⅓ cup freshly grated Parmesan cheese
  Freshly ground black pepper

Make a sponge by first dissolving the yeast in the water, then stirring in 1 cup of the all-purpose flour. Cover the bowl with plastic wrap and let the dough ferment 2 or 3 hours until it is bubbly.

In the bowl of an electric mixer, mix the remaining flour, the cornmeal, 1 teaspoon only of the salt, and 3 tablespoons of the olive oil. Add the sponge and the ver-

mouth and mix well. Add the garlic and herbs and mix again. Knead with a dough hook until the dough is smooth and elastic (about 5 minutes).

Put the dough in a bowl, cover with a damp towel, and let rise in a warm place until doubled (1½ hours because oil-based dough rises slowly).

Preheat the oven to 475 degrees and prepare a baking sheet by sprinkling it with cornmeal.

Punch the dough down and let it rest a couple of minutes. Then pat it into a large circle about ¼ inch thick and place it on the sheet. Indent the dough all over the top with your forefinger. Sprinkle the remaining oil over the top, then the remaining salt. Sprinkle on the cheese, then a few grinds of black pepper from a pepper mill.

Bake the dough for 10 to 15 minutes until brown and crusty.

Lemon Pepper Oregano Bread

MAKES 2 MEDIUM LOAVES

I particularly love flavored yeast breads, like this refreshingly aromatic one I've adapted from Mark Miller's Coyote Café in Santa Fe. To lemon and pepper, I've added dried oregano, which is especially good if you can get the large blossomed kind from Mexico. If you can't get good dried or fresh oregano, try other herbs like marjoram or sage, remembering that a little sage goes a long way.

Serve hot, warm, or sliced and toasted.

2 tablespoons dry yeast
1 cup very warm water
(110 to 115 degrees)
1 cup whole-wheat flour
1 cup freshly ground yellow
cornmeal, fine grind
4 to 4½ cups all-purpose flour
1 tablespoon coarsely ground black
pepper
2 teaspoons salt
2 teaspoons sugar
1 cup milk
2 tablespoons corn oil
2 lemons
4 teaspoons dried oregano or 2
tablespoons fresh

Dissolve the yeast in the warm water in the mixing bowl of an electric mixer. Stir in the whole-wheat flour, cornmeal, 3 cups of the all-purpose flour, the pepper, salt, and sugar and mix thoroughly.

Beat together the milk and oil and add them to the flour mixture. Grate the rind of the lemons and add to the dough, along with the oregano. Knead the dough with the dough hook, adding as much flour as needed to make a smooth and elastic dough (about 5 minutes).

Place the dough in a large bowl, cover with a damp towel, and let stand in a warm place about an hour or more until the dough doubles.

Punch the dough down, shape it into two long loaves, and place them on the baking sheet. Cover lightly with the towel and let the dough rise again about 45 minutes. With a razor blade cut four parallel slashes across the top of each loaf.

Preheat the oven to 400 degrees and prepare a baking sheet by sprinkling it with cornmeal.

Bake for 25 to 30 minutes, spraying the oven with water (with an atomizer) 2 or 3 times during the first 10 minutes to give a good crust. Remove when the loaves are brown and sound hollow when rapped on the bottom.

Sun-Dried Corn and Tomato Bread

MAKES 1 LARGE OR 2 SMALL ROUNDS

Sun-drying tomatoes in the summer for winter use was almost as ancient a New World art as sun-drying "green" corn kernels. Now that we're recovering for modern culinary uses these ancient arts, it's natural to wed corn and tomatoes in a yeasted corn and wheat bread, baptized with tomato juice and blessed with cheese. The tomato juice provides both color and extra flavor. This needn't be a sourdough loaf, but I like the flavor of bread that has taken its own sweet time, 12 to 24 hours, to ferment.

Capitalizing on the color, I've sometimes used this bread for Thanksgiving feasts, inserting the stem of a large pumpkin into the top of the dough to suggest an improbable but very edible "pumpkin." Because of the cheese, you'll get the best flavor if you serve the bread warm. Like any sourdough, the bread keeps very well and is easily reheated.

FOR THE STARTER:

1 tablespoon dry yeast
1 cup very warm water
    (110 to 115 degrees)
1 cup whole-wheat flour
1 cup freshly ground yellow
    cornmeal, medium grind,
    toasted (see page 121 for
    toasting directions)

FOR THE DOUGH:

1 tablespoon dry yeast
¼ cup very warm water
    (110 to 115 degrees)
3 to 4 cups all-purpose flour
2 teaspoons salt
½ cup dried sweet corn kernels,
    soaked an hour in water to cover
½ cup dried tomatoes, soaked an
    hour in water to cover

½ to 1 cup tomato juice, as needed
¼ cup olive oil
1 cup grated Monterey Jack cheese

For the starter, dissolve the yeast in the water and mix in the flour and meal. Cover with plastic wrap and let sit in a warm place for 12 to 24 hours until it has fermented enough to smell yeasty.

When ready to bake, dissolve the second tablespoon of yeast in water and mix in 3 cups of the flour and the salt. Add this mixture to the starter.

Drain the corn and tomatoes over a cup to catch their liquid. Add sufficient tomato juice to make 1 cup total liquid. Add the liquid to the flour mixture, then the oil, and knead until the dough begins to hold together. Add the raw kernels and the tomatoes cut in small pieces. Add the

cheese and additional wheat flour as necessary to make a pliable dough. Knead until the dough is glossy and elastic.

Put the dough in a bowl, cover with plastic wrap, and let it rise for 1 to 1½ hours until doubled.

Prepare a baking sheet by greasing and sprinkling it with cornmeal.

Punch the dough down, shape it into a large round, and place it on the prepared baking sheet. Slash the top of the dough in three parallel lines and let the dough rise a second time, 45 minutes to an hour.

Preheat the oven to 400 degrees.

Put the dough into the preheated oven and bake for 30 to 45 minutes, or until the bottom sounds hollow when tapped. Put the loaf on a rack to cool slightly before cutting.

Black and White Braided Bread
(*Huitlacoche* Bread)

1 16-INCH LOAF

The flavor and color of corn mushrooms (huitlacoche) are so distinctive that they must be handled carefully when it comes to breads. Here I decided to dramatize their earthy brown-black color by braiding dark dough with white dough. Because the corn mushroom gives off a lot of moisture, especially if it's been frozen, it's best to mix in the liquid and knead the two doughs separately in order to control the wetness of the dough. The results are worth the effort because the loaf is an eye dazzler, with a good crust, a nicely moist interior, and the earthy flavor of mushrooms.

1 tablespoon dry yeast

¾ cup very warm water
(110 to 115 degrees)

1 cup freshly ground white cornmeal, medium grind

3½ to 4 cups all-purpose flour

1 teaspoon salt

½ teaspoon coarsely ground black pepper

1 tablespoon dried epazote or dried oregano

3 tablespoons vegetable oil

½ cup coarsely chopped huitlacoche (fresh or frozen, chopped, and drained)

(continued)

In a small cup, dissolve the yeast in ¼ cup of the water.

Mix together the cornmeal, 3 cups of the wheat flour, the salt, pepper, and epazote. Put half of the mixture into the bowl of an electric mixer and add to it half the yeast and the remaining ½ cup of water. Mix the dough and gradually add half the oil (1½ tablespoons). Add more wheat flour as needed to make a soft but pliant dough. Knead the dough about 5 minutes by machine until it is elastic. Shape the dough into a ball and put in a bowl large enough to hold the second ball of dough.

Put the remaining half of the cornmeal and flour mixture into the bowl of the electric mixer. If the corn mushrooms have been frozen, thaw them thoroughly, chop them, and squeeze them over a small bowl to remove excess liquid. Mix the mushrooms into the flour, add remaining oil, and

knead the dough. Add more wheat flour as needed. Knead until the dough is elastic.

Shape into a ball and place the dark dough beside the white one, dividing them with a square of plastic wrap or wax paper. Cover the bowl with plastic wrap and let the dough rise until double (1 to 1½ hours).

Prepare a baking sheet by greasing and sprinkling it with cornmeal.

Punch each dough down and roll each into a cylinder about 16 inches long. Braid the two doughs together and place the loaf on the prepared baking sheet. Cover the loaf lightly with plastic wrap and let rise again (45 minutes to 1 hour).

Preheat the oven to 400 degrees. Bake the bread for 30 to 40 minutes, spraying with water 3 times during the first 10 minutes. When done, the bread will be crusty on top and sound hollow when rapped on the bottom. Let it cool on a rack.

Sourdough Three-Grain Bread

MAKES 1 LARGE ROUND LOAF

The colonists would have called this Thirded Bread, using equal parts of three grains—wheat, rye, and corn. When wheat flour was a rarity on this continent, colonists longed for a bread of sifted bleached flour, sweet with fresh yeast. Three centuries later, in our post-Wonder Bread age, what we long for is a gutsy peasant bread packed with whole grains, the sourer the better. This dough ferments in two stages, first the starter, then the sponge, before the final dough. This is one recipe where I've specified bread flour because the proportion of nonglutenous grain is large.

For a corn event in New York, I was lucky enough to have Tom Cat Bakery make a large round crusty loaf of this dough, decorated with a dough-baked ear of corn on top. Like a birthday cake, it was painful to cut into the design to slice the bread. Two weeks later I was still cutting thick slices of this loaf, which I kept in a paper bag in the refrigerator. Toasting the slices quickly restores flavor and sometimes improves texture.

FOR THE STARTER:

- ½ cup bread flour
- ½ cup rye berries, ground in a blender
- ½ cup freshly ground yellow cornmeal, medium grind
- ¾ cup cold water

FOR THE SPONGE:

- 1¼ cups cold water
- 1 cup bread flour
- ½ cup rye berries, ground in a blender
- 1 cup freshly ground yellow cornmeal, medium grind
- ½ tablespoon salt

FOR THE FINAL DOUGH:

- 1 tablespoon dry yeast
- ¼ cup very warm water (110 to 115 degrees)
- 1½ to 2½ cups bread flour

Mix the ingredients for the starter in a bowl, cover with a wet cloth (secured by a rubber band), and leave in a cool place for 2 days until the starter is yeasty and fermented.

Mix the ingredients for the sponge and add the starter to it. Mix well. Cover the bowl with a plastic wrap (secured with a rubber band) and leave 12 hours or overnight in a cool place.

Dissolve the yeast in the warm water and mix into the sponge. Add bread flour until the dough is the right consistency to knead. Knead the dough in an electric mixer with a dough hook for about 5 minutes (15 minutes by hand or in two batches in a food processor for 2 minutes). When the dough is elastic and nonsticky, shape it into a ball, and put it in a bowl. Cover with a damp towel and put the bowl in a warm place to rise for 1 to 1½ hours until the dough has doubled.

Punch the dough down, shape it into a ball, and put it on a baking tile or sheet sprinkled with cornmeal. Let the dough rise again slightly for 45 minutes to an hour (this is a dense dough so it will spread rather than rise high). With a razor blade, slash a cross on top of the dough.

Preheat the oven to 450 degrees.

For extra crustiness, cover dough with a heatproof earthenware bowl, and bake in the preheated oven for 15 minutes. Reduce heat to 400 degrees, carefully remove the bowl (take care not to burn yourself from released steam), and bake 15 to 20 minutes more, until good and crusty on top and the bottom sounds hollow when rapped with the knuckles. Cool on a rack.

Sourdough Bread with Masa Yeast

MAKES 6 TO 8 SQUARES

A fermented corn bread from West Africa is called Aboloo, and is made, according to Laurens Van der Post in *African Cooking* (1970), from a wild yeast generated by the equivalent of *masa harina*. Africans shape the dough into individual breads like tamales, wrapping them in banana leaves or corn husks (or foil packets) to steam. Because the practice of fermenting dough was so common in ancient America, I decided to add fermented *masa*, as a leavened flavorer, to an ordinary corn bread batter leavened also by baking powder. Why bother? The resulting bread answered my own question because it had character—a chewiness, earthiness, and aftertaste, like wine, that a conventional corn bread often lacks.

I bake this bread, like an ordinary corn bread, in a square pan so that it easily cuts into square portions.

FOR THE STARTER:

- 1 cup *masa harina*
- 1 cup warm water

FOR THE DOUGH:

- 1 cup freshly ground yellow cornmeal, medium grind
- ½ cup all-purpose flour
- 1 teaspoon baking powder
- ½ teaspoon baking soda
- 2 teaspoons sugar
- 4 tablespoons melted butter or vegetable oil
- 2 eggs, beaten
- 1 cup buttermilk

Mix the *masa harina* and water thoroughly in a small bowl, cover with plastic wrap, and let it ferment for 2 or 3 days.

Preheat the oven to 425 degrees and grease a 9 × 9-inch baking pan.

For the dough, sift the dry ingredients together in a large bowl. Beat together the butter, eggs, and buttermilk. Mix the liquid into the flour mixture, add ½ cup of the *masa* starter (keep the rest in the refrigerator for another batch; it will keep for a week), and blend well.

Scoop the batter into the baking pan and bake for 25 to 35 minutes, or until browned and crusty on top.

Sweet Corn Sourdough Bread

MAKES A ROUND LOAF ABOUT 10 INCHES IN DIAMETER

Native Americans both north and south of the Mexican border made much use of fermented corn, both fresh and dried, for food as well as drink. Fermentation both sweetened, flavored, and nutritionally enriched native bread doughs. Since I've long experimented with making yeast from scratch from any number of traditional starters like potatoes, pumpkin, hops, etc., I decided to try fresh corn puree. Certainly both the sugar and starch components of corn would create yeast. The final result was a good spongy dough with a faint whiff of cheese and a heavenly golden color.

Slow fermentation gives bread its best flavor, but obviously the four-step process spread out over 4 days is not recommended to anyone keen on saving time. Like other sourdoughs, the flavor is most pronounced when the bread is sliced and toasted.

STEP 1:

> ½ cup fresh sweet corn kernels,
>   coarsely pureed

Put the puree in a small bowl, cover tightly with plastic wrap, and let ferment 2 or 3 days at room temperature until the puree smells cheesy.

STEP 2:

> 2 teaspoons honey
> ½ cup warm water
> 1 cup freshly ground yellow
>   cornmeal, medium grind
> 1 cup all-purpose flour

Dissolve the honey in the water, add the fermented corn puree, then the cornmeal and flour, and mix well. Knead the dough in a food processor or electric mixer until the dough is elastic. Put the dough in a bowl, cover it with a damp cloth, and let it ferment 8 to 10 hours until it is bubbly and cheesy.

STEP 3:

> 1 teaspoon honey
> ½ cup warm water
> 1 cup all-purpose flour

Dissolve the honey in the water, mix in the flour, add it to the previous dough (in order to "feed" the yeast), cover the bowl, and let the dough ferment again for 4 to 5 hours to keep the bubbles going.

(continued)

STEP 4:

  1 tablespoon dry yeast

  1 cup very warm water

        (110 to 115 degrees)

  ½ cup freshly ground yellow

        cornmeal, fine grind, or corn

        flour

1½ to 2 cups all-purpose flour

  1 teaspoon salt

Dissolve the yeast in the water. Mix in the previously fermented dough. Gradually add the cornmeal, flour, and salt. Knead by hand or with a dough hook in an electric mixer until the dough is satiny and elastic. Put the dough in a bowl, cover it with a damp towel and let rise for 1 to 1½ hours in a warm place until doubled.

Prepare a baking sheet by greasing and sprinkling cornmeal over it.

Punch the dough down, shape it into a high mound, and put it on the baking sheet. With a razor slash a deep cross in the top of the dough, cover the dough with the towel, and let the dough rise again for 45 minutes to an hour.

Preheat the oven to 425 degrees.

Bake the bread for 20 minutes, spraying the oven with water (from an atomizer) 2 or 3 times. Lower the heat to 375 degrees and bake 15 to 25 minutes more, until golden brown on top. The bottom should sound hollow when rapped.

Sweet Dishes

Peach-Corn-Buttermilk Sherbet

Coconut-Corn Caramel Flan

Sweet Corn Custard and
    Moonshine Anglaise

Mexican Chocolate-Chili Cups

Chocolate Popcorn Pudding

Peruvian Purple Corn Dessert
    (*Mazamorra Morada*)

Grape Juice Cornmeal Diamonds

Coconut Polenta
    (*Funche con Leche de Coco*)

Native Indian Pudding

Colonial Indian Pudding

Italian Cornmeal Pound Cake
    (*Amor Polenta*)

Italian Cornstarch Sponge Cake
    (*Torta Sabbiosa*)

Sour Cream Chocolate-Hazelnut Cake

Chocolate-Chili-Orange Corn Cake

Cornmeal Piecrust

Popcorn Piecrust

Kiwi and Starfruit Tart

Plum Cornmeal Torte

Barbados Conkies

Cornmeal Peanut Butter Cookies

Almond-Cornmeal Shortbread
    (*Fregolata Veneziana*)

Piedmontese Horseshoe Cookies
    (*Krumiri*)

Cherry Cornmeal Biscotti

Homemade Cracker Jacks

Sorority Corn Flake Kisses

Taffy Popcorn Apples

I sing the sweets I know, the charms I feel,

My morning incense, and my even meal,

The sweets of Hasty-Pudding.

—*Joel Barlow,* The Hasty-Pudding: A Poem, in Three Cantos, *1793*

There are so many sweets to know, from a traditional Colonial Indian Pudding to a contemporary Native Indian Pudding. Along the way, corn surfaces in crunchy Italian biscotti and cakes, in North American ice creams and Latin American flans, in Scottish shortbreads and Peruvian compotes. Several recipes suggest the ancient and noble Mexican triumvirate of chocolate, chili, and corn, while others are as Made-in-the-U.S.A. as Homemade Cracker Jacks and Sorority Corn Flake Kisses.

I've omitted one bit of Americana, a recipe sent from the spirit world to a true believer in the return of Elvis Presley, one persuaded she can woo him back with chocolate corn bread, made with ½ can Hershey's Chocolate Syrup and 1 box Jiffy Corn Bread Mix. Apostates should give it a try. My personal favorite may seem to be similarly off-the-wall, but this one I beg everyone to try. It's a Popcorn Piecrust using ground popped corn, which lends a deliciously nutty taste and crunch without the calories of nuts.

Peach-Corn-Buttermilk Sherbet

MAKES ABOUT 1 QUART SHERBET

Buttermilk is a simple old-fashioned way to make a refreshing milk sherbet for a hot summer's day, when fresh peaches blush side by side with sweet corn in the market. Besides adding body, the buttermilk has a tang that accents fruit purees, especially delicate ones like peaches, which in any case require an acidic squirt of lemon to bring out their flavor. The pureed corn adds an underpinning of creaminess and, with buttermilk, balances sweet against tart. I've pureed sweet corn with many different kinds of fruits for ice creams and sherbets, including blueberries, coconut, mango, etc., because corn provides a creamy texture without the calories or cooking of an egg-cream custard.

This is good served with a crisp corn cookie like Almond-Cornmeal Shortbread (page 173).

3 to 5 ripe peaches (to make 3 cups puree)
3 tablespoons fresh lemon juice
¾ cup superfine sugar
2 cups buttermilk
2 ears fresh sweet corn
    (to make 1 cup kernels)
¼ teaspoon almond extract

Skin and pit the peaches. Puree the pulp in a food processor with the lemon juice and sugar.

Put the buttermilk in a blender, add the corn kernels and almond extract, and blend to make the mixture as smooth as possible.

Freeze according to directions for an ice cream freezer, or put in a metal container and freeze as quickly as possible. Once the sherbet is frozen and just before serving, put it in a food processor and pulse until the mixture is creamy.

Coconut-Corn Caramel Flan

SERVES 6 TO 8

For those who've loved flan, or custard, since their nursery days, the flavors of this Peruvian version are anything but nursery fare. It calls for Peru's famous brandy, Pisco, but if you lack that, there's always good rum or bourbon to go with the coconut cream, aniseed, and brown sugar. Peru's sugar is *chancaca*, a dark brown molasses-laden cone or square, but our granulated dark brown sugar plus a tablespoon of molasses comes close. Besides adding its own sweet flavor and texture, corn puree cuts down on the usual large number of eggs.

½ cup dark brown sugar

1 tablespoon molasses

2 cups half-and-half

1 cup milk

3 ears fresh sweet corn
    (to make 1½ cups kernels)

¼ cup coconut cream

4 whole eggs

½ teaspoon ground aniseed

1 tablespoon orange or lemon zest

3 tablespoons Pisco brandy or rum

Preheat the oven to 300 degrees.

In a saucepan, put the sugar, molasses, half-and-half, and milk and bring the liquid to the simmer.

Cut the kernels from the ears, add them to the milk mixture, and return to the simmer. Remove from the heat, cover pan with a lid, and let the corn steep for 10 minutes.

Put the mixture in a blender and liquefy. Add the coconut cream and liquefy again until the mixture is as smooth as possible.

Beat the eggs together in a bowl, then pour the hot milk gradually into the eggs, beating steadily.

Add the remaining flavorings and mix well.

Pour the mixture into a baking dish or individual custard cups and set them in a large baking pan filled with an inch of boiling water. Bake for 30 to 45 minutes, depending on the size of the baking dish or cups. The custard is done when a tester put in the center comes out clean.

Sweet Corn Custard
and Moonshine Anglaise

SERVES 8

When Philippe Chin did an all-corn dinner for me at his restaurant Chanterelles in Philadelphia, he ended with a delicate baked custard, thickened with pureed sweet corn and sauced with that soft dessert custard the French call *anglaise*. In honor of corn, he spiked it with moonshine rather than vanilla, but if you don't have a reliable source of quality moonshine, I'd try Maker's Mark bourbon, gold label. Once again, the pureed sweet corn acts as a custard stabilizer as well as a delicate flavorer.

3 cups whole milk
4 ears fresh sweet corn
    (to make 2 cups kernels)
4 large eggs
2 egg yolks
½ cup sugar
1 teaspoon vanilla extract

FOR THE SAUCE:

1 cup milk
3 tablespoons sugar
3 egg yolks
¼ cup moonshine or bourbon
    Ground cinnamon (optional)

Preheat the oven to 325 degrees and butter eight ramekins, 4 inches in diameter, suitable for unmolding.

Bring the milk to the simmer in a saucepan, add the corn kernels, cover with a lid, remove from the heat, and let sit for 10 minutes. Put the mixture in a blender and puree as smooth as possible. Set aside.

With a whisk or electric beater, beat the eggs, egg yolks, and sugar until light and fluffy. Add the vanilla and gradually stir in about a cup of the corn puree. Return the mixture to the blender and blend again to liquefy the corn skins.

Pour the mixture through a strainer into the ramekins, placed in a baking pan. Set the pan on the top rack of the oven and carefully pour in boiling water to a depth of about an inch in the bottom of the pan. Bake for 40 to 50 minutes, or until the custards are set. A knife inserted near the middle should come out clean. Remove the ramekins from the pan and let them cool. Chill them in the refrigerator until ready to unmold.

To make the sauce, bring the milk and sugar to the simmer in a saucepan over medium heat.

In a separate bowl, beat the egg yolks with a whisk or electric mixer until light. Then slowly add the hot milk, beating all

the while. Pour the mixture back in the saucepan and whisk over low heat for about 30 seconds, or until the sauce is thick enough to coat the back of a spoon. (Don't overheat or overcook or the mixture will curdle. Should it start to curdle, pour it into a blender and blend at top speed.)

Remove the sauce from the heat and stir in the moonshine.

When ready to serve, pour some sauce in the middle of each plate, unmold a ramekin on top of the sauce and, if desired, sprinkle the top of the custard with a little cinnamon.

Mexican Chocolate-Chili Cups

SERVES 4 TO 6

This is a very simple cold dessert, a chocolate mousse thickened by sweet corn, that brings a warm response because chili warms the tongue in a surprising aftertaste. Crème fraîche or sour cream increases the creaminess of the corn but you don't have to add it to this unusual but delectable layering of corn, chocolate, coffee, chili, cinnamon, and nuts. Even though I serve this in very small bowls, like pots de crème, I find it ends the meal with an exclamation point rather than a period.

2 ears fresh sweet corn
   (to make 1 cup kernels)
8 ounces bittersweet chocolate
½ cup espresso
1 teaspoon ground cinnamon
4 teaspoons pure ground chili,
   mild to medium hot
½ cup finely ground hazelnuts,
   lightly toasted
½ cup crème fraîche or sour cream
   (optional)

Cut the kernels from the ears, scraping the cobs to remove all the milk, and puree them in a food processor as smooth as possible. Strain the puree through a sieve and discard the skins.

Over a very low flame (or in a double boiler), melt the chocolate slowly with the coffee, cinnamon, chili, and toasted nuts. Add the corn puree, stir well, and remove from the heat. Let the mixture cool for 10 minutes before adding the crème fraîche.

Spoon the mixture into small cups or bowls. Refrigerate for an hour or more.

Chocolate Popcorn Pudding

SERVES 4 TO 6

For those who imagine that the idea of a popcorn pudding is but the latest outrage of a jaded nouvelle cuisine, let me cite *The Kansas Home Cook-Book* of 1874, where Mrs. C. H. Crane of Ossawattomie contributes a recipe for plain popcorn pudding. Even New England's Maria Parloa and Fannie Farmer included pudding recipes for popped corn, which were adaptations of Native American recipes for popped corn boiled with maple sugar and sunflower seed or bear oil.

My "pudding" is not what we usually mean by that word. It's more like a dense soufflé or a spoon bread, baked in individual soufflé dishes, pots de crème, or muffin tins, so that it has a light crispness to it despite the chocolate. The toasted popcorn gives it the taste and texture of finely ground roasted nuts. Serve warm with whipped cream, heavy cream, raspberry sauce, fresh raspberries, etc.

2½ cups popped corn
1 cup half-and-half
½ cup dark brown sugar
Pinch of salt
2 ounces unsweetened chocolate
1 teaspoon vanilla extract
¼ teaspoon almond extract
1 egg

Preheat the oven to 300 degrees.

Spread the popped corn on a large baking pan and toast it for 10 minutes to dry it out. Put the corn in a blender and grind as fine as possible. Raise the oven to 325 degrees.

Put the half-and-half, sugar, salt, and chocolate in a saucepan and bring the mixture almost to the simmer, just long enough to melt the chocolate. Stir frequently. Remove from the heat and add the vanilla and almond extracts.

Pour the chocolate mixture into the popcorn flour in the blender. Blend again. Add the egg and blend until well mixed.

Pour the mixture into 4 soufflé dishes or pots de crème, or 6 cups (filled with paper inserts) in a muffin tin. Cover whatever containers are used with foil.

Bake at 325 degrees for 30 minutes, until mixture is firm.

Peruvian Purple Corn Dessert
(*Mazamorra Morada*)

SERVES 6

One ancient strain of the large-kerneled corn typical of Peru is colored deep purple, or *morada*. For reasons of color the corn is used in the sweetened unfermented corn drink *chicha morada* and in this spectacularly purple dessert of dried and fresh fruits, in a sauce of purple corn sweetened by the molasses-rich sugar called *chancaca* and thickened by sweet potato flour (*harina de camote*). I substitute dark brown sugar with a little molasses for the one and cornstarch or arrowroot for the other. But there's no substitute for the color purple. Interestingly, Germany makes a similar dessert of purple and red berries or other dark fruits, thickened with cornstarch, and called *rote grütze*, or "red grits."

The Peruvian dessert looks a bit like an opaque fruit-laden Jell-O, but the binder has a nice creamy texture varied by the texture of different fruits. Although Peruvians like the dessert on the sweet side, you can make it as tart as you want with lemon juice. Refrigerated and covered with plastic wrap, it will keep well for a week or more.

1 pound dried purple corn
8 cups cold water, or to cover
½ cup dark brown sugar,
    plus 1 tablespoon molasses
1 stick of cinnamon
½ teaspoon aniseed
6 whole cloves
½ cup quartered dried apricots
½ cup raisins
1 cup fresh fruit, such as blueberries
    or cherries or chopped plums,
    peaches, pears, or apples
⅓ cup sweet-potato flour or cornstarch
⅓ to ½ cup fresh lemon juice
    Ground cinnamon for garnish

In a kettle, cover the whole corn cobs with their kernels with 8 cups cold water, allowing a good 4 inches at the top because the corn will absorb liquid. Bring to a boil, cover the pan, and simmer for 30 to 40 minutes. Strain the liquid over a large bowl and reserve. Discard the corn.

Measure 4 cups of the corn liquid and put it in a saucepan with the sugar and spices. Stir well. Bring to the simmer; cover the pan, and simmer for 30 minutes.

Remove the spices with a slotted spoon and discard them. Add the dried fruits. Cover the pan and simmer until the fruits are tender, about 10 minutes. Remove from the heat.

(continued)

Add the fresh fruit to the corn mixture.

Dissolve the sweet-potato flour in ½ cup of the reserved corn liquid (or cold water) and stir until smooth. Add it to the corn mixture and stir it in thoroughly. Put the pan over low heat to thicken the starch, stirring constantly.

When it is thick, add lemon juice to taste. Put the mixture in a bowl and refrigerate until well chilled (it will thicken more when cold).

When ready to serve, sprinkle the top of the bowl with ground cinnamon.

Grape Juice Cornmeal Diamonds

MAKES ABOUT 3 DOZEN PIECES

Sweetening, flavoring, and coloring cornmeal with grape or berry syrup is common to many European countries. In Georgian Russia, according to Darra Goldstein in *The Georgian Feast*, it is a grape-flavored polenta called *pelamushi*. In Italy it is made with the juice of freshly pressed wine grapes called *sapa*. In America, when wild grapes were as abundant as corn, grape juice–flavored mush was called "Porko Afke," according to a 1904 recipe from Tulsa (collected in *Pioneer Cookery Around Oklahoma*).

In this version, I've followed Goldstein's suggestion for using a mixture of both wine and grape juice to deepen flavor. If you have fresh Concord grapes, you can squeeze their juice to make a strongly tart and aromatic fresh juice (3 pounds will make about 3 cups juice). Or you can use bottled forms of unsweetened red or purple grape juice. Whatever you use, you will want to sweeten it to your own taste for this beautifully colored mush.

You can serve the mush hot as a dessert, the way Mexicans serve sweetened *tamal* for desserts. Or you can spread the mush in a pan and cut it in squares or diamonds to serve as a "cookie" or "candy." This makes a delightful, simple, healthy finger-food snack for kids. As with other forms of mush, the flavor and texture are best when served at room temperature, but I have snacked on them with pleasure, not to say addiction, after they have been well chilled in the refrigerator.

3 pounds Concord grapes or 3 cups
   unsweetened grape juice

1 cup Concord grape wine

¼ cup sugar or to taste

1½ cups freshly ground white
   cornmeal, fine grind

½ cup chopped walnuts (optional)

If you are using fresh grapes, chop them in a food processor and push the juice through a strainer. Discard the seeds and pulp.

In a saucepan, combine the grape juice with the wine, taste for sweetness, and add sugar accordingly. Bring the mixture to the boil. Put the cornmeal in the top of a double boiler and pour the liquid gradually into the meal, stirring until smooth.

Place the top over the bottom of the double boiler, covered with an inch or two of boiling water. Steam the meal over medium heat, stirring occasionally, for about 20 minutes, or until thick. Add the chopped nuts and mix well.

Rinse a 9 × 13-inch baking pan with cold water; pour in the cooked cornmeal, smoothing the top. Let it cool at room temperature and cut it into 2-inch diamonds or squares.

Coconut Polenta
(*Funche con Leche de Coco*)

SERVES 6

Puerto Rico provides this variant on the sweetened polenta theme. In this recipe from *Rice and Beans and Tasty Things* by Dora Romano, the cornmeal is boiled in coconut milk. Nothing could be simpler or more delicious once you have your coconut milk.

To me, this kind of milky sweetened mush is comfort food, and I like it for breakfast with a little milk poured over the top, or as a bedtime snack.

1 **fresh coconut**
1 **quart whole milk**
1 **cup freshly ground white cornmeal,**
    medium to fine grind
½ **cup sugar**
  Pinch of salt
1 **stick of cinnamon**
  Ground cinnamon for garnish

Preheat the oven to 400 degreees.

To make the coconut milk, pierce the three "eyes" of the coconut with an ice pick and a hammer, drain off the "water" inside, and reserve. Heat the coconut in the oven for about 20 minutes. Remove the coconut from the oven, cover it with a cloth, and smash it with a hammer to split open the shell.

Separate the meat from the shell with a screwdriver or heavy knife and pare off the brown skin from the white meat with a vegetable peeler. Cut the meat in small chunks and put in a food processor to get 3 to 4 cups grated coconut. Reserve ½ cup of the coconut and set aside.

Bring the quart of milk to the simmer. Process the grated coconut in two batches: add half the milk and half the coconut meat to the processor and process for 2 to 3 minutes. Repeat with the remaining half. When cool enough to handle, pour the coconut and liquid into a clean towel set over a bowl. Squeeze the towel to extract all the liquid. If the liquid measures less than 4 cups, add the reserved coconut "water" or regular cow's milk.

Prepare a double boiler with 1 to 2 inches of boiling water in the bottom pan. Place the cornmeal in the top of the boiler. In a separate pan, combine the coconut milk with the sugar, salt, and stick of cinnamon and bring to the simmer. Remove from the heat and pour the milk into the meal, stirring until the meal is smooth. Cover the top of the boiler and steam for 30 to 40 minutes.

Ladle the mixture into a bowl, sprinkle with the reserved grated coconut and cinnamon, and serve.

Native Indian Pudding

SERVES 8

When New England colonists spoke of "Indian" pudding, they meant a steamed or baked pudding made with Indian meal (cornmeal), instead of with true British flour made of wheat. Such "puddings" might be as wet as porridge, as in "hasty pudding," or as solid as fruitcake, as in "Christmas pudding." Colonists once again were implanting Wheat-culture words and methods on Corn-culture materials.

Instead of sweetening their cornmeal with milk and molasses, native Americans used maple sap, cactus juice, wild berry juice, wild honey. They also added nuts and seeds and native herbs. Here I've used toasted cornmeal with nuts and cranberries, sweetened with maple syrup and cranberry-raspberry juice, and flavored with cinnamon and ginger. Of course you can use other cranberry juice mixtures, but I like the berry taste of this one. You can also use blackberries, loganberries, huckleberries, or any wild berry provided you sweeten them to taste. Slow baking intensifies the already intense fruit and nut taste, which I find delicious topped with sour cream.

2 cups cranberries
2 cups cranberry-raspberry juice
1 cup maple syrup
½ teaspoon ginger
½ teaspoon cinnamon
½ teaspoon salt
⅔ cup finely ground and toasted cornmeal
1 cup coarsely ground walnuts (black walnuts are best)
1 cup sour cream (optional)

Preheat the oven to 300 degrees and butter a baking dish 6 to 8 inches in diameter.

In a saucepan, combine the cranberries, cranberry juice, maple syrup, ginger, cinnamon, and salt. Bring the mixture to the simmer and cook until the berries begin to pop.

In a bowl, combine the cornmeal and nuts. Gradually stir the cranberry mixture into the cornmeal and mix thoroughly.

Scoop the mixture into the dish and bake for about 1½ hours, until the cornmeal has thickened the mixture somewhat. The pudding will thicken more as it cools.

Serve hot or warm in small bowls and pass a separate bowl of sour cream.

Colonial Indian Pudding

SERVES 6, MAKES 1¹/₂ CUPS SAUCE

Our Yankee cookbook author Amelia Simmons gives three variations for A Nice Indian Pudding in her *American Cookery* of 1796, ranging from a pudding bag of plain sweetened meal to one with very little meal but lots of eggs, raisins, butter, and spice. The point was to make it as much like an English Christmas pudding as possible, with chopped suet if you had it, substituting molasses for costly sugar and Indian meal for wheat.

Today we identify the pudding as a rustic one of meal and molasses. But since this is a very wintry dish, I like to return to the colonial tradition of using whatever dried fruits are to hand, such as dried blueberries and cranberries, in addition to raisins. It was the urbane Miss Eliza Leslie of Philadelphia who suggested adding lemon or orange zest, Zante currants, or sultana raisins to her pudding, and of serving the pudding in a hard sauce of powdered sugar, butter, and fresh orange. I've added a bit of bourbon to her sauce.

This version resembles a wet fruit cake, enlivened with fresh ginger and with the citrus juices of the sauce.

2 cups whole milk
1 cup half-and-half
½ cup unsulphured molasses
¼ cup dark brown sugar
6 tablespoons (¾ stick) butter
1 cup freshly ground yellow
    cornmeal, medium grind
1 teaspoon salt
½ teaspoon grated nutmeg
½ teaspoon grated cinnamon
2 tablespoons grated fresh ginger
4 eggs
1 cup dried fruit, such as raisins,
    currants, blueberries,
    cranberries, cherries, chopped
    peaches

FOR THE SAUCE:

4 tablespoons butter, melted
2¼ cups confectioners' sugar
½ cup fresh orange juice
¼ cup fresh lemon juice
¼ cup bourbon

Preheat the oven to 300 degrees, butter a 2-quart baking dish, and boil water for a larger pan to set the dish in.

In a saucepan, bring the milk and half-and-half to the simmer with the molasses and brown sugar, stirring well. Remove from the heat and melt the butter in the hot mixture.

Pour the mixture over the cornmeal and stir until smooth. Mix in the salt and spices and stir again.

In a separate bowl, beat the eggs until light and fluffy. Fold them into the mixture. Fold in the dried fruit.

Pour the mixture into the buttered dish, set it in the larger pan filled with an inch or two of boiling water, and bake for 1½ hours until the mixture is firm in the center. Serve with the sauce.

To make the sauce, beat the melted butter gradually into the sugar, then the orange and lemon juice, and finally the bourbon.

Italian Cornmeal Pound Cake
(*Amor Polenta*)

MAKES 1 8-INCH CAKE OR 1 9×5-INCH LOAF

The Italians have given us many delicious cornmeal cakes and cookies, among them this delightfully named *Amor Polenta*, which I've often made for Valentine's Day. In *The Italian Baker,* Carol Field cites its origin in Varese, around Como and Bergamo, in northern Lombardy bordering the Swiss Alps. And indeed, it's a border cake, adding to the standard European wheat flour pound cake the character of cornmeal and the flavor of maraschino liqueur or almond.

The version I've used here, suggested by New York baker Peggy Cullen, cuts down on the heavy quantity of egg yolks and increases the proportion of cornmeal. Because of its sturdy character, this is a good keeping cake, which might suggest that polenta love, unlike some other kinds, lasts.

12   tablespoons (1½ sticks) unsalted butter, softened
¾   cup superfine sugar
3   eggs, at room temperature
3   egg yolks, at room temperature
½   teaspoon vanilla extract
½   teaspoon almond extract
½   cup all-purpose flour
½   cup freshly ground yellow cornmeal, fine grind
1½   teaspoons baking powder
¼   teaspoon salt
    Confectioners' sugar

Preheat oven to 350 degrees and prepare an 8-inch cake pan or 9- × 5-inch loaf pan by buttering it well and sprinkling the interior with cornmeal.

Cream the butter and sugar together in an electric mixer until light and fluffy. Add the whole eggs one at a time and beat well after each. Add the egg yolks, vanilla and almond flavorings, and beat well again until the mixture is very fluffy.

Sift together the flour, cornmeal, baking powder, and salt and gently fold the dry mixture into the batter. Smooth the top.

Bake for 35 to 40 minutes, or until a tester comes out clean. Cool on a cake rack for 10 minutes, then invert the cake onto the rack and remove the pan. When ready to serve, invert the cake again and sprinkle the top with confectioners' sugar.

Italian Cornstarch Sponge Cake
(*Torta Sabbiosa*)

MAKES 1 9-INCH CAKE

Around the turn of the century, cornstarch was a relatively new product on the domestic front when it was being marketed and sold to women whose principal kitchen pride was baking cakes. Consequently, cornstarch cakes and puddings were much in vogue. A recipe for Cornstarch Cake appears in *Our Women's Exchange*, offered by the ladies of Xenia, Ohio. A similar recipe, except for the telltale anisette or sambuca, I wiggled from an Italian friend and chef, Anna Teresa Callen. This one was called *Torta Sabbiosa*. There's no getting around it. Those who guffaw at a recipe for Cornstarch Cake will rush to their sifters and cake pans to produce *Torta Sabbiosa* (the name means "sandy torte"). And for all those Americans who will down polenta but scorn mush, let's go with the *torta*.

The *torta* tastes like a light Italian pound cake, with a fine crumb. It doesn't matter if the top of the cake cracks, because you'll sift confectioners' sugar over it. Serve slices with a bowl of mascarpone and fresh or poached fruit and toast slices next morning for breakfast.

2 cups confectioners' sugar
1 cup freshly ground corn flour
½ cup all-purpose flour
1 cup cornstarch
1 teaspoon baking powder
½ pound (2 sticks) butter,
    cut into small pieces
4 eggs
1 teaspoon vanilla extract
1 tablespoon anisette or Sambuca

Preheat the oven to 375 degrees. Butter and flour a 9-inch springform pan.

Set aside 2 tablespoons of the confectioners' sugar. Put the remaining sugar in a food processor with the corn flour, all-purpose flour, cornstarch, and baking powder. Pulse to mix.

Add the butter and pulse several times until the butter is cut into the dry ingredients.

Beat the eggs lightly with a fork and add to the processor, along with the flavorings. Pulse until the dough is smooth.

Scoop the mixture into the cake pan and bake for 45 to 50 minutes, until a cake tester comes out clean.

Let the cake cool for 10 to 15 minutes on a rack before removing the springform pan. When ready to serve, sprinkle the reserved confectioners' sugar over the top.

Sour Cream Chocolate-Hazelnut Cake

SERVES 12

This very light and airy cornmeal pound cake is another Italian contribution. A version of it is served at New York's San Domenico restaurant in individual round molds on a chocolate sauce with a flutter of raspberries. Like other cornmeal cakes, it is delicious toasted, and I particularly like to eat it at breakfast.

2 ounces unsweetened chocolate
2 ounces bittersweet chocolate
¼ cup espresso (or other strong) coffee
1 cup finely ground toasted hazelnuts
8 tablespoons (1 stick) butter
1 cup brown sugar
½ cup granulated sugar
4 eggs
½ cup sour cream
1 teaspoon vanilla extract
1 cup freshly ground corn flour, yellow or white
1 cup all-purpose flour
1½ teaspoons baking powder
½ teaspoon baking soda
1 teaspoon ground cinnamon
½ teaspoon freshly ground black pepper
Pinch of salt
Confectioners' sugar or cocoa and cinnamon, or additional toasted hazelnuts (optional)

Preheat oven to 350 degrees. Butter and flour a 9 × 13-inch baking pan.

Melt the chocolate over very low heat with the coffee. Put aside to cool slightly. Mix in the hazelnuts.

In an electric mixer beat the butter with the brown and white sugars until light and fluffy. Add the eggs one at a time, beating a minute each time, until the mixture is thick and lemon-colored. Beat in the melted chocolate.

Mix the sour cream with the vanilla and stir into the egg mixture.

Sift together the flours, baking powder, baking soda, cinnamon, pepper, and salt and fold them lightly into the batter until well mixed.

Pour the batter into the baking pan and smooth the top. Bake for 35 to 45 minutes, until a cake tester comes out clean.

Cool in the pan for 15 minutes. Invert onto a cake rack and remove the pan. Let cool. Sprinkle with confectioners' sugar or cocoa mixed with cinnamon or additional toasted ground hazelnuts.

Chocolate-Chili-Orange Corn Cake

SERVES 12 TO 16

I had my first bite of this dense moist cake, with a surprising zing in the aftertaste, at the Fourth Street Grill in Berkeley when California Cuisine was in its blooming adolescence in the 1970s. I've been fiddling with the cake ever since because it encapsulates what I love about California, the oranges of my childhood, and then the double-barreled Mexican shotgun of chocolate and chili.

I've added cornmeal and pumpkin seeds to give added texture to the complex layering of flavors in this long-keeping cake. I kept one once, well wrapped, for almost 8 weeks in my refrigerator. Like a really good brandied fruitcake, or a well-kept friend, it gets better and better as it ripens.

FOR THE CHOCOLATE SYRUP:

- 2 ounces semisweet chocolate
- 1 ounce bitter chocolate
- 2 teaspoons honey
- 1 tablespoon butter
- ⅓ cup espresso

FOR THE BATTER:

- ½ pound (2 sticks) butter
- 1½ cups sugar
- 5 eggs
- ¼ to ⅓ cup grated orange zest
- 2 tablespoons fresh orange juice
- 1 cup all-purpose flour
- ¾ cup freshly ground cornmeal, fine grind
- ½ teaspoon baking soda
  Pinch of salt
- 1 to 2 tablespoons pure ground chili, medium hot

- 1 cup chopped, toasted pumpkin seeds or walnuts
  Chocolate syrup (see above)

FOR THE GLAZE:

- ½ cup orange or lemon marmalade, melted
- 2 tablespoons fresh orange juice
- 2 tablespoons fresh lemon juice
- ⅓ cup tequila, orange liqueur, or rum
  Confectioners' sugar

Preheat the oven to 350 degrees and prepare a bundt pan or a 9-inch spring-form pan by buttering it and sprinkling it with flour.

To make the syrup, melt the chocolate over very low heat with the other ingredients, stirring until smooth. Set aside.

(continued)

For the batter, cream the butter and sugar in an electric mixer. Add the eggs one at a time and beat until light and fluffy. Add the orange zest and juice and beat again.

Mix the dry ingredients together in a large bowl and stir in the egg mixture. Fold in the pumpkin seeds. Add the chocolate syrup with a rubber spatula and streak the syrup through the batter to make a marbled effect.

Scrape the batter into the prepared cake pan and smooth the top. Bake for 1 to 1½ hours, or until a cake tester comes out clean. Cover top loosely with foil for the first 30 minutes, then remove foil to let the top brown.

Cool the cake in the pan for 15 minutes, then invert it onto a platter (or remove sides of the springform pan).

Prepare the glaze by heating the marmalade until syrupy. Remove from the heat and stir in the juices and liqueur. Pour the glaze over the cake. Scoop up the glaze from the platter and repour until it is all absorbed.

When the cake is cool, wrap it in foil and refrigerate. When ready to serve, sprinkle the top with a thick layer of powdered sugar.

Cornmeal Piecrust

MAKES 2 8- OR 9-INCH PIE SHELLS

One of my discoveries in working with cornmeals is to find how useful corn flour, *masa harina,* or even finely ground cornmeal is in making a crumbly rather than flaky piecrust. The corn gives the crust a slight crunch no matter how juicy or wet the filling. I've found references to mixed-grain crusts in nineteenth-century cookbooks, but in the context of a "Poor Man's Pie," where corn was a stretcher for wheat. Today when wheat is cheap and standardized, we can use corn for extra flavor as well as crunchiness. To underline that texture, add a small quantity of toasted sesame seeds or toasted and finely ground nuts.

With *masa harina* or corn flour, use equal amounts of wheat and corn. With a finely ground cornmeal, use a smaller proportion of corn to wheat (i.e., ¾ corn to 1¼ wheat). I like to use this kind of crust with fruit pies and tarts that are apt to be juicy. Although you can roll out the dough, it breaks so easily that I find it simpler to press the dough into a pan with my fingertips. That means the crust will work best for a one-crust pie or tart. With fruit

tarts I add a little sugar to the crust. But the crust is also good for savory pies, such as quiches, cheese tarts, vegetable tarts, etc., and with those I omit the sugar and add a little cayenne or freshly ground black pepper. Many of the mixtures in Appetizers and Side Dishes could be baked in this crust. See Chili-Corn Ramekin (page 15) or Corn and Goat Cheese Flan (page 16).

1 cup *masa harina* or corn flour
1 cup all-purpose flour
  Pinch of salt
2 tablespoons sugar
8 tablespoons (1 stick) butter, chilled
¼ cup shortening or lard, chilled
4 to 6 tablespoons iced water

Put the *masa harina,* flour, salt, and sugar in a food processor and pulse until mixed.

Cut the butter in 16 cubes and add to the processor. Add the lard, cut in small pieces. Pulse until the butter and lard are in pieces smaller than canned peas.

With the machine running, add 4 tablespoons of the water through the opening in the lid. If the dough is too dry to come together, add the rest of the water as needed, but be careful to pulse only until the dough begins to form a ball. Don't overprocess the dough.

Wrap the dough in plastic or foil and refrigerate for 30 minutes.

When the dough is chilled, roll it out between plastic sheets to fit two 8- or 9-inch pie pans, or press the dough quickly with your fingertips into the pans, making it of even thickness on bottom and sides. Prick the dough with fork tines and refrigerate again, until the dough is chilled (20 to 30 minutes).

To prebake the crust, bake it either in a hot oven (425 degrees) for 8 to 12 minutes, or in a low oven (300 degrees) for 20 to 30 minutes, until lightly toasted.

Popcorn Piecrust

MAKES 1 8- OR 9-INCH PIE SHELL

Even more distinctive than corn flour for taste and texture in a tart crust is toasted and ground popcorn flour, which gives a lovely nutty taste. You can use commercially popped corn, or pop your own (it's fresher and very much cheaper)—1½ cups of popped corn will reduce to about 1 cup of popcorn flour. Spread the popped corn in a single layer on a jelly roll pan, or other large baking pan with slightly raised sides, and toast in a 300-degree oven for 10 minutes. The heat dries the corn so that it will grind fine instead of coarse. Grind the toasted kernels in a blender. If you want to make a large quantity at one time, the popcorn flour will keep well in a jar with a tight lid.

I use this crust for both sweet and savory fillings, adding sugar for fruit tarts and omitting it for savory tarts. This crust is best when baked fully and then filled just before serving because the popcorn will absorb moisture. It is not suitable for custard tarts, but rather for fillings that require no cooking, such as fresh fruit ones, or ones that are already cooked, such as grilled vegetables. See Kiwi and Starfruit Tart (opposite).

1½ cups popped popcorn
  (to make 1 cup flour)
1 cup all-purpose flour
3 tablespoons sugar
  Large pinch of salt
6 tablespoons (¾ stick) butter
1 egg, beaten

Preheat the oven to 300 degrees.

Spread the popped popcorn in a single layer in a baking pan and toast for 10 minutes. Grind it in a blender as finely as possible.

In a food processor, mix the popcorn flour, wheat flour, sugar, and salt. Add the butter and pulse until it is cut into the dry ingredients. Add the egg and pulse until mixture just begins to hold together, as in a graham cracker crust (the dough won't form a ball). Press the mixture into an 8- or 9-inch pie pan. Bake for 30 to 40 minutes, until the crust is lightly toasted. Remove and let the crust cool.

Kiwi and Starfruit Tart

SERVES 4 TO 6

This is a good filling for the Popcorn Piecrust (opposite). Comically, and appropriately for the ambidextrous nature of popcorn and cornmeal crusts, this exotic fruit filling began as a green tomato and sweet bell pepper tart. But in Manhattan such down-home produce as green tomatoes is harder to get than kiwis, imported from California, and starfruit (or carambola), imported from Florida, Hawaii, or the Caribbean.

The contrast of color and shape makes this tart visually striking, but there are many combinations of fruits and vegetables that display well in a prebaked crusty tart shell. Consider diced red tomatoes, sliced oranges, sliced avocados, mangoes, green or ripe papayas. How much sweetening you add in this tart depends on the fruit; starfruit comes in both tart and sweet varieties, so taste it first. Since kiwi is relatively bland, it takes well to a highly spiced tart glaze that also binds the flavors of the fruits together.

6 kiwi

2 starfruit

1 cup orange or lemon marmalade

1 teaspoon grated fresh ginger

1 teaspoon pure ground chili,
    New Mexican type

2 tablespoons orange liqueur
    Honey

1 8- or 9-inch baked Popcorn Piecrust
    (opposite) or Cornmeal Piecrust
    (page 166)

Peel the kiwi by cutting off both ends, running a sharp knife just inside the brown skin all the way around, and popping the fruit out. Slice crosswise. Cut the starfruit crosswise into $\frac{1}{4}$-inch slices.

Melt the marmalade with the ginger, chili, and liqueur. Add honey if the starfruit is very tart. Spread three-quarters of the mixture over the bottom of the tart crust. Layer the kiwi with the star fruit in overlapping slices. Dribble the remaining marmalade over the top as a glaze.

Plum Cornmeal Torte

SERVES 8 TO 12

Next time Italian plums are in season and your mouth begins to water for a classic plum torte baked in a springform pan and indulgently heaped with whipped cream, try this batter, which includes cornmeal as well as flour. The meal absorbs the plum juice and gives another layer of texture to the torte.

15 Italian prune plums

1½ cups sugar

½ pound (2 sticks) butter

1 cup all-purpose flour

1 cup freshly ground cornmeal, fine grind

2 teaspoons baking powder
   Pinch of salt

4 eggs, beaten

2 teaspoons vanilla extract

½ teaspoon almond extract

2 teaspoons ground cinnamon

2 teaspoons sugar

Preheat the oven to 350 degrees.

Split the plums and remove the pits. Set aside.

Put the sugar and butter in a food processor and process until well mixed.

Mix the flour, cornmeal, baking powder, and salt together and add to the processor. Pulse until mixed.

Add the eggs, the vanilla and almond extracts, and pulse just until the mixture comes together.

Scoop the batter into a buttered 9- or 10-inch springform pan. Lay the plums skin side up on top of the batter. Sprinkle cinnamon and sugar over the top.

Bake for about 60 minutes, or until a cake tester poked into the middle comes out clean. Let the torte cool in the pan 15 minutes, then remove the pan and cool thoroughly.

Barbados Conkies

MAKES 16 SMALL SQUARES

Célestine Eustis, in her *Fifty Valuable and Delicious Recipes Made with Corn Meal for 50 Cents* (1917), calls them West Indies Cookies but she has Americanized the word "conkies." Historians have traced the Bajan word to Africa, where *kenkey* is a fermented cornmeal bread steamed in leaves. I've had prolonged tastings and discussions of "true conkies" with my Bajan friend Wendy Wickham, who wrote home for this recipe provided by her friend Janet Hunt.

What is wonderful about these conkies is their crunchiness and natural sweetness, from the combination of grated raw pumpkin, coconut, sweet potato, and cornmeal, enriched with milk, butter, and raisins. Banana leaves or green corn husks give extra flavor in the baking but foil will substitute nicely. I cut them in small squares and eat them as cookies. They also make a filling and vitamin-rich snack for children. Wrapped in foil and refrigerated, the conkies keep well for at least a week.

1 cup grated raw pumpkin

1 cup grated fresh or dried coconut meat (see page 158 for instructions on fresh coconut)

1 cup grated raw sweet potato

1 cup freshly ground cornmeal, medium grind

½ to 1 cup sugar

½ teaspoon salt

½ teaspoon nutmeg

¼ teaspoon allspice

½ teaspoon almond extract

1 cup sultana raisins

8 tablespoons (1 stick) butter, melted

½ cup evaporated milk

Banana leaves, green corn husks, or aluminum foil for wrapping

Preheat the oven to 300 degrees.

In a bowl mix the pumpkin, coconut, and sweet potato with the cornmeal, sugar, spices, and almond extract.

Add the raisins, butter, and milk and mix thoroughly.

Line a 9 × 9-inch baking pan with banana leaves, green corn husks or aluminum foil cut to shape. Spread the dough on the leaves (husks or foil) and cover it with another layer of leaves, sealing the dough inside.

Bake for 1½ hours until firm. Let the pan cool for 10 minutes before removing the top leaves. Serve hot, warm, or cold.

Cornmeal Peanut Butter Cookies

MAKES ABOUT 4 DOZEN SMALL COOKIES

When I was a child, peanut butter cookies never lasted longer than it took to remove them from the oven. I've never outgrown my taste for them, but now I want them less bland, with a lot more crunch and pep. Instead of using peanut butter, I begin with chopped peanuts and underscore the crunch with cornmeal. For pep I add molasses and black pepper. For extra texture, I add rolled oats. It's still a kid's cookie but designed for adults who've been around the cookie block more than once.

1 cup roasted salted peanuts
12 tablespoons (1½ sticks) butter
1 cup dark brown sugar
2 eggs
1 tablespoon molasses
1 teaspoon vanilla extract
1½ cups all-purpose flour
½ cup freshly ground cornmeal, medium grind
1 teaspoon baking powder
¼ teaspoon baking soda
½ teaspoon freshly ground black pepper
¼ teaspoon salt
½ cup rolled oats

Preheat the oven to 350 degrees.

Chop the nuts coarsely in a food processor. Remove half of the nuts (½ cup) and reserve.

Add the butter and sugar to the nuts in the processor and process until well mixed. Add the eggs, molasses, and vanilla and process until smooth.

Mix together the flour, cornmeal, baking powder, baking soda, pepper, and salt and add to the processor. Pulse until the dough is just mixed. Put the mixture in a bowl and fold in the rolled oats and remaining peanuts.

The dough is very soft, but you can make blobs the size of walnuts and place them on a greased cookie sheet about an inch apart. Dip the back of a fork into a saucer of flour and press the top of each blob to flatten it. Bake for 15 to 20 minutes until lightly browned.

Almond-Cornmeal Shortbread
(*Fregolata Veneziana*)

MAKES 8 PIECES

Shortbreads are easier to make than cookies because you don't have to shape them individually; you just press the dough into a pie pan and bake it. I'm fond of shortbreads because they're not very sweet and I'm especially fond of nut shortbreads because of the crunchy texture. I know there are people who like chewy cookies but I am not one of them. Cornmeal once again underscores the crunch.

Venetians blanch their almonds for this traditional shortbread, which I've adapted from a version in Carol Field's *The Italian Baker,* but I prefer the coarse texture and the flecked color you get by leaving the almond skins on. Shortbread keeps well in a cookie or biscuit tin.

1 cup unskinned almonds
½ cup plus 2 tablespoons sugar
½ cup freshly ground cornmeal, fine grind
½ cup all-purpose flour
Pinch of salt
8 tablespoons (1 stick) unsalted butter, chilled
2 egg yolks, beaten
1 teaspoon vanilla extract
¼ teaspoon almond extract
1 to 1½ teaspoons grated zest of lemon or lime

Preheat the oven to 350 degrees and butter an 8- or 9-inch pie pan.

Grind the almonds in a food processor, remove half of them, and set them aside. To the remaining half, add the ½ cup sugar, cornmeal, flour, and salt and pulse until mixed.

Cut the butter in 8 pieces and add to the processor. Pulse until barely mixed, as if making piecrust.

Beat the egg yolks with the vanilla and almond extracts and the lemon zest. Add to the mixture in the processor and pulse again to mix.

Press the dough into the pie pan. Cut the top (but not all the way through) into 8 segments. Sprinkle dough with the remaining almonds and sugar.

Bake for 20 to 30 minutes. Let cool before cutting all the way through.

Piedmontese Horseshoe Cookies
(Krumiri)

MAKES ABOUT 4 DOZEN

From the Piedmont come these traditional buttery cornmeal cookies shaped like horse-shoes. If you're a professional Italian baker, you'll pipe these out with a pastry tube, but for home cooks it's easier to shape the dough individually by hand. Or you can simply roll the dough into a cylinder, an inch or two in diameter, chill, and cut into slices ¼ inch thick to bake. Here I've used the proportions of an excellent professional baker, Nick Malgieri.

Cookies as light and simple as these are particularly good with tea or coffee, wine or champagne. They'll keep well in a cookie tin but should be eaten within a week to get the fresh taste of the butter.

½ **pound (2 sticks) unsalted butter**
⅔ **cup sugar**
3 **egg yolks**
1 **teaspoon vanilla extract**
1½ **cups all-purpose flour**
1 **cup freshly ground yellow**
   cornmeal, medium grind

Preheat the oven to 325 degrees and line two cookie sheets with parchment paper (or butter and flour them).

In an electric mixer, whip the butter with the sugar until light and fluffy. Add the egg yolks, one at a time, beating well after each one. Beat in the vanilla.

Mix the flour with cornmeal and add to the mixer, beating a few seconds only until the dry ingredients are just barely mixed. Finish mixing by hand with a spatula.

Pinch off a walnut-sized piece of dough and roll it into a log, then bend it into a horseshoe shape on the cookie sheet. Place the cookies an inch apart. Repeat until all the dough is used.

Bake for about 15 minutes, until the edges begin to brown. Remove the cookies with a spatula while they are still warm (and soft).

Cherry Cornmeal Biscotti

MAKES 3 DOZEN BISCOTTI

Biscotti, as the name indicates, are twice-baked and made without fat so that they will keep "eternally," like old-fashioned ship's biscuits. Adding a small proportion of cornmeal, as they do in the corn belt of northern Italy, underlines their dry texture. Adding a variety of dried fruits and nuts radically improves flavor and texture. I like to use dried cherries in biscotti I flavor with a cherry liqueur such as Maraschino or Kirschwasser, or with almond-flavored Amaretto, to intensify the taste of the almonds as well as of the cherries. In an airtight tin, these will keep for weeks.

2 cups all-purpose flour
½ cup freshly ground cornmeal, medium grind
1 teaspoon baking powder
  Pinch of salt
½ teaspoon freshly ground black pepper
2 cups sugar
1½ cups unskinned almonds, toasted
3 eggs, beaten
1 tablespoon cherry liqueur
1 cup dried cherries

Preheat the oven to 325 degrees and prepare a baking sheet with a strip of parchment paper, or grease the pan and sprinkle flour over it.

In the bowl of an electric mixer combine the flour, meal, baking powder, salt, pepper, and sugar and mix well.

Add the almonds and mix until they are slightly broken. Add the eggs and liqueur and mix well. Stir in the cherries.

On a piece of plastic wrap or wax paper, divide the dough in half and shape each half into a cylinder about 2 inches in diameter. Put the cylinders on the baking sheet with at least 2 inches between.

Bake for 35 to 40 minutes, until they are somewhat browned. Let the cylinders cool for 15 minutes, then cut them on the diagonal into 1-inch slices and lay the slices flat on the sheet.

Lower the heat to 300 degrees and bake the slices for another 15 minutes until browned. Cool them thoroughly on a rack, then store in a cookie tin.

Homemade Cracker Jacks

MAKES 12 LARGE BALLS, 24 SMALL ONES, OR 8 QUARTS CARAMEL CORN

Decades before a pair of Chicago entrepreneurs named Frederick William Rueckheim and Louis Rueckheim packaged molasses-sweetened popcorn as Cracker Jack (after the confection was sold at the 1893 Columbian Exposition in Chicago), mothers in their home kitchens had been sticking popcorn together with nuts and candies in a molasses glue to delight the children at their apron strings. Sometimes they shaped the popcorn into balls, other times they made it like a peanut brittle and called it "crystallized popcorn." There were a great many recipes for it at the turn of the century, mixing molasses and sugar or corn syrup. The version here is a modern one that I've adapted from the Junior League of Denver's *Crème de Colorado,* which combines the popped corn with a caramel butterscotch.

You can use commercial popped corn but freshly popped corn will taste better.

1	**cup kernels**
	(to make 8 quarts popped corn)
½	**pound (2 sticks) butter**
2	**cups dark brown sugar**
¼	**cup dark corn syrup**
¼	**cup water**
½	**teaspoon salt**
1	**teaspoon baking soda**
2	**teaspoons vanilla extract**

Preheat the oven to 250 degrees.

Spread the popped corn on 2 ungreased cookie sheets and toast for about 15 minutes to crisp. Transfer to a bowl or pan large enough to hold the popcorn.

Melt the butter over low heat. Mix in the sugar, syrup, water, and salt and bring to the boil. Boil about 5 to 8 minutes until the caramel reaches the hard-ball stage (260 degrees on a candy thermometer). Remove from the heat and beat in the baking soda and vanilla.

Immediately pour the caramel over the popped corn and stir it gently with wooden spoons to coat all the kernels with the mixture.

To make popcorn balls, as soon as the mixture cools enough to handle without burning your fingers, butter your hands well and shape the corn into large or small balls.

Sorority Corn Flake Kisses

MAKES 2 DOZEN KISSES

The popularity of Kellogg's new machine-made corn flakes in the first decade of this century coincided with the popularity of home candy making. Corn flakes were seen to be a natural adjunct to other crunchy sweets like coconut and no candy recipe was more popular than meringue kisses, especially among young collegians. Here's one such recipe contributed by Lois Tennant Pennock to the *Delta Gamma Cook Book,* published in Minneapolis in 1922.

Meringues are not hard to make except in damp or humid weather. Best to wait until the weather is dry. Once made, the meringues will keep for weeks in an airtight tin.

4 egg whites, at room temperature
Pinch of salt
1 cup sugar
¾ cup grated coconut
2 cups corn flakes

Preheat the oven to 250 degrees; cover 2 cookie sheets with parchment or brown wrapping paper.

Beat the egg whites until they form soft peaks. Add the salt and beat the sugar in gradually, a tablespoon at a time, to form a stiff meringue.

Fold in the coconut and corn flakes and drop the mixture by spoonfuls on the cookie sheets.

Bake the kisses for 1 hour until firm and dried. Turn off the heat and leave them in the oven for 12 hours or overnight to dry further, without opening the oven door. Keep them, for nibbling, in an airtight cookie tin.

Taffy Popcorn Apples

MAKES 6 POPCORN APPLES

T he advent of commercial corn syrup, marketed as Karo by the Corn Products Refining Company of New York, boosted the candy division of the American sweet tooth by a thousand percent. The syrup was a boon to the home candy maker because it didn't crystallize the way sugar syrup was wont to do. Karo became an integral part of the taffy world and opened the door to such new taffy uses as apples stuck with skewers and dipped into a taffy vat. This is a basic recipe of the 1920s published by the Corn Products Refining Company to push not only Karo but Mazola corn oil. I've added the popcorn for fun.

You do need good teeth to bite into these apples when they're on a stick, but you can always cut the apple into quarters once the taffy coating is chilled.

4 cups popped corn (to make 2 cups coarsely chopped popcorn)
1 cup brown sugar
½ cup granulated white sugar
½ cup light corn syrup
½ cup water
1 tablespoon corn oil or butter
¼ teaspoon salt
1 teaspoon vanilla extract
6 red eating apples

Chop the popped corn in a food processor and set aside.

In a heavy saucepan, boil the brown and white sugars, corn syrup, water, oil, and salt together until a candy thermometer registers 300 to 310 degrees, to make a hard crack brittle. Remove pan from the heat and mix in the vanilla.

Stick a wooden skewer in the stem end of each apple and dip the apple into the pan of taffy to coat it evenly all around. Then dip the apple into the chopped popcorn. Since the taffy will take some time to dry, you need to set the apples upright in an inverted cardboard box (like a shoe box), in which you've cut six holes spaced far enough part to hold the 6 skewered apples. Set the box in the refrigerator to fully harden the caramel.

Snacks

Crazy for Corn

POPCORN SNACKS

Garlic-Parmesan Popcorn

Patti's Old Bay Popcorn

Snail-Butter Popcorn

CHIPS AND SALSAS

To Make Deep-Fried Corn Chips

To Make Oven-Baked Corn Chips

Sweet Corn Salsas

Cranberry-Jalapeño

Black Bean, Mango, and Sweet Red Pepper

Salsa Verde with Corn

Creamy Corn Salsa

Charred Corn and Poblano Salsa

Corn and Cactus

CORN RELISHES

Corn Chowchow

Sweet, Hot, and Sour Corn Relish

Cumin Corn Nuts

Mexican *Esquites*

Sweet Corn Poker Chips

Sweet Corn Clam Cakes

Cheese-Chili Corn Squares

Miss Sarah's Corn Oysters

Indonesian Corn-Shrimp Fritters
   (*Pergedel Jagung*)

Little Pig BBQ Hush Puppies

Corn-Fried Oysters

Mini Corn Dogs

Buttery Corn Crackers

Rosemary-Garlic Crisps

Blue Corn "Papadums"

Desert Wafers

Polenta Crostini

Fried Grits

Empanaditas with Picadillo

Crazy for Corn

Ideally, [popcorn] should be crisp but not tough. It should shear off cleanly and compress easily as you chew, but not pack the teeth too much. Once chewed, it should be easy to swallow, leaving few crumbled bits in the mouth.

—Consumer Reports, *June 1989*

America takes its snacks seriously, so seriously that *Consumer Reports* defines standards and lists comparative ratings of such multimillion-dollar snacks as popcorn and corn chips. It's fitting that the primary finger-food snacks of the Americas should be made of corn because corn from the beginning was born to travel. The Indians' "journeying" corn provided finger-food snacking for tribes that were constantly on the move. The Hopi's "piki" bread, that paper-thin wafer baked on a hearthstone and rolled up like a scroll, was a more elegant snack but a finger-food snack nonetheless for travelers.

You can't eat popcorn or corn on the cob without fingers, any more than you can eat parched corn kernels or corn fritters or corn chips. Corn was meant to be fingered—and seasoned and salsa-ed and battered and fried. One time in Dallas, I bought, on a stick, a whole ear of corn coated with batter and deep-fried and called "Dixie Corn." It was the ultimate in fast-food finger food and it was the Texas equivalent of a steak the size of half a steer. And why not? Corn is carnival food, party food, drink food, play food, joke food, and the snacks in this section are just the tip of the iceberg.

POPCORN SNACKS

Can you imagine life in America without popcorn? Movie theaters would empty, circuses would close, baseball parks would shut, couch potatoes would go berserk, dieters would grow fat, ex-smokers would hit the weed, beer drinkers would fall down drunk, compulsive snackers would starve.

Since popping corn is an ancient form of cooking in this hemisphere, you don't need any gimmicky equipment to pop corn. You don't even need oil or fat. All you need is a seasoned cast-iron, or any kind of nonstick, skillet. Heat the skillet over medium heat and pour in a single layer of corn kernels (⅓ to ½ cup for a 12-inch skillet). Put a lid on but leave it slightly ajar so that steam can escape, even if the odd popped kernel does too. As soon as you hear kernels begin to pop against the lid, shake the pan gently back and forth to keep the popped kernels from scorching. Continue shaking until the popping sounds stop. That's it. If that's too much work, you can always pay fancy money for an air popper or a microwave pack, but some of us crave the ritual. For some of us the pleasure of popcorn is in the popping, in the shimmy and the shake.

If you make popcorn too far ahead on a wet day or if you have leftover popcorn, you can always reheat it in a low oven (200 or 250 degrees) for 20 or 25 minutes to recrisp it.

Once a jar of popcorn is opened, kernels may dry out and refuse to pop. The best way to store opened popcorn is in the refrigerator. If you've got a longtime opened jar of popcorn in the cupboard, add a tablespoon of water to the jar, shake it, and give the kernels a day to absorb the moisture.

Since a popped kernel is really fiber-wrapped air, many of my friends eat popcorn all day long as a way of pleasuring themselves while maintaining their daily diet. There is even a book called *The Popcorn Diet*. But I'm one of those for whom popcorn without butter and salt is like Trinity without the the Holy Ghost. I recognize that such tastes are as old-fashioned as my analogy, but when I eat popcorn I know that I'm eating 5,000 years of American history and my buttered popcorn childhood belongs to that history.

Garlic-Parmesan Popcorn

MAKES 4 QUARTS

Although garlic nowadays is as much a staple of the American cupboard as a jar of popcorn kernels, time was when garlic popcorn was so macho and adventurous that Charles Baker put it in his 1939 *The Exotic Cookery Book, The Gentleman's Companion.* The care with which he handled this culinary grenade measures how far we've come in garlic years: "To one cup butter allow one finely chopped garlic clove. Simmer these two very gently for 5 minutes, put through a fine sieve to eradicate the chopped lily, then pour the aromatic fluid over our bowl of fresh popcorn, tossing diligently the while to insure equitable distribution."

Today, we play down the butter and play up the garlic. There is even a *Garlic News,* put out by the Fresh Garlic Association of California, which urges us on to untold garlic heights. Of course if you're dead set against butter, you can always use a little olive oil instead.

10 cloves garlic, minced
8 tablespoons (1 stick) butter or 2 to 3 tablespoons olive oil
1 teaspoon lime juice
4 quarts popped corn
1 cup freshly grated Parmesan cheese

Sauté the garlic in the butter for 3 to 5 minutes until the garlic turns golden. Stir in the lime juice.

Pour the garlic butter onto the popped corn and, as soon as the corn is cool enough to handle with your fingers, toss the kernels to coat them evenly with butter. Sprinkle on the cheese and toss again.

Patti's Old Bay Popcorn

MAKES 4 QUARTS

When Patti Rucidlo was helping me research corn, she confessed a weakness for popcorn sprinkled lavishly with Old Bay Seasoning. Old Bay is put out by the Baltimore Spice Company in Maryland and they recommend it for seasoning Chesapeake Bay delights like steamed crabs, but the combination of celery salt, mustard, pepper, laurel leaves, cloves, pimiento, ginger, mace, cardamom, cassia, and paprika perks popcorn up no end, just as any poultry seasoning or crab-boil or Cajun hot seasoning would. The advantage of a good seasoning is that you can make the kernels tasty without butter or oil.

½ cup kernels
   (to make 4 quarts popped corn)
1 tablespoon Old Bay Seasoning or
   any mixed spice seasoning

Heat a heavy iron skillet over medium heat for 3 or 4 minutes. Add the corn kernels in a single layer. Cover the pan with the lid slightly ajar. As soon as you hear the corn begin to pop, shake the pan gently and continue to shake until the popping stops.

Pour the popped corn into a large bowl and toss with the seasoning.

Snail-Butter Popcorn

MAKES 4 QUARTS

While I have many friends who wouldn't touch a buttered or oiled kernel, insisting on the chaste white low-caloric purity of air-popped corn, I revel in corn so lavishly buttered that it dribbles down the chin. Where once I ordered escargots with abandon in order to sop up with a baguette the six little pools of garlic-parsley butter in an escargot tin, now I use popcorn as the sop and a wet towel to mop up the dribbles.

1	whole head of garlic
1	teaspoon olive oil
8	tablespoons (1 stick) butter
¼	cup minced fresh parsley
	Grated peel of 1 lemon
	Salt and freshly ground black
	pepper to taste
4	quarts popped corn

Preheat oven to 400 degrees.

Roll the garlic head in the olive oil, wrap it in foil, and roast in the preheated oven for 15 minutes, or until the pulp of the cloves is soft enough to squeeze from the skins.

Melt the butter and mash the garlic pulp into it. Add the parsley, lemon peel, and seasonings and mix well.

Toss the popcorn in the butter mixture.

CHIPS AND SALSAS

On supermarket shelves today, corn chips seem to have raided the territory of potato chips, just as salsas have shot up the ketchup corral. So quickly have commercial chips proliferated that you have to pay assiduous attention to the fine print to make sure you've not got a no-salt when you wanted salt or a no-fat when you wanted fried or a guacamole-cheese-onion-chili-flavored chip when you wanted plain corn. But no store-bought chip is as good as the one you make at home from fresh (or frozen) tortillas, yellow, blue, or white, cut in quarters, quickly deep fried, and lightly salted.

To Make Deep-Fried Corn Chips

MAKES 48

A dozen fresh tortillas
Oil for deep frying
Salt

Cut the tortillas in quarters with a pair of kitchen scissors (if they're very large, you may want to cut them in sixes).

In a wok or heavy skillet, heat the oil until it is hot but not smoking. Add the tortilla quarters a few at a time so that they will curl and crisp quickly without burning.

Remove chips quickly with a slotted spoon and drain them well on paper towels. Salt them while they are still warm.

Resist eating them as you go so that you will have some left to serve with any good salsa, spread, or dip.

To Make Oven-Baked Corn Chips

MAKES ABOUT 9 DOZEN CHIPS

This is one way to make corn chips at home without deep frying them. Try different kinds of cornmeal, from the *masa harina* that is used for tortillas to blue corn meal, toasted cornmeal, white flint cornmeal, etc. You may need to adjust the amount of liquid, depending on the absorptive powers of the cornmeal. For *masa harina* or for corn flour, you'll probably need ¼ cup additional liquid. For blue corn, you'll need to add ½ teaspoon baking soda to stabilize the color blue. Whatever meal you use, make sure it is fresh.

1 cup cornmeal
2 tablespoons corn oil
½ teaspoon salt
1 cup boiling water

Preheat the oven to 200 degrees.

Mix the meal with the oil and salt. Pour the water gradually into the meal, stirring constantly to avoid lumps. If the batter is too thick to spread, add more water.

Spread the batter as evenly and thinly as possible (no more than ⅛ inch thick) on parchment paper on a baking sheet (batter should make a rectangle about 16 × 11 inches).

Bake for 45 minutes, until the batter is set. With a sharp knife, cut the dough in strips: for example, fourteen strips ¾ inch wide can then be cut into 1-inch lengths. Return the pan to the oven and cook about 15 minutes more, until the strips are dry and crisp.

Cool and store chips in an airtight container for a week or so. These chips will taste best if heated before serving.

SWEET CORN SALSAS

There are now dozens of canned or bottled commercial salsas that taste good, but I like fresh salsas. The crunch and sweetness of raw or roasted corn complements the fire and tartness of most salsa ingredients, and here are a few combinations to provoke your own experiments in the salsa line.

Cranberry-Jalapeño

MAKES 3 CUPS

Here is one place you can use the fresh sweet corn we now get in winter to advantage, because the juiciness of the cranberries and orange compensates for the slightly drier texture of the corn.

1 cup fresh raw cranberries
1 jalapeño chili, seeded and chopped
2 teaspoons chopped fresh cilantro
2 to 3 teaspoons honey
1 navel orange, peeled and sectioned
1 cup fresh corn kernels

Chop the cranberries coarsely in a food processor. Add the jalapeño, cilantro, and 2 teaspoons of the honey; pulse to mix well.

Add the orange sections and pulse 2 or 3 times to chop in the orange but not pulverize it into juice.

Stir in the corn kernels. Taste for seasoning and add more honey if desired.

Black Bean, Mango, and Sweet Red Pepper

MAKES 3 CUPS

If you live in Dallas, as Stephan Pyles does, the combination of corn, beans, and mangoes is natural and he makes a good relish at Routh Street Café to prove it. Where I live in Manhattan, mangoes are costly, so I use sweet red peppers to guarantee color and juice, and if a mango comes my way, so much the better. The four-way color is great.

2 ears fresh sweet corn
    (to make 1 cup kernels)
1 sweet red pepper
1 cup cooked black beans
½ mango, diced (optional)
1 clove garlic, minced
4 scallions, chopped (white part only)
1 serrano chili, seeded and minced
2 teaspoons chopped fresh cilantro
3 tablespoons olive oil
1 teaspoon fresh lime juice
   Salt and freshly ground black
     pepper to taste

Preheat the oven to 400 degrees.

Roast the corn in its husk in the preheated oven for 5 minutes. Remove husks and cut the kernels into a bowl.

Char the red pepper directly over a stove-top flame or under a broiler, turning it to blacken the skin evenly. As soon as it is cool enough to handle, remove the skin, take out the stem and seeds, and chop the flesh in small squares. Add to the corn.

Add beans and the mango, garlic, scallions, chili, and cilantro.

Beat the oil with the lime juice and seasonings and pour over the ingredients in the bowl. Cover with plastic wrap and let sit for an hour.

Salsa Verde with Corn

MAKES ABOUT 3 CUPS

Thank goodness tomatillos, those small green tomato-like vegetable-fruits that come wrapped in papery husks, are being grown now throughout the Southwest so that they are no longer an exotic Mexican import. Old-fashioned green tomatoes are harder to come by than tomatillos but can readily be substituted for them in this salsa.

1 clove garlic, mashed
2 to 3 serrano chilies, seeded and chopped
12 tomatillos, husked and cut in quarters
1 teaspoon chopped fresh cilantro
2 teaspoons fresh lime juice
½ teaspoon sugar

Salt and freshly ground black pepper to taste
½ to 1 cup fresh sweet corn kernels

Put all the ingredients but the sweet corn in a food processor and pulse until they are chopped fine and well mixed.

Turn the mixture into a bowl and add the sweet corn. Let sit for half an hour.

Creamy Corn Salsa

MAKES ABOUT 3 CUPS

This one is very quick, very easy, and very tasty.

½ cup good mayonnaise
¼ cup crème fraîche or sour cream
1 tablespoon Dijon mustard
1 teaspoon freshly grated horseradish
½ teaspoon freshly ground cumin seeds

Freshly ground black pepper and cayenne to taste
2 cups fresh sweet corn kernels

Beat together all the ingredients but the corn. Fold in the corn and chill until ready to use.

Charred Corn and Poblano Salsa

MAKES ABOUT 3 1/2 CUPS

Of course you can use other kinds of chilies, but the dark green thick-fleshed poblano is a Southwest favorite. Roasted, it underscores the flavor of roasted corn.

2   poblano chilies
2   cups fresh sweet corn kernels
2   cloves garlic, skin on
2   tablespoons olive oil
½   small onion, chopped fine
2   teaspoons chopped fresh oregano
1   teaspoon fresh lime juice
½   teaspoon balsamic vinegar
    Salt and freshly ground black
        pepper

Roast the chilies over a stove-top flame or under a broiler until the skins are evenly charred. When cool enough to handle, remove the skin, stems, and seeds. Chop the flesh in small dice and put them in a bowl.

Heat a heavy skillet until it begins to smoke. Add the corn kernels and dry roast them for 6 to 8 minutes, stirring, until the corn is well browned. Remove and add to the chilies.

In the same skillet, heat the garlic cloves until their skin is charred. Remove them and when the cloves are cool enough to handle, squeeze out the flesh and mash it. Set aside.

Heat the olive oil in the same skillet and brown the onions. Add to the garlic and mix well. Add to the corn mixture.

Stir in the remaining ingredients and taste for seasoning. Cover and refrigerate for a couple of days to let the flavors ripen.

Corn and Cactus

MAKES 4 CUPS

The flat green pads of prickly pear cactus called *nopales* appear in specialty foodstores now, I'm happy to say, with the prickles already removed. They should be cut in strips and blanched quickly with a little baking soda to eliminate any sliminess, then drained and rinsed well. They are a gentle companion to corn.

2 sweet bell peppers
    (yellow or orange)
1 jalapeño chili, seeded and minced
1 cup finely diced blanched nopales
1 cup fresh sweet corn kernels
1 ripe tomato, seeded and diced
4 scallions, chopped fine
1 teaspoon chopped fresh cilantro
1 teaspoon fresh lime juice

Roast the peppers over a stove-top flame or under a broiler. When they are cool enough to handle, remove skins, stems, and seeds, and dice the flesh.

Combine all the remaining ingredients and taste for seasoning. Cover and let sit at least half an hour.

CORN RELISHES

These relishes are simply a winter version of summer sweet corn salsas, cooked to preserve color, taste, and texture with vinegar, brine, sugar, or some combination of the three, to liven meats and fish and fowl when fresh ingredients are not available.

....

Corn Chowchow

MAKES ABOUT 2 QUARTS

Cabbage was always and corn was sometimes a part of the pickled multi-vegetable mixture Americans called "chowchow," pidgin English from the Mandarin word *cha,* which means mixed. The American use of the word dates from the 1840s when large numbers of Chinese were imported to work on the Pacific railroads. Apart from the name, however, this thickened sweet-sour relish is strictly in the Anglo-Indian culinary tradition of chutneys and piccalillis, translated to British shores and eventually to American ones.

My recipe here is a scaled-down version of one recorded in 1925 by the ladies in the Rector's Guild of St. Paul, Minnesota, under the rubric *Reliable Recipes.* Where they chopped the ingredients for their Chowchow in a meat grinder, we can do the work quickly in a food processor.

This is a good relish to serve with ham or roast meats at a large buffet.

12 ears fresh sweet corn (to make 6 cups kernels)	½ teaspoon powdered mustard
2 green bell peppers	½ teaspoon turmeric
2 red bell peppers	¹⁄₁₆ teaspoon cayenne
½ small cabbage (to make 2 cups chopped)	3 cups good cider vinegar
2 large onions	1 cup brown sugar
6 celery stalks	2 tablespoons salt
⅓ cup flour	½ teaspoon celery seed
	1 teaspoon mustard seed
	¼ cup olive oil

(continued)

Cut the kernels from the cobs and put them in a large pan. Cut the remaining vegetables in fairly uniform chunks and chop them coarsely in a food processor. Add them to the corn.

Dissolve the flour, mustard, turmeric, and cayenne in a little of the vinegar and mix until smooth. Add the remaining vinegar, sugar, salt, celery seed, and mustard seed. Pour the mixture over the vegetables and mix well. Bring the liquid to the boil-

ing point, cover, and simmer for about 10 minutes. Stir in the olive oil and mix thoroughly.

To preserve the old-fashioned way, put the mixture in sterilized glass jars and lids, then process jars for 20 minutes in a boiling water bath. It's easier just to rinse the jars and lids in boiling water, then fill and seal them, and put the sealed jars in the refrigerator, where they will keep well for at least a month.

Sweet, Hot, and Sour Corn Relish

MAKES ABOUT 2 QUARTS

This flavor threesome is not a crowd but a company that sparks a chutney or piccalilli or ketchup or relish no matter what you call it and no matter what fruits and vegetables you use. Think of green mangoes, watermelon rinds, honeydew melons, sugar pumpkins, quinces, apples, red tomatoes, and green tomatoes—corn will consort with any and all of them with pleasure. I've used green tomatoes and quinces here because I found them together in Union Square Greenmarket when the last of the sweet corn suggested it was time to think of preserves.

2 to 3 green tomatoes, diced
      (about 1½ pounds)
  1 quince
  ¼ cup salt
  2 cups water
  1 red onion, diced
  1 sweet red pepper, seeded and diced
  1 small red or green hot chili pepper,
      seeded and minced
  1 cup currants or raisins
  3 cups cider vinegar
  3 cups sugar
1½ teaspoons ground ginger
  1 stick of cinnamon
  6 whole cloves
  1 smoky dried chili, like chipotle
  4 ears fresh sweet corn
      (to make 2 cups kernels)

Cut the quince in eighths, peel, and core.

Sprinkle the tomatoes and quince with half the salt, cover, and let sit for 12 hours or overnight to draw out moisture. Rinse well and put the tomatoes in a large bowl.

Put the remaining salt in a pan with 2 cups of water and bring to the boil. Add the quince. Simmer for 3 to 5 minutes until tender but still firm, drain, and rinse under cold water. When the segments have cooled, cut them in small dice.

Add the onion, the sweet and hot peppers, and the currants to the tomatoes and quince.

In a saucepan mix the vinegar, sugar, and spices.

Heat the chipotle chili briefly (in a preheated low oven or skillet), remove stem and seeds, chop the flesh in small pieces, and add to the vinegar mixture.

Bring the liquid to the boil. Add the vegetable-fruit mixture and simmer for 5 minutes. Add the corn kernels and bring quickly back to the simmer.

Remove the pan from the heat, cool, and put the relish in screw-top jars in the refrigerator to mellow.

Cumin Corn Nuts

MAKES 2 CUPS

When Leah Holzel was helping me research the world of corn, she was also working for Yura Mohr's Catering Company in New York City, and one of Yura's specialties was caramelized salted almonds flavored with cumin. Since Leah and I both loved the combination of sugar, cumin, and salt, we tried the caramel process with the parched dried kernels marketed as snack food under the name Corn Nuts, produced from a variety of the big-kerneled Peruvian corn called Cuzco. Health food stores carry Corn Nuts in bulk, usually salted but sometimes unsalted. If you buy them unsalted, add 2 tablespoons of sea salt to the seasoning mixture of sugar and cumin.

¼ cup freshly ground cumin seeds
2 cups sugar
1 teaspoon vegetable oil
2 cups salted Corn Nuts

Heat the cumin for a minute or two in a heavy skillet, then mix it with 1½ cups of the sugar in a large bowl.

In the same skillet, heat the oil to coat the pan. Add the corn with the remaining ½ cup of sugar. Caramelize the sugared corn over medium-high heat for about 5 to 8 minutes. Be patient and make sure all the sugar has liquefied before stirring briskly to coat the kernels with caramel.

Turn the corn quickly into the bowl of seasonings and toss until each kernel is coated with dry sugar. When the kernels are cool enough to handle, pull apart any that have stuck together. When they are thoroughly cooled, sift out the extra seasoning.

Mexican *Esquites*

MAKES 8 SERVINGS

In summertime when the first tender ears of young or "green" corn come to the market in Mexico City, you can find street-sellers ladling tender buttery kernels into little paper cups. Traditionally the kernels are heated in lard and seasoned with hot chili and the distinctively pungent herb epazote, which in this country we pull with disdain from our gardens as "pigweed" or "stinkweed."

When corn season comes to New York City, Josefina Howard of Rosa Mexicano serves *esquites* with sweet corn kernels tossed in butter and seasoned with epazote and jalapeño peppers "chopped very very fine." It's her version I include here. Put the mixture in small glasses or cups and eat with a spoon.

8	**ears fresh sweet corn** **(to make 4 cups kernels)**
8 to 10	**tablespoons (1 to 1¼ sticks) butter**
2	**jalapeño chilies, seeded and minced**
⅓ to ½	**cup finely chopped fresh epazote** **Salt**

Cut the kernels from the cobs.

In a large skillet, heat the butter until bubbling. Add the corn, then the jalapeños, half of the epazote, and salt to taste. Add just enough boiling water to cover and simmer a few seconds only. Taste to sample the strength of the epazote.

Ladle the mixture into small glasses or cups and garnish, if desired, with the remaining epazote.

Sweet Corn Poker Chips

MAKES ABOUT 2 DOZEN SMALL CAKES

This is a simple batter made of pureed sweet corn, eggs, and corn flour without any additional leavening. I vary the seasoning of salt, black pepper, and some variety of chili pepper according to what I want to mix with the batter or tuck inside it as a filling between two layers as it cooks.

I've tried this batter with little squares of smoked salmon topped with salmon caviar, smoked tuna, smoked sturgeon topped with black caviar, all delicious. I've also tried the batter with little rounds of fresh goat's cheese, with grated aged goat's cheese, and with strips of roasted poblano pepper. My favorite variation is this one, where I add diced poblanos to the batter, along with a smoky chipotle chili. In addition I dry roast the corn in a skillet to intensify all these dark earthy tastes and to give the corn a dark golden color.

4 ears fresh sweet corn
    (to make 2 cups kernels)
½ teaspoon freshly ground chipotle
    chili
2 eggs
2 tablespoons *masa harina* or
    corn flour
½ poblano chili, roasted (see Note,
    page 5), seeded, and chopped
4 ounces goat's cheese (chèvre), cut in
    small pieces

Husk ears and cut the kernels from the cobs. In a heavy skillet, dry roast the kernels over high heat for 2 or 3 minutes, stirring to cook evenly. Add the ground chili powder and mix well.

Put the kernels in a food processor with the eggs and the *masa harina* and puree. Add the poblano chili and mix well.

Heat a griddle or heavy iron skillet over medium heat. Drop the batter onto the griddle by the teaspoonful. Lay a small piece of cheese on top of each and cover with another spoonful of batter. Flatten the cake slightly.

Brown the cakes on both sides, turning them once.

Sweet Corn Clam Cakes

MAKES ABOUT 3 DOZEN SMALL CAKES

Chopped clams or oysters, crabmeat, flaked poached cod, or salmon (or even that cupboard staple—canned tuna) are also delicious with fresh corn kernels, bound together in a corn batter and fried into little cakes. I've used clams here because the batter tastes especially good with clam juice. If you want a really spicy fish cake, add crab-boil or Cajun seasoning or any of your favorite hot chilies. Use freshly shelled clams if you can. If you can't, substitute canned chopped clams.

4 ears fresh sweet corn
    (to make 2 cups kernels)
½ cup clam juice
2 eggs
2 tablespoons butter, melted
1 cup *masa harina* or corn flour
1 teaspoon baking powder
1 teaspoon salt
¼ teaspoon freshly ground black
    pepper
    Several dashes of Tabasco
¼ cup minced red onion
1 cup finely chopped clams

In a food processor, puree half the corn kernels. Add the clam juice, eggs, and butter and puree.

In a bowl, mix together the *masa harina*, baking powder, salt, pepper, and Tabasco and add to the processor. Pulse to mix well.

Remove the batter to a bowl and fold in the onions, clams, and the remaining corn.

Heat a heavy skillet or griddle, film with a little butter, and drop the batter by the teaspoonful onto the skillet to make little cakes about an inch or so in diameter. Brown on both sides.

Cheese-Chili Corn Squares

MAKES 6 TO 7 DOZEN SQUARES

This is one of those blessedly easy to make and to eat snacks that can be done in quantity for hungry mobs.

3 ears fresh sweet corn
    (to make 1½ cups kernels)
3 jalapeño chilies, seeded and
    chopped
1 pound Monterey Jack cheese, grated
6 eggs, beaten
    Salt and freshly ground black
      pepper to taste

Preheat oven to 350 degrees.

Cut the kernels from the ears into a large bowl. Add the chopped peppers, grated cheese, eggs, and seasoning.

Butter heavily a 9 × 9-inch baking pan. Pour the mixture into the pan and bake for 30 minutes until the top is nicely browned.

Let the mixture cool until it hardens enough to cut in 1-inch squares.

Miss Sarah's Corn Oysters

MAKES ABOUT 1½ DOZEN FRITTERS

Corn oysters began as a Southern joke, in which a poor man's knobbly corn fritter was passed off as a rich man's batter-fried oyster. Too often today what passes for corn oysters are leaden and greasy lumps that would horrify Charleston's Sarah Rutledge, who compiled *The Carolina Housewife* in 1847. Attention must be paid, said Miss Rutledge, from grating the corn, to beating the whites and yolks separately, to frying the "oysters" delicately. You can point up the "oyster" joke by serving the fritters in oyster shells. These are best served piping hot.

6 **ears fresh sweet corn**
    (to make 3 cups kernels)
2 **eggs, separated**
¼ **cup corn flour**
¼ **cup Wondra flour**
1 **teaspoon baking powder**
½ **teaspoon salt**
½ **teaspoon sugar**
¼ **teaspoon freshly ground black**
    pepper
    Cayenne to taste
2 **tablespoons butter, melted**
    Vegetable oil for deep frying

Cut kernels from the cobs and scrape the cobs down with a knife to capture all the milk. Puree half the kernels in a food processor.

Add the egg yolks to the processor and mix well.

Mix the 2 flours, baking powder, salt, sugar, and both peppers and add them to the processor. Add the melted butter and pulse until well mixed.

Stir the mixture into the reserved kernels.

Beat the egg whites until stiff but not dry, and gently fold them into the batter. If the batter seems too soupy to hold shape, add a little more Wondra flour.

Heat the oil in a wok or heavy skillet until hot but not smoking. Drop in the batter from a heaping teaspoonful (the fritters should be small, about 1 to 1½ inches in diameter). Fry no more than two or three at a time, and turn them to brown quickly on both sides. Drain well and serve hot.

Indonesian Corn-Shrimp Fritters
(Pergedel Jagung)

MAKES 2 TO 3 DOZEN

The traditional pairing of sweet corn and shrimp in America's Deep South takes on new flavor with garlic and coriander in the Deep South of Asia. I first tasted these fritters when the Time/Life *Foods of the World* series provided a culinary travelogue for homebound cooks. While seasonings vary from version to version, and country to country, mine is a fairly classic rendition of the Pacific Rim fritter, inspired by Sri Owen's *Indonesian Food and Cookery.* These are good hot or at room temperature.

6 ears fresh sweet corn
    (to make 3 cups kernels)
1 hot red chili pepper
4 scallions
2 cloves garlic
½ pound fresh shrimp, shelled and deveined
1 teaspoon freshly ground coriander seeds
    Salt and freshly ground black pepper
1 egg
    Vegetable oil for frying

Cut the kernels from the cobs.

Chop the chili pepper, scallions, and garlic coarsely and put them in a food processor with the shrimp and seasonings. Pulse 3 or 4 times. Add the corn and pulse again until the mixture is coarsely chopped. Add the egg and pulse again until the mixture holds together.

Heat the oil in a wok or heavy skillet until it is hot but not smoking. Drop the mixture by spoonfuls into the oil, a few at a time. Brown for 2 or 3 minutes on each side and drain the fritters well on paper towels.

Little Pig BBQ Hush Puppies

MAKES ABOUT 3 DOZEN

These tasty little cornmeal fritters are an American Deep South version of England's fish and chips, since at traditional Southern fish fries the corn batter was fried in the same lard as the catfish, and was flavored thereby with both fish and pork. Today look for hush puppies at barbecue joints like the Little Pig in Asheville, North Carolina, where they make them in 20-pound cornmeal batches, shape them with an ice cream scoop, fry them in peanut oil, and dispense about a thousand puppies a day to hungering multitudes.

The addition of grated or minced onion distinguishes hush puppies from other kinds of corn fritters, so if you happen to have a Vidalia or some other sweet onion on hand, so much the better. I make them as small as I can and serve them as hot as I can.

Lard, shortening, or vegetable oil
for frying
1½ cups freshly ground cornmeal,
medium grind
½ cup all-purpose flour
2 teaspoons baking powder
½ teaspoon baking soda
½ teaspoon salt
½ teaspoon sugar
¼ teaspoon freshly ground black
pepper
⅛ teaspoon cayenne
½ cup grated onion
1½ cups buttermilk
1 egg, beaten

Preheat the oven to low.

Heat the oil for deep frying in a wok or heavy skillet, until it is hot but not smoking.

Meanwhile, mix the dry ingredients thoroughly. Combine the onion, milk, and egg. Toss the two mixtures together lightly.

When the oil is hot, drop the batter into the oil from the tip of a spoon to make small puffy round fritters about 1 inch in diameter. Fry a few of them at a time, remove them with a slotted spoon, and drain well on paper towels. Keep warm in the preheated oven while finishing the batch.

Corn-Fried Oysters

MAKES 2 DOZEN

The best of all cornmeal batters for coating shellfish, fish, or chicken makes use of the toasted finely ground corn flour that they use in Mexico and the Southwest for the drinks called *atole* or *pinole*. To make your own, grind cornmeal in a blender or grain mill, then toast it in a low oven or a large heavy skillet.

1 cup toasted corn flour
1 teaspoon salt
1½ teaspoons pure ground chili,
    New Mexican type
½ teaspoon freshly ground black
    pepper
3 eggs, separated
1 cup beer (or other liquid like fish or
    chicken stock)
2 dozen freshly shucked oysters
   Oil for deep frying

Mix the dry ingredients together. Beat in the egg yolks and the beer. Let the batter sit for half an hour.

Beat the egg whites until stiff but not dry and fold them into the batter.

Heat the oil in a wok or heavy iron skillet until hot but not smoking.

Coat the oysters with the batter, then drop them into the oil. Turn to brown them quickly, no more than a minute or two, on both sides. Drain well on paper towels.

Mini Corn Dogs

MAKES 30 CORN DOGS

All through the Corn Belt, north to south, no respectable county fair or carnival fails to serve up corn dogs, the one and only way to get a hot dog in a decent-tasting bun. The "bun" is a cornmeal batter that neatly encloses a hot dog skewered on a stick. The dogs are deep-fried, then dipped, according to the connoisseurship of the customer, in the condiment of his choice—mustard, ketchup, chili sauce, pickle relish—and handed over with a sturdy paper napkin around the stick.

Perhaps the best corn dog I ever ate was cooked by Michael Lomonaco of New York's 21 Club, when he slyly put on the dog in an uptown way by substituting foie gras for frankfurter. The result was unspeakably delicious, but not for every day.

⅔ cup freshly ground cornmeal,
     medium grind
⅓ cup all-purpose flour, plus extra
     flour for coating
1 teaspoon salt
⅛ teaspoon cayenne
1 egg, beaten
2 tablespoons olive oil
½ cup beer
10 good quality hot dogs
30 wooden skewers
     Oil for deep frying
     Dijon mustard for dipping sauce

Combine the cornmeal, ⅓ cup flour, salt, and cayenne in a large bowl.

Mix together the egg, oil, and beer; add them to the dry mixture and blend well.

Cut the hot dogs in thirds and skewer each piece. Roll the pieces in the additional flour, then dip each into the cornmeal batter.

Heat the oil in a wok or heavy skillet until it is hot but not smoking. (The shape of the wok is particularly useful when frying skewered foods.) Fry the dogs a few at a time, turning them to brown on all sides. Lift them with a slotted spoon and drain them well on paper towels. Arrange the skewers on a platter around a little bowl of mustard for dipping.

Buttery Corn Crackers

MAKES 35 CRACKERS

Cornmeal requires the addition of wheat flour to turn a coarse corn chip into a fine thin cracker. *Masa harina* or finely ground corn flour works best here in a cracker made crisp and mouth-melting with butter. The trick is to spread the batter as thin as possible in the pan. This is a nonsweet version of a recipe Maida Heatter calls Corn Melba. I serve it with herbed cheese, with shrimp butter, or on its own, since its flavor is delicate.

5 tablespoons butter
1 egg
1 cup all-purpose flour
1 teaspoon baking powder
⅓ cup *masa harina* or corn flour
½ cup milk
½ cup water
Salt in a shaker

Preheat the oven to 375 degrees.

Cream the butter with the egg in a food processor.

In a separate bowl, sift the dry ingredients together, then add them to the processor and pulse gently until the butter is mixed with the flour. Add the milk and water and pulse again until the batter is smooth.

Butter a standard jelly roll pan (10½ × 15½ inches). Spread the batter with a rubber spatula as evenly and thinly as possible.

Sprinkle the surface lightly with salt.

Bake 5 minutes to set the batter, then cut it with a sharp knife into 35 squares.

Return the pan to the oven and bake for 15 to 20 minutes more, removing the crackers to a wire rack as they brown. Crackers at the edge of the pan will brown faster than the ones in the middle.

Rosemary-Garlic Crisps

MAKES 2 DOZEN SMALL OR 1 DOZEN LARGE CRISPS

This is a tasty Italian-flavored cocktail cracker, savory with roasted garlic and fresh rosemary, and sharpened with hot pepper and Parmesan cheese. Pureed sweet corn lends its own flavor and, along with the egg whites, enables the cornmeal to stick together without the addition of wheat.

2 garlic cloves, peeled
2 tablespoons olive oil
2 ears fresh sweet corn, husks on (to make 1 cup kernels)
2 egg whites
2 tablespoons fresh rosemary leaves
½ cup *masa harina* or corn flour
½ teaspoon salt
Large pinch of cayenne
½ cup freshly grated Parmesan cheese

Preheat oven to 400 degrees.

Dip the garlic in the oil and wrap the cloves in foil. Roast about 15 minutes, until they are soft.

Roast the corn in their husks in the oven for about 5 minutes. Remove the husks and cut off the kernels with a sharp knife.

Puree the corn with the olive oil and garlic in a food processor. Add the egg whites and pulse until mixed. Add the *masa harina,* salt, and cayenne and pulse again.

Drop by small spoonfuls 3 inches apart on a buttered baking sheet. Wrap the bottom of a drinking glass in plastic wrap and press the spoonfuls flat. Sprinkle the top of each with Parmesan cheese.

Bake in the preheated 400-degree oven for 25 to 30 minutes. After 15 minutes, turn them over with a spatula to crisp the underside. Their edges should be browned and crisped when they are done.

Blue Corn "Papadums"

MAKES 4 LARGE WAFERS OR "PAPADUMS"

East Indian papadums are made of a lentil (dal) dough seasoned generously with black pepper. The dough is then rolled very thin and dried before the plate-sized rounds are crisped in hot oil. Because corn dough will dry crisp in an oven without any need to fry it, I decided to try a Western "papadum" made from a mixed corn and wheat dough, seasoned with black pepper and cumin. You can serve them, as you would papadums, in plate-sized rounds to be broken into pieces. These are wonderful with drinks because the pepper is a good thirst provocateur.

½ cup freshly ground blue cornmeal, fine grind
½ cup all-purpose flour
1 teaspoon baking powder
¼ teaspoon baking soda
1 tablespoon coarsely ground black pepper
1 teaspoon cumin seeds
½ teaspoon salt
½ cup warm water
1 cup sour cream
1 egg, beaten
2 tablespoons corn oil
1 to 2 teaspoons butter

In a food processor, mix the dry ingredients: cornmeal, flour, baking powder, baking soda, pepper, cumin, and salt. Add the water, sour cream, egg, and oil, and pulse until the mixture is well mixed.

Heat a griddle or crepe pan, brush it with a little butter and pour on ½ cup of the batter to make a thin 8- to 10-inch crepe. Turn once to brown lightly on both sides.

Spread the circles on a baking sheet and dry them in a 200 degree oven for 1 to 1½ hours to become thoroughly crisp and golden brown. Serve hot or cold.

Desert Wafers

MAKES ABOUT 4 DOZEN

The natives of America, before Columbus, ground seeds and nuts to produce a kind of butter. Our American Southwest was rich in the seeds of pumpkins and sunflowers and the little white seeds concealed in the cones of pine trees that we call piñons, or pine nuts. Combined with blue corn and seasoned with desert sage and chili, these wafers suggest the colors of the New Mexican desert. Although they have the heft of trail-pack food, they evoke for me the high plateaus of the Zuni and Acoma, particularly if accompanied by a pitcher of margaritas.

They'll keep for several days in an airtight tin.

½ cup pumpkin seeds
½ cup sunflower seeds
5 eggs
⅓ cup corn oil
1 cup freshly ground blue cornmeal, fine grind
1 cup all-purpose flour
1 teaspoon salt
½ teaspoon baking soda
1 tablespoon dried sage leaves
2 tablespoons pure ground chili, New Mexican type
1 teaspoon water
½ cup pine nuts

Preheat the oven to 300 degrees. Grease a baking sheet for the wafers.

Mix the pumpkin and sunflower seeds in a shallow baking pan and toast them lightly in the oven for 8 to 10 minutes.

Put the seeds in a food processor, add 4 of the eggs and the oil; pulse a few times.

In a separate bowl, mix the meal, flour, salt, baking soda, sage, and chili. Add the mixture to the processor and pulse until the mixture is blended and the seeds are coarsely chopped.

Shape the dough into balls the size of small walnuts and place them 2 inches apart on the baking sheet. Take a square of heavy plastic wrap (like a freezer bag), lay it on top of a ball, and flatten it with the bottom of a heavy glass (or other flat surface). Repeat with all the balls.

Beat the reserved egg with a teaspoon of water to make an egg wash for the pine nuts to stick to. Brush the top of each ball with the wash, then decorate each by pressing 3 pine nuts into the center like a petaled flower.

Bake for 20 to 25 minutes, until the wafers are firm and crisp. Remove them carefully with a spatula while they're hot and put them on a cake rack to cool.

Polenta Crostini

MAKES ABOUT 1½ CUPS TAPENADE, MAKES ABOUT 150 SQUARES

Because of the way polenta, or cornmeal mush, becomes as firm as bread once it is cooked and chilled, it is one of the best materials for shaping finger-food appetizers. With a knife, you can cut the chilled polenta into diamonds, rectangles, squares, circles, crescents, or whatevers with biscuit or cookie cutters. Top the crostini with any good savory, from Gorgonzola to sautéed wild mushrooms, pesto genovese or the Provençal tapenade that I've used here.

FOR THE POLENTA:

- 1½ cups freshly ground yellow cornmeal, medium grind
- Salt and freshly ground black pepper
- 4 cups chicken broth, boiling
- 4 tablespoons butter

FOR THE TAPENADE:

- ¼ cup olive oil
- 2 cloves garlic
- 6 anchovy fillets
- 1 cup Mediterranean olives, such as Niçoise, pitted
- ¼ cup chopped basil leaves
- 2 tablespoons capers
- 1 teaspoon Dijon mustard
- Freshly ground black pepper

In a heavy saucepan, scald the cornmeal (and seasoning) with the boiling broth, pouring it in gradually and stirring constantly. Bring the mixture to the boil, stirring all the while.

Reduce heat and stir in the butter. Cover the pan with a lid and place it over the bottom of a double boiler, filled with an inch or two of boiling water, to steam the polenta for 20 to 30 minutes. The meal should be thick enough for a spoon to stand upright. If it is too thin, cook the polenta with the lid off until it thickens.

Pour the polenta into a standard jelly roll pan to make a layer ½ inch thick. Smooth the top with a spatula, cover with plastic wrap and chill thoroughly.

In a food processor, coarsely chop all the tapenade ingredients. They should remain chunky, not smooth.

When the polenta is cold, preheat the oven to 325 degrees. Cut the polenta into diamonds, triangles, or squares about an inch wide. Place the pieces on a baking sheet and heat in the preheated oven for about 10 minutes, or until the polenta is heated through. Put a dab of tapenade on top of each piece and serve.

Fried Grits

MAKES ABOUT 6 DOZEN TRIANGLES

In the days when Creoles set the finest tables in New Orleans, grits—or ground hominy—was as essential as polenta to north Italy or hasty pudding to New England. Leftover grits were used in all kinds of breads and cakes, but one Creole favorite was cold grits cut into squares and fried. What a Southerner today calls Fried Grits, a Creole would have called Saccamité Frite, which better describes its cultural richness. These can be made well ahead and reheated in a hot oven.

1 cup water
2 cups milk
1 cup freshly ground white grits, medium to fine grind
1 teaspoon salt
¼ teaspoon freshly ground black pepper
4 ounces goat's cheese (chèvre)
1½ cups all-purpose flour
4 eggs, well beaten
2 cups fine bread crumbs
Vegetable oil for frying

In a saucepan bring ½ cup water and 2 cups milk to the boil.

In the top of a double boiler, soften the grits in the remaining ½ cup of water. Then gradually pour in the hot milk, stirring the while. Add the seasonings and mix well.

Cover the top of the double boiler and set it over the bottom, filled with one or two of inches of boiling water. Steam for 45 minutes to an hour. If the mixture is not so thick that a spoon will stand upright in it, remove the lid and cook until the grits thicken.

Add the cheese and mix thoroughly.

Butter or grease a jelly roll pan and scoop in the grits. Smooth them with a spatula, cover with plastic wrap, and chill.

When the grits are cold, cut them into 2-inch squares and then into triangles. Lightly dredge each triangle with flour, dip in the eggs, then dredge in the bread crumbs.

Heat a ¼-inch film of oil in a heavy skillet and, when it is hot but not smoking, fry the triangles until golden brown on both sides.

Empanaditas with Picadillo

MAKES 2 DOZEN TURNOVERS

T he meat- or cheese-filled turnovers called empanadas by much of Latin America, when made small are empanaditas. Small ones are somewhat labor intensive but the rewards of a buttery pastry of corn and wheat flours, stuffed with a traditional picadillo, are large. Picadillo is a sweet and savory mixture of spiced meats, currants, capers, olives, and anything else you choose to put in. Although the ingredient list is long, it's very simple to make.

FOR THE PASTRY:

- 2½ cups all-purpose flour
- 1 cup *masa harina* or corn flour
- ½ teaspoon salt
- 12 tablespoons (1½ sticks) butter, chilled
- 1 egg
- 1 egg yolk
- ⅓ cup ice water

FOR THE FILLING:

- 2 tablespoons currants
- 1 teaspoon cider vinegar
- 1 tablespoon olive oil
- 2 tablespoons finely chopped onion
- 1 teaspoon minced seeded hot chili pepper
- 1 clove garlic, minced
- ¼ pound ground beef
- ¼ pound ground pork
- ¼ cup chopped stuffed green olives
- 1 tablespoon tomato puree
- 1 teaspoon drained capers
- ¼ teaspoon ground cumin seeds
- ¼ teaspoon dried oregano
- A pinch of cinnamon
- A pinch of cloves
- Salt and freshly ground pepper

To make the pastry, mix the flours and salt together in a food processor.

Cut the butter in thirds lengthwise, then in ¼-inch slices to make small pieces of uniform size. Add the butter to the processor and pulse until the butter is cut into the flour in pieces about the size of small peas.

Mix the egg and egg yolk; add to the flour-butter mix and pulse 4 or 5 times. Add the ice water and pulse again until mixture just begins to hold together. If the mixture is too crumbly, add a little more water. Wrap the dough in plastic and put in the freezer to chill quickly.

Once the dough is chilled, roll it out ¼ inch thick on a floured board (or sheet of plastic) and cut it in circles 2 to 3 inches in diameter. On a pair of baking sheets, place the rounds with enough space between them to flatten each with the bottom of a chilled glass. The rounds should be about ⅛ inch thick.

Put the baking sheets in the freezer for 10 minutes.

Make the picadillo filling while the dough is chilling. Soak the currants in the vinegar and add enough water to cover.

In a skillet, heat the oil and sauté the onions, pepper, and garlic for 2 or 3 minutes until slightly softened. Then add the ground meat and brown it lightly.

Add the remaining ingredients, including the currants and their liquid. Cover the skillet and simmer for 5 minutes, then remove the lid and cook another 5 to 10 minutes to evaporate the liquid.

Remove the dough from the freezer and put a dab of filling in the center of each round. Fold the pastry in half and with the tines of a fork seal the half-moon edges together.

Return the baking sheets to the freezer to chill the dough once more.

Preheat the oven to 400 degrees. Bake the turnovers for 10 to 15 minutes, until the edges just begin to brown.

Drinks

Southwestern Toasted Corn Drink
(*Atole*)

Guatemalan Toasted Corn Drink
(*Batido Atol*)

Corn Tea

Purple Corn Drink
(*Chicha Morada*)

Peruvian Corn Beer
(*Chicha de Jora*)

Kentucky Mint Julep

Green Corn Vinegar

As to the meals which they ate in the time of their antiquity, they eat the same today. Thus is corn boiled in water and crushed. When made into dough, they dissolve it in water for a drink, and this is what they ordinarily drink and eat. An hour before sunset it was their custom to make certain tortillas of the said dough. . . . This was the only time they ate during the day, for at other times they only drank the dissolved dough mentioned above.

—*Friar Diego de Landa,* Yucatán Before and After the Conquest, *1566*

The use of corn in drinks, unfermented and fermented, is so important in the practice of corn cuisine that I must include a few, although I've omitted recipes for ordinary home-brew beer or moonshine or bourbon whiskey from scratch. Such recipes are available elsewhere and require skill and apparatus beyond the narrow means of my New York apartment. I have, however, included a recipe for Peruvian beer and for some traditional unfermented corn drinks common to Latin America, as well as one celebrating that full-throated king of American whiskeys, bourbon.

Southwestern Toasted Corn Drink
(*Atole*)

MAKES A LITTLE LESS THAN A QUART

Toasting very finely ground corn is the secret to how Native Americans both ate and drank corn. Often the corn was toasted and reground several times to make it finer and finer, like an instant flour today. Toasting also preserved it so that the corn would keep without spoiling while tribes were traveling or fighting or migrating.

Today, toasting cornmeal and corn flour is a revelation of full-bodied nutty flavor. You can buy already toasted cornmeal or flour, but you can easily toast it in a skillet over low heat or in a medium oven, stirring it occasionally to prevent scorching.

Even without toasting, you can dissolve *masa harina* or fresh *masa* in whatever liquid you choose, water or milk or fruit juice, to make a corn drink.

Seasonings vary widely, but some favored combinations are powdered green or red chili, epazote, bitter chocolate from ground cacao beans, dried jasmine flowers, cinnamon, sugar, honey, in varying combinations. The recipe here is standard in the Southwest for those who, like myself, are addicted to the combination of hot-bitter-sweet.

¼ cup cocoa powder

2 tablespoons pure ground chili, New Mexican type

1 teaspoon ground cinnamon

½ teaspoon salt

1 cup freshly ground blue, white, or yellow cornmeal, toasted, fine grind

⅓ cup honey, or to taste

1 quart boiling water or milk

Mix the cocoa, chili, cinnamon, and salt with the toasted corn flour in a saucepan. Stir the honey into the boiling liquid and add it gradually, stirring the while, to the meal. Simmer the liquid 5 or 10 minutes until it is silky. Serve hot or cold. (You may need to add more liquid if you serve it cold, because it will thicken as it cools.)

Guatemalan Toasted Corn Drink
(Batido Atol)

MAKES A QUART

One of my favorite drinks comes from Antigua in Guatemala, where the markets abound in tropical fruits such as star apple, soursop, zapote, tamarind. I've chosen tamarind here because it's available in the form of tamarind paste in both Caribbean and Oriental food markets in the States. The lemony taste of tamarind, accented by a little fresh ginger, balances well with the sweet nutty flavor of corn.

¼ cup toasted white or yellow cornmeal, fine grind	Put all the ingredients into a blender and mix well. Taste, and if the mixture is too sour, add a little more sugar. If it is too thick, add a little more water (or milk).
¼ cup brown sugar	
3 tablespoons tamarind paste	
2 to 3 teaspoons grated fresh ginger root	
4 cups boiling water	

Corn Tea

MAKES ABOUT A QUART

For a New England version of this native drink, try this recipe from Miss Maria Parloa's *The Appledore Cookbook* of 1872. She recommended it among her many "Dishes for the Sick." "This is very light and nutritious," she advised, "and can be taken where the patient is very weak." As a medicine, "cornmeal water" is even today recommended in northern Greece, of all places, as a way to lower cholesterol.

4 cups boiling water	Gradually pour the water into the meal and let it steep for 15 minutes.
1 cup freshly ground yellow or white cornmeal, toasted, fine grind	

Purple Corn Drink
(*Chicha Morada*)

MAKES ABOUT 2 QUARTS

In Peru, everybody drinks chicha, which is made of different kinds and colors of corn, flavored with sugar and spices and often fresh fruit. Cesar Morales of the Peruvian Import Co. in New Jersey gave me his recipe for a chicha that uses purple corn. The corn is here principally to color and give a light body to a fruit punch. You can use other dried corn of other colors but purple is best.

1 pound dried purple corn kernels
 and cobs
4 quarts cold water
2 sticks of cinnamon
6 whole cloves
¾ cup dark brown sugar
½ cup fresh lemon juice
1 cup fresh orange juice
 Fresh sliced fruit, such as oranges,
 strawberries, pineapples,
 for garnish

Cover the corn with water in a large kettle. Add the cinnamon and cloves and bring the water to the boil over high heat. Lower the heat, cover the kettle, and simmer 40 to 50 minutes, or until the corn has softened.

Strain the liquid into another pot and discard the corn and spices. Dissolve the sugar into the hot liquid. Add lemon and orange juices and taste for sweetness.

Chill thoroughly. When ready to serve the drink, garnish with sliced fruit.

Peruvian Corn Beer
(*Chicha de Jora*)

MAKES ABOUT 4 QUARTS

This is a very light home-brewed corn beer, which everybody drinks in Peru, children included. The recipe here I've taken from the late Felipe Rojas-Lombardi, with whom I had long discussions about chicha and who fortunately wrote down his own formula in *The Art of South American Cooking*. Although Felipe claimed that "chicha is very easy to prepare," I've found home brewing in a New York apartment fascinating but not at all easy.

You must start with *jora,* which are sprouted kernels that are dried and then crushed (see Note). You must continue with pot, strainer, and a container of ceramic, porcelain, or glass to prevent wild yeasts from souring your brew. You must end with a dark storage place that is neither too cold nor too hot, but just right for fermentation. If you like experimenting, this is for you. If you like a sure thing, stick to unfermented drinks.

1 **pound dried corn kernels**
     (**to make** *jora*) (**see Note**)
8 **allspice berries**
8 **quarts cold water**
2 **cups packed dark brown sugar**

To make the *jora,* soak the kernels 2 or 3 days in cold water. Rinse 2 or 3 kitchen towels in cold water and wring them out. Lay the wet towels on a baking tray and spread the drained kernels on top of them. Cover with a double layer of dampened cheesecloth (or more towels) and put the tray in a dark place. Spray the cheesecloth with water regularly (keep it damp but not wet) for 8 to 10 days until the kernels sprout. Put the sprouted corn on a dry tray and dry the kernels in a very low oven or over a radiator for a day or two. When they are thoroughly dry, crush them in a processor or with a rolling pin.

In a large stainless-steel pot, combine the *jora* and the allspice, and cover with 8 quarts of cold water. Let soak for an hour. Bring the pot to the boil over medium heat, lower the heat, and simmer for 4 to 5 hours, stirring occasionally. If you have less than 4 quarts at the end, add enough boiling water to make it up. Let the pot sit for an hour off the heat without stirring.

Strain the corn through a stainless-steel strainer lined with a double layer of cheesecloth into a ceramic (porcelain or glass) container. Twist the cloth to squeeze out all the corn juice.

Drop the sugar in. *Don't* stir it. Cover the container with a dry cloth and place it in a dark, warm, and draft-free spot. Let it ferment for about a week, then chill it thoroughly. The longer it sits unchilled the stronger it gets. It should develop a thick foam on top as it ferments.

Note: Dried *jora* is usually available through Inca's Food and avoids having to sprout the kernels oneself. (See A Source List, page 223.)

Kentucky Mint Julep

MAKES 1 SERVING

The Southern mint julep is not an invention of the distillers of bourbon whiskey, but rather a descendant of a long line of flavored and sweetened brandies called "cordials." Mary Randolph in *The Virginia Housewife* of 1825 begins her recipe for "Mint Cordial" with the instructions, "Pick the mint early in the morning while the dew is on it, and be careful not to bruise it." The housewife was to put two handfuls of mint in a quart of French brandy, let it stand overnight, repeat twice more with fresh mint, then dilute it with water and sweeten it with powdered loaf sugar.

Cordials were suitable for ladies as well as gentlemen, as are mint juleps today, undiluted except with ice. After knocking back two of them in a bar on Derby Day outside of Louisville, Kentucky, once upon a time, I recall with perfect clarity the taste of the juleps and the winner of the race but nothing of driving across the border to Tennessee. Definitely the designated driver should take his mint in lemonade.

5 **sprigs fresh mint**
1 **teaspoon sugar**
2 **ounces bourbon whiskey**

In the bottom of a 12-ounce frosted mint julep cup or glass, bruise 4 sprigs of the mint with the sugar. Fill the cup half full of finely cracked ice. Pour on the whiskey, stir, and fill to the top with ice. Garnish with the final sprig of mint.

Green Corn Vinegar

MAKES ABOUT 3 QUARTS

This is not properly a drink, but it was a common American way of fermenting corn juice to make vinegar the way apple juice made cider vinegar. This recipe I took from *America Cooks,* by Cora, Rose, and Bob Brown, an invaluable anthology of recipes they collected from "the 48 states" in 1940.

12 ears fresh sweet corn
(to make 6 cups kernels)
2 cups sugar
1 gallon rainwater

To get what the Browns call "green corn juice," grind the corn kernels in a food processor. Put the mash in a kitchen towel and squeeze hard to extract all the juice into a large container.

Add the sugar to the corn juice and stir in the rainwater or other purified water.

Cover the container with a damp clean cloth and let the mixture ferment for about a month in a warm draft-free place.

APPENDIX

A Source List

Corn Seeds:

CORNS
Carl and Karen Barnes
Route 1, Box 32, Turpin, OK 73950
(405/778-3615)

CRESS
Eastern Native Seed Conservancy
P.O. Box 451, Great Barrington, MA
01230 (413/229-8316)

NATIVE SEEDS/SEARCH
2509 North Campbell Avenue, No. 325,
Tucson, AZ 85719
(602/327-9123)

SEED SAVERS EXCHANGE
3076 North Winn Road, Decorah, IA
52101 (319/382-5990)

SEEDS OF CHANGE
P.O. Box 15700, Santa Fe, NM 87506-
5700 (800/957-3337)

SOUTHERN EXPOSURE SEED EXCHANGE
P.O. Box 170, Earlysville, VA 22936
(804/973-4703)

Dried Corn and Cornmeals:

Millers who sell whole-grain quality corn and
cornmeals by mail order:

ADAMS MILLING CO. (yellow and white cornmeals; white grits)
Route 1, Box 248, Midland City, AL
36350 (205/983-4233)

CARPENTER'S GRIST MILL (Whitecap flint cornmeal)
Moonstone Beach Road, Perryville, RI
02879 (401/783-5483)

CASADOS FARMS (white and blue corn posoles;
chicos; white and blue cornmeals, plain
or toasted; blue corn *masa harina*
[*harinia*] plain or toasted [for *atole*])
Box 852, San Juan Pueblo, NM 87566
(505/852-2433)

JOHN F. COPE CO. (dried sweet corn, whole
kernel)
Manheim, Lancaster County, PA 17545
(717/665-6440)

GALLINA CANYON RANCH (red corn posole;
red corn *masa harina;* all kinds of
chilies)
144 Camino Escondido, Santa Fe, NM
87501 (505/982-4149)

GRAY'S GRISTMILL (Whitecap flint and yellow meals)
P.O. Box 422, Adamsville, RI 02801 (508/636-6075)

GREAT VALLEY MILLS (coarse and fine yellow cornmeals; toasted cornmeal; dried sweet corn)
RD 3, County Line Road, Box 1111, Barto, PA 19504 (800/688-6455)

HOPPIN' JOHN'S (white corn flour; white and yellow cornmeals; white speckled heart grits)
30 Pinckney Street, Charleston, SC 29401 (803/577-6404)

KENYON CORNMEAL CO. (white and yellow cornmeals)
Glenrock Road, Usquepaugh, West Kingston, RI 02892 (401/783-4054)

MORGAN MILLS (white and yellow cornmeals; yellow corn flour)
Route 2, Box 115, Union, ME 04862 (207/785-4900)

NORA MILL GRANARY (white and yellow cornmeals; white and yellow speckled heart grits)
P.O. Box 41, Sautee, GA 30571 (800/927-2375; 706/878-2375)

OSCEOLA MILL COUNTRY INN (yellow cornmeal)
Steele's Tavern, VA 24476 (703/377-6455)

THE TEAGUE MILL (yellow and white cornmeals; speckled heart grits)
155 Texas Lane, Gatlinburg, TN 37738 (615/436-9563)

WAR EAGLE MILL (yellow and white cornmeals; grits)
Route 5, Box 411, Rogers, AK (501/789-5343)

YELLOW DOG MILLING CO. (yellow cornmeal and grits)
Box K, Highway 49 South, Greenwood, MS 38930 (601/455-4742)

DISTRIBUTORS OF SPECIALTY CORN PRODUCTS:

BURNS FARM (grows and markets *huitlacoche* [corn mushrooms])
16158 Hillside Circle, Montverde, FL 34756 (407/469-4490)

DEAN & DELUCA (Molini Nicoli polentas, will mail-order)
560 Broadway, New York, NY 10012 (212/431-1691)

DON ALFONSO FOODS (white and blue posole; blue cornmeal, *masa harina*)
P.O. Box 201988, Austin, TX 78720 (800-456-6100)

FRIEDA'S BY MAIL (dried corn husks; chilies)
P.O. Box 58488, Los Angeles, CA 90058 (800/241-1771)

INCA'S FOOD (Peruvian purple corn on the cob; Peruvian dried white whole-kernel hominy; dried *jora*)
Peruvian Import Co., P.O. Box 469, Mahwah, NJ 07430 (201/773-6705)

KITCHENS OF NEW YORK (blue cornmeal; posole; *masa harina*; chilies; red corn)
218 Eighth Avenue, New York, NY 10011 (212/243-4433)

MARIA AND RICARDO'S TORTILLA FACTORY (quality white and blue tortillas from fresh *masa*)
Harbar Corp., 30 Germania Street, Jamaica Plain, MA 02130 (617/524-6107)

NATIVE SEEDS/SEARCH (Hopi and Pueblo blue cornmeal; white and blue posole; toasted blue corn *masa harina*)
(see address above)

PUEBLO FOODS (fresh *masa*)
75 Jefferson Street, Passaic, NJ (201/473-4494)

RF NATURE FARM FOODS (blue cornmeal)
925 S Street, Lincoln, NE 68508 (402/474-7576)

Note: Most health food stores carry whole-grain cornmeals, of which Arrowhead Mills is the best known. Arrowhead, started thirty-four years ago by a farmer in Deaf Smith County, Texas, uses local organic corn and grinds it with an impact or "hammer" mill that eliminates heat.

ALL-CORN MENUS

With corn, as with Cleopatra, "She makes hungry where most she satisfies." No matter how many corn recipes I've tested or how many cobs I've chewed, I am always hungry for more. And I am always eager to discover new possibilities that I haven't tested, tasted, or chewed. My first all-corn tasting menu for the James Beard House in 1990 was for me a revelation of corn's infinite variety. I now know that I, or anyone else, could plan an all-corn dinner 365 days of the year and not once repeat a dish. I wanted to include five of these menus and their evolution from seminar to banquet to show that the hunger for corn is a passion not to be toyed with and to prove that Cleopatra had nothing on corn.

THE FIRST CORN SEMINAR AND TASTING, JULY 24, 1990

My corn megalomania turned what was meant to be an informative slide-lecture, followed by a few nibbles, into a monster twenty-dish buffet with four kinds of corn drinks. Since I'm a home cook, not a restaurant cook, I asked for help—*help!*—from a number of professional chefs who turned corn chaos into a feast. With the help of Rosa Ross, Bobby Flay, Stuart Taborin, Ruth Bronz, Josefina Howard, and Leah Holzel, these are the dishes we set out:

Corn Nuts and Spiced Popcorn

Sweet Corn on the Cob, with Seasoned Butter or Lime and Chili

Corn Oysters

Indonesian Shrimp Fritters

Polenta French Fries

Posole

Shrimp-Garlic Tamales

Grits-Cheese Soufflé

Salt Cod Stew

Blue Corn Bread

Yellow Corn Bread

Tortillas with Corn Salsa

Rhode Island Jonnycakes

Tomato-Corn Salad

Peruvian Corn Pudding

Popcorn Pudding with Red-Corn Pinole

Barbados Conkies

Peruvian Fruit Dessert

Parched Corn Ice Cream

Corona Beer

Jack Daniel's Bourbon

Chicha Morada

Chicha de Jora

Blue Corn Chocolate Atole

....

THE SECOND CORN WORKSHOP AND TASTING, AUGUST 7, 1991

By now even I knew that the tasting of corn was as primary as lust. We called the evening "A Celebration of Sweet Corn," and I got David Turk, of Indiana Market and Catering, with his chef Stephen Evasew, to select an orderly menu that we could serve to celebrants sitting at tables in the back garden of the James Beard House. This time there were good white wines, along with the beer, and "Tomato Bob" Polanz did a comic turn on corn farming.

Carolina Corn Oysters

Blue and White Corn Cups with Corn Salsa

Corn on the Cob Two Ways, with Chili Butter and Poblano Puree

Peruvian Fresh Corn Tamales

Southern Style Shrimp and Green Corn Soufflé

Zuni Summer Succotash

Huitlacoche Sauté with Chèvre/Corn Sauce

Fresh Corn Sticks

Molded Corn on the Cob Ice Cream with Caramel Corn Sauce

Pueblo Corn/Piñon Wafers

Maker's Mark Bourbon

THE THIRD ANNUAL CORN TASTING, AUGUST 19, 1992

Despite the name, the event was now an informally formal dinner with a well-known and much-praised chef who knew his corn, Brendan Walsh. Brendan had brought the Southwest to Manhattan at Arizona 206 before he left to start his own restaurants, chiefly North Street Grill, in Long Island. On the information side, Donald Prostak, a geneticist from Cook College at Rutgers University in New Jersey, supplied diners with a comparative tasting of thirteen different absolutely fresh-from-the-field sweet corns. That was for starters. Beer was out. Brendan offered us seven Long Island wines.

Sweet Corn for Mondawin
Huitlacoche Polenta Gratin
Grilled Summer Fish over Hominy Poblano and Roast-Pepper Stew
Chicken Sausage with Fresh Bean Succotash
Fresh Fruit Atole

....

THE FOURTH ANNUAL CORN DINNER, AUGUST 12, 1993

On the fourth round, we had graduated to an eight-course uptown dinner, commanded by Michael Lomonaco of the 21 Club, with five wines and wine expert Gerry Dawes to explain them. You might say that things were getting out of hand, but such good things were going from hand to mouth that no one regretted corn's going uppity. The menu tells all.

Foie Gras "Corn Dogs"
Corn Fried Oysters and Ancho Chile Sauce
BBQ Monkfish and Corn Bread
Indonesian Shrimp and Corn Fritters
Corn Silk Cured and Smoked Trout
Fresh Maine Lobster and Quick-Cooked Sandbar Corn Chowder
Popcorn-Crust Soft-Shell Crabs with East-Indian Piccalilli
Poached Salmon Salad with Roasted Corn Vinaigrette and Bucks County Greens
Roasted Quail with Walnut-Gorgonzola Polenta and Baked Figs
Black Angus Rib Steak with Felipe Rojas-Lombardi's Giant Vegetable Tamale
Fresh Steamed Corn on the Cob
Chocolate-Chile Cupcakes with Corn and Bourbon Sauce

THE FIFTH ANNUAL CORN DINNER, AUGUST 31, 1994

By now, the notion that corn could be as urbane as a "foie gras and corn terrine" or as a "corn silk tea and nasturtium granité" was an established fact. Ali Barker of Piperade in Cleveland, Ohio, furthered the sophistication of corn with a number of courses that might have surprised corn eaters in Ohio a century ago. Note that corn husks are now a form of "papillote." We finished this dinner off with port.

Shaker Corn "Oysters" with Crème Fraîche and Caviar

Blue and Red Corn-Fried Shrimp, Clams, Oysters, and Calamari with Harissa

Corn Blini with Lobster

Corn Chips with Three-Onion Dip

Hudson Valley Foie Gras, Prosciutto and Corn Terrine with Green Corn Piccalilli and Cornichons

Sea Scallops Piperade Steamed "en Husk Papillote" with Red and Yellow Peppers, Corn, Black Beans, Garlic, and White Wine

Corn Silk Tea and Nasturtium Granité

Corn Cob–Smoked Duck Breast with Polenta and Bourbon Demi-Glace

"Corn" Brûlée

A List of Corn Cookery

Besides books mentioned in the text, I've included books that have some interesting corn recipes or corn talk and some books that have nothing but corn recipes.

Bailey, Lee. *Corn* (New York: Clarkson Potter, 1993).

Baker, Charles H., Jr. *The Exotic Cookery Book, The Gentleman's Companion* (New York: Derrydale Press, 1939; Crown, 1946).

Bayless, Rick, and Deann Groen Bayless. *Authentic Mexican* (New York: Morrow, 1987).

Benitez, Ana M. de. *Cocina prehispánica* (Mexico City: Ediciónes Euroamericanas, 1976).

Brown, Cora, Rose Brown, and Bob Brown. *America Cooks* (Garden City, N.Y.: Doubleday, 1940).

Buff, Sheila. *Corn Cookery* (New York: Lyons & Burford, 1993).

Carnacina, Luigi. *La Polenta* (Milan: Fratelli Fabbri Editori, 1973).

Child, Lydia Maria. *The Frugal Housewife* (Boston: March & Capen, 1829).

Coe, Sophie D. *America's First Cuisines* (Austin, Tex.: University of Texas Press, 1994).

Cox, Beverly, and Martin Jacobs. *Spirit of the Harvest* (New York: Stewart, Tabori and Chang, 1991).

Cushing, Mrs. C. H., and Mrs. B. Gray. *The Kansas Home Cook-Book* (Leavenworth, Kans.: J. C. Ketcheson, 1874; Arno Press, 1973).

Cushing, Frank Hamilton. *Zuni Breadstuff,* reprint of 1920 ed. (New York: Museum of the American Indian Heye Foundation, 1974).

Deerfield Parish Guild. *The Pocumtuc Housewife* (Deerfield, Mass.: Deerfield Parish Guild, 1805).

Eustis, Célestine. *Fifty Valuable and Delicious Recipes Made with Corn Meal for 50 Cents* (Aiken, S.C.: 1917).

Field, Carol. *The Italian Baker* (New York: Harper & Row, 1985).

Flay, Bobby, and Joan Schwartz. *Bobby Flay's Bold American Food* (New York: Warner Books, 1994).

Frank, Lois Ellen. *Native American Cooking* (New York: Clarkson Potter, 1991).

Fried, Michelle O. *Comidas del Ecuador* (Quito: n.p., 1986).

Goldstein, Darra. *The Georgian Feast* (New York: HarperCollins, 1993).

Greenspan, Dorie. *Waffles from Morning to Midnight* (New York: Morrow, 1993).

Heatter, Maida. *New Book of Great Desserts* (New York: Knopf, 1982).

Hultman, Tami. ed., *The Africa News Cookbook* (New York: Viking Penguin, 1985).

Humphrey, Richard. *Corn, The American Grain* (Kingston, Mass.: Teaparty Books, 1985).

Jaffrey, Madhur. *A Taste of India* (New York: Crown, 1988).

Junior League of Denver, *Crème de Colorado* (Denver: Junior League of Denver, 1987).

Kamman, Madeleine. *Madeleine Kamman's Savoie* (New York: Atheneum, 1989).

Karoff, Barbara. *South American Cooking* (Berkeley, Calif.: Addison-Wesley, 1989).

Kavasch, Barrie. *Native Harvests* (New York: Random House, 1979).

Kennedy, Diana. *The Art of Mexican Cooking* (New York: Bantam Books, 1989).

Lambda Nu Chapter, *Delta Gamma Cook Book* (Minneapolis: Lambda Nu Chapter, 1922).

Ledford, Ibbie. *Hill Country Cookin' and Memoirs* (Gretna, La.: Pelican, 1991).

Leslie, Eliza. *The Indian Meal Book* (Philadelphia: Carey and Hart, 1847).

New Receipts for Cooking (Philadelphia: T. B. Peterson, 1854).

The Maize Board. *Maize on the Menu* (Pretoria, South Africa: Muller & Retief, 1971).

Malgieri, Nick. *Great Italian Desserts* (Boston: Little, Brown, 1990).

Marks, Copeland. *False Tongues and Sunday Bread* (New York: M. Evans, 1985).

Martinez, Zarela. *Food from My Heart* (New York: Macmillan, 1992).

McNair, James. *Corn Cookbook* (San Francisco: Chronicle Books, 1990).

Miller, Mark Charles. *Coyote Café* (Berkeley, Calif.: Ten Speed Press, 1989).

Mirodan, Vladimir. *The Balkan Cookbook* (United Kingdom: Lennard Publishing, 1987).

Murphy, Charles J. *American Indian Corn* (New York and London: Putnam, 1917).

Ortiz, Elizabeth Lambert. *The Book of Latin American Cooking* (New York: Random House, 1979).

Our Women's Exchange (Xenia, Ohio.: Xenia Republican Press, 1910).

Owen, Sri. *Indonesian Food and Cookery* (London: Prospect Books, 1986).

Parker, A. C. *Iroquois Uses of Maize and Other Plants* (Albany: University of the State of New York, 1910).

Parloa, Maria. *The Appledore Cookbook* (Boston: Graves & Ellis, 1872).

Miss Parloa's New Cook Book (Boston: Estes & Lauriat, 1881).

Pascale, Celine-Marie. *The Blue Corn Cookbook* (Albuquerque, N.M.: Out West Publishing, 1990).

The Picayune's Creole Cook Book (New Orleans: The Picayune, 1901).

Pyles, Stephan. *The New Texas Cuisine* (New York: Doubleday 1993).

Randolph, Mary. *The Virginia Housewife* (Washington, D.C.: Way & Gideon, 1825).

Rector's Guild of St. Paul, *Reliable Recipes* (Minnesota: Rector's Guild of St. Paul, 1925).

Redenbacher, Orville. *Popcorn Book* (New York: St. Martin's 1984).

Rhett, Blanche S., Lettie Gay, Helen Woodward, and Elizabeth Hamilton, *200 Years of Charleston Cooking* (Columbia, S.C.: University of South Carolina Press, 1976; first published in 1930).

Rivieccio, Maria Zaniboni. *Polenta, Piatto da Re* (Milan: Idealibri, 1986).

Robbins, Maria Polushkin. *American Corn* (New York: St. Martin's 1989).

Roberts, Michael. *Secret Ingredients* (New York: Bantam Books, 1988).

Rojas-Lombardi, Felipe. *The Art of South American Cooking* (New York: HarperCollins, 1991).

Romano, Dora. *Rice and Beans and Tasty Things* (Hato Rey, Puerto Rico: Ramallo Bros., 1986).

Rosser, Linda Kennedy. *Pioneer Cookery Around Oklahoma* (Oklahoma City: Bobwhite Publications, 1978).

Rutledge, Sarah. *The Carolina Housewife* (Charleston, S.C.: W. R. Babcock & Co., 1847; first published anonymously).

Sahni, Julie. *Classic Indian Vegetarian and Grain Cooking* (New York: Morrow, 1985).

Sanchez, Irene Barraza, and Gloria Sanchez Yund. *Comida Sabrosa* (Albuquerque: N.M.: University of New Mexico Press, 1982).

Sedlar, John. *Modern Southwest Cuisine* (New York: Simon & Schuster, 1986).

Simmons, Amelia. *American Cookery* (1796) Facsimile ed: Ed. M.T. Wilson (New York: Oxford University, Press, 1958).

Smith, Mary Stuart. *Virginia Cookery Book* (New York: Harper & Bros., 1885).

Spitler, Sue, and Nao Hauser. *The Popcorn Lover's Book* (Chicago: Contemporary Books, 1983).

Stapley, Patricia. *The Little Kernel Cookbook* (New York: Crown, 1991).

Sunset Mexican Cookbook (Menlo Park, Calif.: Lane Books, 1993; first published 1969).

Valldejuli, Carmen. *Puerto Rican Cookery* (Gretna, La.: Pelican, 1975).

Van der Post, Laurens. *African Cooking* (New York: Time-Life Books, 1970).

Velázquez de León, Josefina. *Tamales y Atoles* (Mexico: J. Velázquez de León, 1974).

Von Bremzen, Anya, and John C. Welchman. *Please to the Table,* (New York: Workman's, 1990).

Wade, Mary L. *The Book of Corn Cookery* (Chicago: A. C. McClurg, 1917; reissued Glenwood, Ill.: Meyerbooks, 1990).

White, Jasper. *Jasper White's Cooking from New England* (New York: Harper & Row, 1989).

Woodier, Olwen. *Corn Meals & More* (Pownal, Vt.: Storey Communications, 1987).

Woody, Laurie. *Corn-of-Plenty Cookbook* (Des Moines, Iowa: Pioneer Hi-Bred International, 1986).

INDEX